REPRESENTING GOD

Representing God

CHRISTIAN LEGAL ACTIVISM IN CONTEMPORARY ENGLAND

Méadhbh McIvor

PRINCETON UNIVERSITY PRESS

PRINCETON & OXFORD

Copyright © 2020 by Princeton University Press

Requests for permission to reproduce material from this work
should be sent to permissions@press.princeton.edu

Published by Princeton University Press
41 William Street, Princeton, New Jersey 08540
6 Oxford Street, Woodstock, Oxfordshire OX20 1TR

press.princeton.edu

All Rights Reserved
ISBN 9780691193625
ISBN (pbk.) 9780691193632
ISBN (e-book) 9780691211619
LCCN 2020942223

British Library Cataloging-in-Publication Data is available

Editorial: Fred Appel and Jenny Tan
Production Editorial: Debbie Tegarden
Jacket/Cover Design: Chris Ferrante
Production: Erin Suydam
Publicity: Kathryn Stevens
Copyeditor: Jay Boggis

Jacket/Cover Credit: St. Paul's Cathedral in London /
Songquan Deng / Alamy Stock Photo

This book has been composed in Classic Miller

Printed on acid-free paper. ∞

Printed in the United States of America

10 9 8 7 6 5 4 3 2 1

CONTENTS

ACKNOWLEDGEMENTS

THIS BOOK WOULD NOT HAVE BEEN POSSIBLE without the generosity of my interlocutors at both Christian Concern and Christ Church, who welcomed me into their respective communities with patience, honesty, and unswerving good humour. At Christian Concern, special thanks are owed to Andrea Minichiello Williams, Andrew Marsh, Ade Omooba, and the Christian Legal Centre (CLC) clients who took the time to share their stories with me. Andrea, Andrew, and Pastor Ade—and, indeed, the entire staff team, particularly those referenced within as Annabelle, Carrie, Grace, Jake, John, Louise, and Maria—enabled this project from its earliest stages, opening their doors and giving me access to the world of Christian activism. This act of bravery is one I appreciate deeply.

At Christ Church, thanks are owed to the church staff; to Lucy, who first introduced me to the congregation; to Carol and Leah, with whom I spent so much time studying the Bible; and to Hannah, who went out of her way to introduce me to friends and colleagues. Special thanks also to the members of my women's Bible study group, who welcomed me with such warmth.

I have had incredible mentors in Fenella Cannell, Matthew Engelke, and Winnifred Fallers Sullivan, all of whom have been incredibly supportive of this project and my career (and me personally, of course). My work has benefitted hugely from their feedback and critique; I hope they recognise their influence on this text. They are the kind of scholars I hope to be.

Fred Appel, Jenny Tan, and the team at Princeton University Press have been enormously helpful in bringing this book about, not least for organising the reviews that so improved the final product. Special thanks to these anonymous reviewers, whose reports strengthened my analysis in myriad ways.

I am grateful to my friends and peers at the London School of Economics, particularly Agustín Diz, Katharine Fletcher Wolstenholme, Juli Qermezi Huang, Megan Laws, and Philip Proudfoot, who offered helpful feedback in seminars and (more often) at the White Horse during my doctoral studies. Thanks also to colleagues at University College London, particularly Timothy Carroll, Lewis Daly, Ashraf Hoque, Dalia Iskander, and Aaron Parkhurst, who encouraged me as I wrote the proposal, and to Alanna Cant and Miranda Sheild Johansson for emotional support (and comic relief) during the wrapping up phase. Finbarr Curtis, Abby Day, Rosalind Hackett, and Anna Strhan all offered helpful feedback at different stages.

My colleagues at the Centre for Religion, Conflict and Globalisation— Brenda Bartelink, Kim Knibbe, Julia Martínez-Ariño, Brenda Mathijssen, Joram Tarusarira and Erin Wilson—have been hugely supportive of this project. I appreciate them immensely, both for the community they've created and the wonderful work they do. Similarly, my students at the LSE, UCL, and the University of Groningen continue to inspire me with their enthusiasm, commitment, and good humour; working with them has made me a better scholar.

My greatest debt is owed to those bound by ties of friendship so deep it is kinship and kinship so deep it is friendship. My parents, Bernadette and Peter, have always encouraged my love of books; the fact that I've now written one is testament to the three decades of love, support, and encouragement I have received from them. Thank you both for everything. The research on which this book is based would not have been possible without Otso, who not only supported and sustained me in the field but hosted dinner parties, attended church, and generally integrated into my field site. I honestly couldn't have done it without you. *Kiitos kaikesta.* Lisa stuck with me from start to finish, from helping me find a field site to talking through each chapter I produced. Marie, Jean-Yves, Dáire, Kimberly, Clémentine, Constance, and Agathe provided endless support (and welcome distraction). Thank you all. Finally, special thanks are owed to Richard, who read every draft twice and reads me more generously than anyone. (I guess it's finally true that you've been 'reading a lot of anthropology lately'.)

This research was made possible by grants from the Economic and Social Research Council and the London School of Economics.

Thanks for your patience, everyone! Now that the book is done, I promise to be more fun at parties . . .

REPRESENTING GOD

Palm Fronds in the
Public Square

'NOW LOOK, LOOK, if I can manifest my faith publicly with a *donkey*, seriously, what do the rest of you want to do?'

So asked Anirban Roy, a parishioner of St Martin-in-the-Fields, Trafalgar Square, to a packed lecture hall at the University of York. It was July 2012, and Mr Roy was one of almost five hundred delegates at a meeting of the Church of England's General Synod, the governing association of England's established church. A tricameral organisation made up of the Houses of Bishops, Clergy, and Laity, Synod is the Church's law-making body. Its members meet at least twice yearly to debate and amend ecclesiastical legislation. As a legislative body, Synod mimics the conventions and formalities of the United Kingdom's Houses of Parliament: members put forward draft measures, proposed amendments are discussed, and procedural rules are scrupulously observed. Once they have received Royal and parliamentary assent, the Canons and Measures it passes have the effect of state law. When, that is, it manages to pass anything at all. With its conservative, liberal, and Anglo-Catholic wings often in disagreement over matters of doctrine, liturgy, and the 'mission' of the nation's established church, achieving consensus at Synod is no easy task.[1]

Mr Roy, a lay member of the Church, had stood to speak to a Private Member's Motion put forward by the Reverend Stephen Trott, a conservative evangelical representative of the House of Clergy. Although a temperate summer's evening—the perfect weather for a stroll around the University's campus lake—the entry of the St Martin's donkey into discussion signalled that the debate on Motion GS1859A was about to heat up.

The innocuously titled Motion read:

That this Synod express its conviction that it is the calling of Christians to order and govern our lives in accordance with the teaching of Holy

Scripture, and to manifest our faith in public life as well as in private, giving expression to our beliefs in the written and spoken word, and in practical acts of service to the local community and to the nation.

On the face of it, GS1895A was uncontroversial. Many members of Synod welcomed Rev. Trott's intervention, agreeing that the Church should, in the words of one supporter, 'share [Jesus] forth in the public square'. Others questioned the necessity of the Church of England affirming its commitment to living in light of Holy Scripture. One speaker referred to it as 'an apple pie Motion', the sort of thing that no one—*well, no one who was a member of the Church's General Synod*—could sensibly argue against.

Yet argue they did. Defending the Motion, Rev. Trott spoke of 'very determined attempts' to remove Christianity from the public square: '[Christians are no longer] permitted to manifest our faith or to live and work according to our conscience as Christians, because to do so is increasingly, and mistakenly, classed by Government and by the courts as "discriminatory."' He deemed the Motion necessary on the basis that, if passed, those who faced opposition in their efforts to live 'according to [their] conscience as Christians' could point to it as evidence of the inherently public-facing nature of their faith. A growing number of Christians, he argued, now faced this challenge, citing as evidence a recent increase in the number of cases alleging anti-Christian discrimination in the English courts.

Indeed, the claimants from two such cases had come to Synod to highlight this need. Gesturing towards two women sitting behind him on the stage, Rev. Trott explained that they were clients of the Christian Legal Centre, an organisation founded to protect the rights of Christians to manifest their faith in public life. These women were, he assured the audience, 'real people' facing real problems.

For Anirban Roy, however, Rev. Trott's analysis did not ring true. Why, he wondered, did some members of the established church view themselves as 'persecuted minorities'? From where had this defensive attitude come? It was the sense of 'victimhood' underpinning the Motion that led him to counter:

> I go to St Martin-in-the-Fields. We know all about the public square. We are in Trafalgar Square in the middle of London. I wonder if I might give an example of how, as a church, we are able to manifest our faith in public life. Now look, on Palm Sunday, the ten o'clock congregation at St Martin's takes to the streets. And we are able to manifest our faith publicly by marching round Trafalgar Square, singing hymns and waving palm fronds. And do you know what, we do that with the Salvation Army brass band and a donkey. Now look, look, if I can manifest my faith publicly with a *donkey*, seriously, what do the rest of you want to do?

What indeed?

Notwithstanding the comic intent behind Mr Roy's rhetorical flourish, nor the whoops of appreciative laughter with which it was met, the question he raised was a serious one. After all, Rev. Trott was not alone in his fears. Many members of Synod were equally concerned by what he framed as a creeping pressure to 'hide away any evidence of our faith while at work or in public and only practise it, as they used to say, as consenting adults in private'. Too often, it seemed, the Christian faith was approached as a problem to be managed, not a gift to be shared. And yet, the setting in which these fears were voiced—a meeting of the legally established, taxpayer-supported,[2] legislation-passing state church—seemed to complicate, if not contradict, any suggestion that Christianity had been ousted from public life. More so even than the paschal perambulations of the St Martin's donkey, the spirited discussions, interminable disagreements, and uncomfortable stalemates for which Synod had become known were evidence not only of Christianity's ongoing role in the life of the nation, but of its highly contested nature.

As for the two Christian Legal Centre clients on stage—Caroline Petrie, a nurse who had been disciplined for offering to pray for an elderly patient, and Olive Jones, a teacher who had been temporarily suspended for speaking of her belief in miracles to a pupil undergoing treatment for cancer[3]—they too embodied these contradictions. To some Synod members, these women were victims of a creeping anti-Christian bias in contemporary Britain, living, breathing examples of the challenges faced when sharing one's faith in a hostile public square. To others, they were confirmation of internalised Christian privilege, proof that members of England's majority religion felt so *entitled* to broadcast their beliefs that even a minor limitation felt like persecution.

Or, perhaps, they were both and neither, simultaneously embodying the ongoing presence of Christianity in the public square and heralding a pluralistic public's changing attitudes towards it.

༄

This book offers an ethnographic account of the disputed place of 'public' Christianity in twenty-first-century England.[4] It focuses on those addressed by Mr Roy's question, that is, those (primarily Protestant) Christians who actively experience and/or discursively construct English public life as hostile to manifestations of their faith, and who work to counter this perceived hostility through sustained engagement with Parliament and the courts. Drawing on twenty-two months of dual-sited fieldwork split between a multidenominational Protestant Christian lobby group and a conservative evangelical Anglican church, I explore this activism as an element of England's shifting secular settlement (or the relationship between church and state).

In a rapidly changing religious landscape, Protestant Christianity—although it remains both legally and culturally established—has become relativised. This relativisation is, in many ways, the product of centuries' worth of political dispute and interreligious negotiation, as the legal privileges associated with established religion (and the penalties associated with its non-established variants, which have historically included dissenting Protestantism, Judaism, Catholicism, and other minority traditions) have been diluted. Yet it has taken on a particular salience in recent years, one which I date to a seismic shift in the state's regulation of religion: English law's transition from viewing 'religious freedom' as a negative civil liberty to ensuring it as a positive human right.[5] For the first time in English legal history, Article 9 of the Human Rights Act 1998 enshrined a positive right to religious freedom in a domestic statute. This turn to rights-based law both marked and inaugurated a new relationship between religion and the state, with Christianity now governed both as a national, established faith and as merely one religious option among others.

The resulting 'juridification' of religion[6]—its regulation under anti-discrimination and rights-based law, and its interaction with other identity markers governed by these instruments, such as race, sexuality, and gender—has had significant consequences for English Christians. These have been felt particularly acutely among the socially and theologically conservative Protestants with whom I carried out fieldwork, both Anglican and independent. Their understanding of the world, much of which was previously shared (or was assumed to be shared) by their non-churchgoing peers, is now markedly different from that of 'the culture' at large. While many such Christians have responded to these changes with resignation, some have embraced modes of legal and political engagement born of very different church-state paradigms, including a litigiousness more often associated with the United States. Armed with law degrees, evangelical conviction, and 'a passion to see the United Kingdom return to the Christian faith',[7] these activists lobby and litigate to contest what they see as Christianity's ousting from the public square.

This book argues that a willingness to take on legal challenges to protect Christian values risks those same values' marginalisation, as moralities previously woven into the fabric of national life are filtered out from their quotidian context and rebranded as 'religion' or 'religiously motivated'. That which might once have been understood as majority culture comes to be seen as the particular concern of a minority group. By framing the beliefs and practices for which they seek protection as specifically *Christian*, these cases and campaigns function to remove those same beliefs from the realm of cultural common sense, such that efforts to reclaim Christianity's place in the public square might well result in its relegation to the cultural sidelines. Thus, while it is true that this activism is, in part, a *response* to the changing place of majority religion in the life of the nation, I offer an ethnographic account of the ways in which conservative Christian politico-legal engagement is, somewhat para-doxically, also *constitutive* of this very shift.

Contemporary Christian Establishment

My interest in Christian legal activism stemmed from the media prominence of a narrative that appeared, from the outside, to contradict itself: how was it that members of England's majority religion could see themselves, as Mr Roy put it, as 'persecuted minorities'? After all, according to the 2011 census, which was taken just before I began my fieldwork with Christian activists in 2012, almost 60 percent of residents in England and Wales identify as Christian (the census does not distinguish between denominations). Although fewer than 5 percent of the population regularly attend church services (with under 1.5 percent attending services of the established Church of England),[8] Christianity remains legally and culturally privileged in a number of ways. Since the Church of England's founding in 1534, when King Henry VIII broke with the Roman Catholic Papacy and established himself as the governor of an independent national church, the monarch has been head of both Church and state. Five hundred years later, the two remain closely linked.

Nor is this relationship merely symbolic. Twenty-six Anglican bishops sit by right in the House of Lords (the upper chamber of the Houses of Parliament), thereby forming part of the legislature. And, as we have already seen, the Church of England's governing body passes measures that have the effect of state law. While these constitutional privileges are restricted to the Church of England (as opposed to the wider category of 'Christian', upon which I elaborate below), its historic hegemony means that (Protestant) Christianity as a whole is typically met with greater understanding and tolerance than comparable religious traditions. Moreover, 'cultural' Christianity is visible at every turn: in state-funded schools named for particular saints; in the recognition of the Christian Sabbath as a day of rest; in the Christian prayers read to open the day's sitting in Parliament; in the Queen's annual Christmas message; in national holidays that were once 'holy days'.

Yet among English Christians (particularly certain groupings of conservative Protestants), the view that Christianity is under threat has fairly widespread purchase. A 2011 survey of self-identified Christians carried out by Premier Christian Media Trust, for example, found that while only 12 percent of respondents claimed to have experienced discrimination on account of their faith, 63 percent claimed to have 'observed [the] marginalisation' of Christianity in British public life,[9] while a 2012 report by the Equality and Human Rights Commission refers to the 'Christian "marginalisation" narrative' as being 'exceptionally high profile in contemporary public and media debate'.[10] Those who answered Premier's survey are, of course, self-selecting; their perception of marginalisation may tell us more about their subjectivity than anything else. (As has been noted in relation to race and gender, dominant groups sometimes experience efforts to 'level the playing field' as a kind of discrimination against them.) Yet these feelings are deeply held.

Indeed, so prominent had this narrative become by 2011 that Christians in Parliament, an all-party parliamentary group of Christian politicians from across the political and theological spectrum, launched a fact-finding inquiry framed around the question: 'Are Christians marginalised in the UK?' The inquiry, published under the title *Clearing the Ground*, was prompted by the fact that 'recent high profile [legal] cases have demonstrated how Christian believers have increasingly found themselves in conflict with some elements of the UK's new legal landscape'. It identified extensive media coverage of these cases as a key factor in the 'widespread perception [among Christians] that they are being marginalised'.[11]

The cases to which the *Clearing the Ground* report refers are part of a growing body of Christian-interest litigation in the United Kingdom. Over the past two decades, increasing numbers of Christians—primarily, but not exclusively, conservative Protestants—have taken to court to enforce what are framed as 'religious rights' under both European and domestic law. These cases, which typically involve those who have been penalised for seeking faith-based exemptions from their conditions of employment—registrars who claim a conscientious objection to registering the marriages or civil partnerships of same-sex couples, for example, or employees who ask for exceptions to be made to uniform policies that forbid the visible wearing of jewellery, including crosses and crucifixes—often captivate the public imagination, highlighting the uneasy truce between law and religion in a country that maintains an established church but is wary of those looking to 'do God' in public.[12] English courts struggle to determine what protecting these religious rights might reasonably involve: the recognition of a distinctive communal identity? The broadcasting of belief? Exemptions from the state's quotidian regulation of family life? Judges dabble in theology as they seek to define and police the messy reality of claimants' religious worlds.[13] But courts of law are rarely equipped to balance the significance of commitments that are seen to be, in the words of the aptly titled Lord Justice Laws, 'necessarily subjective'[14] against their objective impact on everyday life. What counts, from the perspective of the law, as religion? What *should* count? And how far should this '"legal" religion' be accommodated by the state?[15]

Taking these cases, the debates they spark, and the narrative of which they are a part as its objects of ethnographic inquiry, this book explores what Winnifred Fallers Sullivan, Robert Yelle, and Mateo Taussig-Rubbo call the 'awkward incapacity of secular law' to engage with religion as it is lived.[16] Based on multi-sited comparative ethnography carried out at a Christian lobby group and a conservative evangelical church, it attends to the values, desires, and goals of those seeking to live out their faith in a context they paint as hostile to it. (I elaborate on both my choice of field sites and my rationale for choosing multi-sited fieldwork below.) The dual-sited nature of my research reflects the multiple avenues of action available to such Christians, with my activist and church-based interlocutors modelling different, if intersecting, strategies of public engagement. In particular, it focuses on the mobilisation of legal categories in this process of engagement, highlighting the complex interaction of quotidian religious practices (forms of dress, prayer, and personal witness) and 'secular' law in a nation where Christianity is both state apparatus and countercultural movement. As such, it is a contribution to the anthropologies of law, (counter)public religion, and socio-political activism, but also to theoretical investigations of secularism as an historical, cultural product. In this understanding, national secular settlements are rooted in local particularities even as they emerge out of transnational discourses on the relationship between 'law' and 'religion'—and the proper regulation of the latter by the former.[17]

Examining data from a lobby group and a church in tandem reveals the impact of religion's juridification at both macro and micro levels, that is, in terms of both public policy and individual experience. Those chapters that focus primarily on Christian activism are based on the work of Christian Concern and the Christian Legal Centre (CLC),[18] a dual lobby group and legal aid centre where I carried out fieldwork between 2012 and 2014, most intensively during the six-month period from July to December 2012. Christian Concern and the CLC litigate many of the Christian-interest cases that have made headlines in recent years (including those of Caroline Petrie and Olive Jones, the women who joined Stephen Trott on stage at the Church of England's General Synod). Christian Concern is controversial both within and without the broader Christian community, with some commentators viewing it as a harbinger of the 'Americanisation' of religio-political life in Britain. As I show, these legal activists view the law as an evangelistic vehicle, a bureaucratic means of broadcasting the gospel message. From this perspective, a high-profile legal case or political campaign is a public crusade to change private convictions.

Equally, this book is an account of those who already hold these Christian convictions, who sometimes struggle to express them in such a way that they are accessible to those lacking an evangelical hermeneutic. This struggle is the primary ethnographic concern of those chapters focusing on the members of Christ Church, a conservative evangelical Anglican community located in Greater London, where I carried out sixteen months of fieldwork between January 2013 and April 2014. For those at Christ Church, the evangelical experience is equally one of joy and contentment—the result of one's sure and certain knowledge of salvation—and anxiety and guilt, the result of a conviction that countless others, including those to whom one may be intimately connected through kinship or friendship, do not share this heavenly eternal destiny. These evangelicals want (or feel they *should* want) to help others on their journey to faith, but they worry that non-Christians experience preaching and proselytism as unwelcome, perhaps even aggressive. This colours their understanding of the legal cases and campaigns run by Christian activists. As with those at Christian Concern, the members of Christ Church mourn the state of the nation, and fear for what will become of it. Yet they also express unease about the instrumentalisation of the law in the service of evangelism, not least because doing so seems to circumscribe Christianity to a relatively limited set of concerns: sexual ethics; abortion; Sabbath observance.

While the term 'Christian' encompasses a wide range of theological traditions, those I worked with at both Christian Concern and Christ Church are perhaps best identified as socially conservative evangelical Protestants. Since its emergence in the 1730s, evangelicalism has gone through many permutations, and it remains a cross-denominational movement today. Although evangelicals make up only 3 percent of the population, they represent approximately 27 percent of British Christians, spread throughout both established and independent churches.[19] As such, although all of my interlocutors can broadly be termed 'evangelical', this does not mean there are no differences between them: while the members of Christ Church are part of the white-majority 'conservative evangelical' wing of the established Church of England, the *evangelicalisms* represented at Christian Concern are much more varied. During my time there, Christian Concern staff members worshipped at Anglican, Baptist, Pentecostal, and independent churches, including West African-, West Indian-, and white-majority congregations. Despite some differences in theology and worship styles, they are united by their shared commitment to a conservative reading of the Bible (and the socio-political positions understood to flow from it, including opposition to abortion and LGBTQ+ marriage rights); a belief in the necessity of being 'born again' through Jesus Christ; and the conviction that Christians have a duty to share the gospel with others in the hopes of their too receiving salvation through Christ.

Thus, while I reference various denominations throughout the book, unmarked references to 'Christians' in general ought to be taken to mean the socially and theologically conservative Protestants with whom I spent the majority of my fieldwork, who differ in their preferred modes of worship but share a similar orientation to what they view as biblical mandates. While this use of 'Christian' is, admittedly, something of a fudge, I believe it is the best way to handle a recurrent tension in the term's use. As I explain below, my interlocutors tend to self-describe simply as 'Christian' rather than Anglican, Baptist, and so forth, a move which works to mask theological difference even as it assumes a sectarian understanding of what a 'true Christian' is. This is an effective movement-growing tool: although those most heavily involved in Christian lobbying and legal activism are conservative Protestants, their cases and campaigns also receive support from self-identified Christians with different church backgrounds (including those—such as Catholics—who might not always be counted as 'true Christians' by the movement's conservative Protestant majority). I ask readers to keep this tension in mind as they progress with the book.

My interlocutors' religious worlds must be situated within a particular moment in English legal history. As I outline in more detail below, the incorporation of the European Convention on Human Rights (ECHR) into domestic law means that the state has recently moved from what legal scholar Russell Sandberg calls the 'passive toleration' of religious difference to the 'active promotion' of freedom of religion.[20] Under this new legal regime, Protestant Christianity's establishment fails to offer all of the privileges it once did. (In Julian Rivers' terms, the Church of England is now 'barely established'.[21]) Somewhat paradoxically, then, the strengthening of rights-based law is experienced by some evangelicals as a threat to their religious liberty. As I suggest throughout the book, this is because it requires the rebranding of values that were previously shared by the public at large as now being the interests of a religious minority; interests that then come to seem ever more rarefied and distinct from 'secular', everyday life. In other words, the more Christianity is contested in the English courts, the more it is differentiated from English culture.

Indeed, by relying on legislation that requires them to frame their moral commitments and behavioural norms in specifically *religious* terms, the legal strategies adopted by my interlocutors as they seek 'to infuse a biblical worldview into every aspect of society'[22] can be seen as both an answer to and generative of the secularisation they seek to challenge. The secular, here, is less a *Weltanschauung* against which a named religion competes, and more a way of knowing the world; an 'epistemic regime', as Richard Amesbury puts it, through which the category of religion has become an object of fascination, concern, and—increasingly—regulation.[23] European and American case law suggests that non-Protestant claimants are particularly likely to fall foul of these regulations, which tend to assume that religion is (or ought to be) primarily about belief, not practice.[24] Yet, as this work shows, even those who subscribe to an interiorised, immaterial, conscience-based approach to the religious life—what Sullivan calls the 'small "p"' protestant definition of much legal religion,[25] and one which ought not trouble the implicitly Christian framing of the English legal system—find themselves caught up in the 'secular cunning', in Mayanthi Fernando's words, of the law.[26]

Evangelical Activism at Home and Abroad

What does it mean, in practice, to 'infuse a biblical worldview into every aspect of society'? At Christian Concern, this aim is pursued through both Parliament and the courts. Christian Concern is often spoken of in terms of its perceived importation of a confrontational, 'American' approach to public engagement, with its political lobbying and 'swift recourse to legal action' dubbed 'a carbon copy' of the way American organisations are thought to operate.[27] Parallels are sometimes drawn, for example, between Christian Concern and the Moral Majority, the Christian campaign organisation at the heart of America's 1980s 'Religious Right'.[28] It is worth remembering, however, that English evangelicals have a long history of involvement in socio-political activism, having campaigned from the 1700s to the present on issues ranging from prison reform, to the temperance movement, to the sexual revolution. Indeed, the historian David Bebbington designates 'activism', that is, 'the expression of the gospel in effort', as one of the defining traits of evangelical Christianity.[29]

Today's activists view themselves as the legitimate descendants of this tradition. Indeed, Andrea Minichiello Williams (hereafter, simply Andrea), Christian Concern's CEO, once gifted me a biography of Lord Shaftesbury, the nineteenth-century evangelical politician and moral reformer, in hopes of helping me understand the motivation behind their work.[30] To Andrea's mind, legislation that is 'permissive' of sinful behaviour is, quite simply, 'bad law'. The cases she litigates are 'the culmination' of these bad laws, laws that undermine Britain's historic Christian foundation and the freedoms that flow from it. As such, and as with the political lobbying of their eighteenth- and nineteenth-century forerunners—including the anti-slavery, anti-child labour, and anti-ritualism campaigns of evangelical heroes such as William Wilberforce and Lord Shaftesbury—Christian Concern's most high-profile policy initiatives are framed in terms of the sins (from their perspective) to which they are opposed: abortion, same-sex marriage, embryonic stem-cell research.

Although the prominence of evangelical reform movements had declined by the late Victorian era, the changing mores of the 1960s prompted something of a revival amongst England's activist-minded Christians. It is here that the more immediate roots of Christian Concern's work can be found. As with earlier campaigns, twentieth-century evangelicals targeted what they saw as state-sanctioned immorality. Mary Whitehouse's National Viewers' and Listeners' Association (NVLA), for example, founded in 1965 to campaign against the casualisation of sex and violence in the media, had a significant Christian component among its 20,000 members.[31] Its predominantly Anglican base supported the Association's goal of 'moral regeneration' and the 're-establishment' of Christian society.[32] Evangelical-led anti-pornography campaigns followed in the 1970s.[33] By the 1980s, Christians were mobilising against plans to relax England's strict Sunday trading laws, which limit the number of hours shops can stay open on Sundays. (Paul Diamond, a barrister who often represents the Christian Legal Centre's clients in court, first became involved in evangelical activism when he joined the 'Keep Sunday Special' movement in 1988.)

Although these campaigns had some success,[34] they did little to stem the changing moral tide. By the time Mary Whitehouse retired in 1994, sex and swearing were commonplace on Britain's national broadcaster, supermarkets could open on Sundays, and Britain was increasingly recognised as a multi-faith society. (In the 2011 census, Muslims formed the second-largest religious community at 4.8 percent of the population. Those identifying as Hindu, Sikh, Jewish, Buddhist, or 'Other' constituted 4 percent, while almost a quarter espoused no religious affiliation.) By contrast to the situation in the United States, where evangelicals have constituted a serious political force since the 1970s, politicians in England feel little need to pander to the 'Christian vote'. (This is not necessarily the case in other parts of the UK, such as Northern Ireland, where religious identity can play a significant role in parliamentary elections.) Still, evangelicals continue to agitate for moral reform, even if the nation-shaping impact of figures like William Wilberforce seem a distant memory.

If English evangelicals have a long legacy of political activism, they also have a long history of collaboration with their American peers. This history stretches back to the movement's advent in the 1730s, when fomenters of the (North American) Great Awakening and the (UK) Evangelical Revival communicated through visits, personal letters, and the circulation of evangelistic literature. Eighteenth-century English evangelist George Whitefield preached throughout the American colonies, while John and Charles Wesley, the founders of English Methodism, sent evangelical ministers to what would later become America's Episcopal Church. Such figures ensured the presence of a strong evangelical wing within the Church of England,[35] both in Britain and in the lands it colonised. Nor was this influence unilateral. The American Jonathan Edwards' fiery 1741 sermon, 'Sinners in the Hands of an Angry God', had a significant impact in England, as did Charles Finney's 1835 *Lectures on Revivals of Religion* (not least, as Bebbington notes, 'because it was adapted for the British market by removing . . . strictures on drinking tea').[36] English abolitionists of both evangelical and Quaker persuasion campaigned alongside their American peers to outlaw the transatlantic slave trade in the eighteenth and nineteenth centuries (while other Christians, including evangelicals, fought to preserve it).[37] More recently, American evangelicalism has influenced its English cousin through the work of missionaries such as Billy Graham, whose many UK crusades shaped the evangelical faction of the Church of England in the latter half of the last century. Outside of the established church, transatlantic charismatic and evangelical networks—such as the Vineyard Movement and the 'Emerging Church'—bring UK and US congregations together.[38]

English evangelical activism, then, is well established, as is the relationship between English and American evangelicalism(s). Yet there *are* elements of both novelty and American inspiration in the way certain English activists now pursue these longstanding reformist goals. This is primarily so in terms of the specifically *legal* approach to social change with which this book is concerned (and which, it is worth pointing out, is also relatively new in the US context).[39] Christian Concern and the Christian Legal Centre's willingness to argue freedom of religion test cases is a recent development that mirrors the headline-grabbing, strategic litigation promoted by their US counterparts, including Arizona-based Alliance Defending Freedom, which has been at the forefront of 'Christian freedom' litigation in the United States.

Given the very different understandings of freedom of religion in the UK and US, it is, perhaps, somewhat surprising that English evangelicals would adopt the legal strategies of their American peers.[40] In the UK, the history of religious liberty is deeply bound up with church establishment. It has taken English law nearly five centuries to move from religious discrimination (when the established church was recognised at the expense of other Christian denominations), to non-discrimination (in which multiple religions were 'tolerated'), to anti-discrimination, in that the incorporation of the European Convention into domestic law created a positive obligation on the part of the state to ensure freedom of religion.[41] (Prior to the ECHR's incorporation as the Human Rights Act 1998, no domestic legislation guaranteed a positive right to religious freedom in the United Kingdom.[42]) This move from negative liberty to positive right,[43] set within the context of an established, law-making Christian church, is fundamentally different from the US context, in which religion is constructed as outside the bounds of legal regulation.

By contrast to its English variant, American religion is disestablished. Indeed, in Sullivan's terms, it is *radically* disestablished.[44] The First Amendment to the Constitution, which prohibits Congress from passing laws 'respecting an establishment of religion, or prohibiting the free exercise thereof', is a core component of American national identity.[45] Britons may be proud of their tradition of civil liberties, but they have no comparable ideology of religious freedom. Given that the rites of the Church of England have historically constituted both theology and law,[46] English religion appears to be doubly unfree, at least in American terms: it fails both the 'establishment' and 'free exercise' clauses outlined in the First Amendment. As such, it is not immediately obvious why Christian activists in England would adopt the legal strategies of their peers in the United States. Cases that might well be won in American courts are unlikely to pass muster in England, just as public displays of religiosity that might be at home on Main Street USA would seem out of place on the British High Street.

Part of the explanation for Christian Concern's ostensibly 'American' approach to law and politics may lie in co-founder Andrea's personal testimony, which blends her conversion narrative with English legal history and American-inspired public engagement.[47] In a rhetorical move that echoes her own genealogy of Christian activism as much as it does Britain's changing attitudes to sexuality and family life, Andrea's 'State of the Nation' address—her default presentation for church groups interested in the work of Christian Concern and the Christian Legal Centre, which lays out the moral depravity of twenty-first-century Britain before asking the audience to stand up against it—begins by painting the passage of the Abortion Act 1967 as the crossing of a national moral boundary.[48] As with the role played by *Roe v Wade* in the American pro-life movement, Andrea holds up the Abortion Act as a symbol of both moral and legal depravity around which Christians should unite.

While the US Christian Right's coalescence around *Roe v Wade* meant that, by the 1980s, most conservative Protestants in the United States were convinced 'that a strict pro-life position was both God's word and the traditional Christian position',[49] conservative Protestants in Britain have never conflated pro-life convictions with the core of their faith. Media interest in the religious regulation of fertility has traditionally focused on those Christian who take their cues from the Vatican rather than Lambeth Palace (that is, Catholics rather than Protestants).[50] Yet the elision of Christianity with what Susan Harding calls 'the pro-life gospel' forms an important part of Andrea's activist testimony.

For Andrea, the critical moment came when she and her husband moved to Atlanta, Georgia, in the mid-1990s (a decade before she founded Christian Concern and the Christian Legal Centre). She describes herself as having come to America with all of the '"prejudices", in inverted commas, of a Brit going to the States' (those same 'prejudices' that continue to influence many Britons' reception of Christian Concern and the Christian Legal Centre's work). But she quickly warmed to Atlanta's 'blue skies and sunshine and "have a nice day", big smiles, painted nails, and big hair'. Although not every Georgian had a personal relationship with Jesus Christ, the entire state seemed to have been 'infused' with Christian language: '"You be blessed now", "have a blessed day", you know, there was a sense in which the language was infused with Christian values and Truths. And it felt good for the community.'

It was at an Atlanta megachurch that Andrea first met Karen Black, a pro-life campaigner, who was then looking for volunteers to offer 'sidewalk counselling' outside local abortion clinics.[51] Although she had always felt that abortion was wrong, the thought of praying outside a clinic made her uncomfortable. Still, she decided to sign up and find out more: 'I found myself listening . . . and before I knew it I found myself down on a sidewalk in Atlanta. And actually, that day, I saw women turn away from the clinic.' It was this experience that prompted her to reconsider her bias against Christian activism: '[women] were saved and their babies were saved'.

Andrea speaks of her time in America as a time of preparation for her work with Christian Concern (the founding of which I explore below). Not only had she seen the physical fruits of Christian activism, but the common grace evident in Georgia's biblically-infused language made the paucity of this grace in England all the more apparent. The contrast between the blue sky thinking of Atlanta and the grey realities of the church in London proved difficult to adjust to:

> Those two years had had the most profound effect on me. In America, I mean, the church, it was big, you know, there was no such thing as 'we can't do that'. I got back and it felt a bit flat. The sky was grey again and everything felt a bit flat, and I thought, 'Where's the energy? What are we going to do?' And I was probably quite unbearable, but I found it quite hard to recover.

This lack of 'energy' might be better understood as an aversion to contentious politics. Overcoming this aversion is particularly difficult in England, where notions of reserve and restraint continue to be positively associated—albeit in a self-conscious, ironic way—with middle-class manners (and, as the sociologist Anna Strhan has argued, with the secular norms of public speech that many metropolitan evangelicals have imbibed).[52] Andrea is, of course, cognisant of this barrier. Her testimony begins by positioning her former self on the side of the divide that finds sidewalk counselling to be in poor taste. She describes her initial decision to volunteer with Karen Black as having been 'un-British', in that it required her to shed her reserve and insert herself into a stranger's life. (To understand just how 'un-British' this action was, it is worth remembering that Andrea moved to Atlanta just two years after Don Treshman, an American anti-abortion activist with the campaign group Rescue America, found himself threatened with deportation for bringing his American-style picketing to UK soil.[53]) But the Rubicon from discomfort to urgency was crossed when she saw those strangers' lives 'saved'. By recounting the successes she experienced on that Atlanta sidewalk, Andrea invites her listeners to make this conceptual leap with her, raising up godly men and women to fight against sin-normalising laws. In this sense, Christian Concern and the Christian Legal Centre can be understood as a manifestation of English evangelicalism's long-running interest in the state's regulation of (im)morality.

Yet by seeking to ensure protections for religiously-motivated actions, Christian activists inevitably succumb to the hegemonic power of the not-quite-secular state: the law's power to circumscribe and police the legitimate limits of religious expression, and its prerogative to reject certain forms of religiosity as not quite religious *enough* to be protected under laws guaranteeing religious freedom.[54] As I argue throughout the book, this both emerges from and generates ambivalence towards the very category to be protected, an ambivalence that is equally rooted in evangelical theology and England's religio-legal history. Evangelicals frequently reject the language of 'religion' as regards their own beliefs and practices, preferring to view Christianity as a *relationship with God*, something fundamentally different (in their eyes) from the kinds of creeds and ritual systems typically labelled 'religious'. In this sense, to rely on the right to freedom of religion as a Christian is to relativise one's faith, accepting that it is merely one religious option among others. But in England—with its 'Christian heritage' and established church—it is also to sift Christian values out from the national fabric, portraying the moral norms that evangelicals believe to have *universal* application as the *particular* interests of a minority group. In other words, challenges to the liberal consensus on religion—the idea that it ought to be accommodated so long as it is spatially interior, a phenomenon largely reducible to claims of conscience—can shore up its power even as they reveal its potentially oppressive force.

Legal Theology: Fieldwork at Christian Concern and the Christian Legal Centre

While Lord Justice Laws, quoted above, presumes a distinction between the 'necessarily subjective' faith of a religious claimant and the objective reality of statutory law, anthropology's theoretical and ethnographic record suggests that law and religion—in so far as one can define or distinguish either—are often interlinked. For Émile Durkheim, for example, law and morality were 'born from religion, have long been confused with it, and remain imbued with its spirit'.[55] In this understanding, both legal and religious norms are reflective of the values of the moral community, and thus form the basis of social solidarity and stability. Given the discipline's early interest in this presumed stability (and the law's role in ensuring it), it is, perhaps, unsurprising that many of the classic texts in the anthropology of law ascribe legal weight to the religious, the spiritual, and the magical. Bronisław Malinowski's *Crime and Custom in Savage Society*, for example, speaks of black magic as being both 'an instrument of crime' and a 'genuine legal force',[56] while Karl Llewellyn and Edward Hoebel's *The Cheyenne Way*, which stresses the religious elements of dispute resolution, features a chapter titled 'Homicide and the Supernatural'.

What is true of the Trobriand Islanders and the Cheyenne is equally true of the modern nation state. Despite efforts to disentangle 'law' and 'religion', the two remain stubbornly interlinked. As John Comaroff puts it, 'modern secular law, born of the separation of *lex naturae* from *lex dei*, has always had the quality of a fetish', appearing as 'an abstraction made real, ascribed a life force of its own, and attributed the mythic, numinous capacity to configure relations and transactions in its own image'.[57] Indeed, even the promotion of an ostensibly neutral, 'secular' law as a 'one size fits all' approach to managing diversity in multicultural states can be seen to draw its power from the universalism of salvific religion.[58] But while it is clear that religion and law have always been mutually implicated, it is also true that the late twentieth- and early twenty-first centuries have seen an increase in religious groups and individuals turning to law to protect or extend their place in what are otherwise described as 'secular' societies.[59] With political claims increasingly formed in terms of identity, religious communities are ever more willing—or ever more obliged—to deploy what Comaroff terms 'legal theology' in their search for state recognition of their distinctive lifeways (or what might be called, in liberal parlance, the 'tolerance' of their difference). Others go beyond this quest for mere recognition. For some, recourse to the law is a means of transforming the world, with secular law the instrument 'by which civil society is to be remade in the image of the sacred'.[60]

This is the position of Christian Concern and the Christian Legal Centre, where I carried out fieldwork between 2012 and 2014. Together, these sister organisations form a paradigmatic example of what José Casanova famously called 'public religion', evidence of the ways in which religious conviction can be critical in 'the very struggles to define and set the modern boundaries between the private and public . . . between legality and morality, between individual and society'.[61] Christian Concern and the CLC were founded by Andrea, introduced above, and Pastor Ade Omooba, an evangelical minister with over twenty years of experience in social activism, particularly in the areas of racial justice and youth work. (Andrea herself is a qualified, albeit non-practising, barrister and former Director of Public Policy for the Lawyers' Christian Fellowship, or LCF.[62] Prior to her time in the United States, after which she worked with the LCF, she had practiced at the Bar.) The two began working together to oppose the Racial and Religious Hatred Act 2006, which they believed could have been used to prevent Christians from criticising other religions. Andrea opposed the then bill from within the LCF while Ade worked to mobilise black-majority churches against it. They went on to found Christian Concern together in 2008.

Based on a belief that Britain is in the process of abandoning its traditional Christian heritage, Christian Concern and the CLC exist, as their website put it during my fieldwork (the site has recently been updated), 'to be a strong Christian voice in the public sphere, arguing passionately for the truth of the gospel and defending the historic freedoms that we have enjoyed in this nation for so long'.[63] They are run from shared offices in Wimpole Street, in central London's fashionable Marylebone. During my fieldwork, they had a combined total of approximately fifteen full and part-time staff (plus occasional interns and volunteers), with perhaps seven to ten staff members present in the office on any given day.

In terms of division of labour, the CLC is the arm of the organisation that litigates Christian-interest legal cases, while Christian Concern is primarily concerned with lobbying, political campaigning, and church outreach events. In practice, however, and in terms of both staff and policy interests, there is a great deal of overlap between the two. As such, I tend to refer to them somewhat interchangeably. Both campaign on a variety of policy areas deemed of interest to Christians (by which, as noted above, they usually mean theologically conservative Protestants). These include sexual ethics, 'life' issues (including abortion, embryology, and assisted suicide), religious freedom, and what is referred to as 'the challenge of Islam'. Although sometimes dismissed by the press as a 'fringe group',[64] they have a number of high-profile supporters, including Baroness Caroline Cox of the House of Lords; Fiona Bruce, Conservative Member of Parliament; and Michael Nazir-Ali, former bishop of Rochester. Moreover, co-founder Ade Omooba was recently awarded an MBE (Member of the British Empire) by the Queen in recognition of his social outreach and voluntary work.

It was at their Wimpole Street offices that I spent the most intensive period of my fieldwork at Christian Concern, where participant observation took the shape of an unpaid internship carried out from July to December 2012. Christian Concern often takes on interns during the summer months. As such, although my status as a research student marked me out as different from my peers, I was but one of a number of twenty-something interns based at the organisation in the summer of 2012. I had first been put in touch with the group by a contact working at an evangelical charity, who knew the leadership team from the evangelical 'circuit'. Given Christian Concern's staunch theological conservatism, this contact had warned me that the staff were unlikely to welcome the presence of a non-Christian researcher. (Although I was raised Catholic, my interlocutors did not read me as 'Christian'.) Bucking these expectations, the Christian Concern staff were enthusiastic about my project. They were keen to support academic research in this area, perhaps hoping that my work would raise awareness of Christian-interest litigation.[65] Indeed, I was not the only researcher with whom Christian Concern was in contact during this period: during a trip to the European Court of Human Rights in September 2012 (which I discuss in chapter 2), our party shared a meal with two British philosophers who had explored the CLC's cases as part of a philosophical study of religious symbols. Thus, although I am often met with surprise when I recount the relative ease with which my access to the group was initially negotiated, I have come to think that this says as much about the assumptions and anxieties of my 'secular' networks as it does my interlocutors' wariness of non-evangelical outsiders.

This is not to say that my presence was never controversial within the organisation. I was not privy to the initial board meetings in which my project was discussed, and so am unable to comment on the internal debates that may have taken place in relation to my proposed fieldwork. I was not invited to fundraising events aimed at high-level donors, for fear that the presence of a researcher might be off-putting to them. Whether by accident or design, I spent more time with some staff members than others; perhaps some were wary of my ever-present notebook. In spite of these limitations, however—and aided by my colleagues' desire to evangelise, which both eased and complicated my experience of fieldwork—those with whom I spent my internship were open and gracious, both in response to my presence and in their answers to my never-ending questions. The path these discussions took often depended on personality; some colleagues relished the chance to debate controversial issues with an 'outsider', while others sought to find common ground.

While other researchers have gained access to Christian Concern staff to conduct formal and semi-formal interviews,[66] my internship enabled me to immerse myself in the organisation over a sustained period, giving me privileged access to its day-to-day workings and overall strategic aims. This immersion formed a useful corrective to outside images of the organisation. Despite its reputation for controversy and confrontation, Christian Concern functions much like any other mid-size office (albeit with more frequent prayer meetings). During my internship, I undertook light legal research; compiled initial draft responses to government consultations on issues ranging from Internet pornography to the use of mitochondrial replacement therapy; drafted news pieces for the Christian Concern website (a task at which I was usually found wanting: none of my pieces were posted without heavy editing); put together countless information packs to be distributed at Christian Concern speaking engagements; and participated in demonstrations, prayer rallies, and Christian conferences. It was as a guest of Andrea that I was able to attend the July 2012 meeting of the General Synod, during which Motion GS1895A was so hotly debated.[67] More informally, I got to know my colleagues over the innumerable cups of tea and coffee that punctuate the workday in any London office.

Outside of business hours, I accompanied them to church, socialised over shared meals, and attended weddings and birthday parties. I was also present at a number of court hearings with the CLC team. This took me from the sparkling glass facade of Strasbourg's European Court of Human Rights, to the Gothic grandeur of London's Royal Courts of Justice, to the squat, humble concrete of Brighton Magistrates' Court. While my internship, and thus the most intensive period of fieldwork among my activist interlocutors, ended in December 2012, I continued to return to the office over the following year to conduct interviews, meet CLC clients, and catch up with former colleagues.

Andrea is the public face and primary directive force behind both Christian Concern and the CLC. Both were born from her public policy work at the Lawyers' Christian Fellowship, from which she had been running Christian-interest cases from as early as 2004. When her LCF colleagues expressed concern that the cases were politically polarising, thereby undermining the LCF's primary function as a fellowship (not to mention risking its charitable status), the CLC was founded as an independent body. It has since become the UK's premier Christian liberties legal fund.[68] It provides advice and representation to a wide variety of claimants, including those who have been asked to remove Christian symbols, those who have been disciplined for praying or witnessing at work, and those who have expressed conscientious objections to working with LGBTQ+ customers or clients. Many of their cases are argued under Article 9 of the Human Rights Act 1998 (the domestic equivalent of the European Convention), which protects the right to freedom of thought, conscience, and religion. Unlike not-for-profit legal centres that rely on government funding and prioritise cases with the best chance of success, the CLC tends to be principled rather than pragmatic in its willingness to litigate, prioritising what they see as the pursuit of justice over likely outcome. It is perhaps this result-blind ethos that explains the Centre's track record. Despite recent successes in employment tribunals and hate speech cases, it has historically lost most of its cases (although it is worth pointing out that those cases that go to court are, almost by definition, those that are particularly difficult to resolve; cases that are settled behind the scenes do not make the headlines).[69] Similarly, and despite its significant media presence (Christian Concern spokespeople are regular contributors to television and radio news programmes, including on the national broadcaster, the BBC), its lobbying has had little impact on legislation related to, say, abortion or LGBTQ+ rights.

The staff and clients of the CLC are racially and ethnically diverse and represent a range of church backgrounds, including Anglican, Baptist, and independent. This diversity is reflective of conservative Protestantism in an increasingly multicultural and multi-ethnic Britain, one aspect of what historian David Martin has called 'the religious implications of the migratory backflow of empire'.[70] During my tenure, most staff members attended either conservative evangelical or Pentecostal churches. (Andrea, for example, attends an independent conservative evangelical church in Sussex. She previously worshipped at a conservative Anglican congregation in London that is strikingly similar, in both theology and socio-economic make-up, to Christ Church, my second field site.) Although they typically prefer to describe themselves simply as 'Christians', all staff members and clients with whom I had contact also identify, so far as I am aware, as Bible-believing Protestants. Their use of the term 'Christian', then, is exclusivist, and the fact that they are a multidenominational organisation should not be taken to mean that they are uninterested in theological distinctions. (As an opinion piece on the Christian Concern website states, 'When we are on TV, radio, or even in court we are often told that our brand of Christianity is not what lots of other Christians think.'[71]) While they support the Catholic Church's official opposition to abortion and LGBTQ+ rights, none of their high-profile cases have involved Catholic or Orthodox claimants,[72] and they do not recognise, for example, Jehovah's Witnesses or the Church of Jesus Christ of Latter-Day Saints as Christian churches. Local ecologies of conflict exist between churches that endorse Christian Concern's conservative worldview and those that do not. This conflict cuts both ways: just as those opposed to the trappings of 'Christendom' reject the public activism of their conservative peers,[73] the CLC often criticises liberal Christians (and particularly the liberal wing of the Anglican Church).

Due to the political nature of the work they undertake, neither Christian Concern nor the CLC is eligible for charitable status under UK law. Nor, however, do they operate as 'for profit' businesses. Both rely on donations to fund their work. Their legal services are offered free of charge to their clients, and the two bodies (and their charitable arm, Faith, Truth & Hope Ltd) have an annual turnover of well over £1 million pounds.[74] While they do occasionally receive large one-off gifts—in an interview with the think-tank Theos, Andrea acknowledged that they had 'very [occasionally]' received cheques of up to £50,000[75]—the majority of their funding comes in the form of the small donations I saw trickling through the letterbox during my fieldwork: a standing order for £5 a month; a one-off gift of £20.

Christian Concern also receives some funding from international donors, including from para-church organisations in the United States. Among these is Alliance Defending Freedom (ADF), a multimillion-dollar organisation based in Scottsdale, Arizona, which has contributed to some of their legal cases. ADF pioneered the use of strategic Christian-interest litigation in its efforts to counter what it frames as 'threats' to religious liberty: 'As secular forces chip away at our nation's Judeo-Christian roots, religious freedom is increasingly threatened.'[76] Paul Diamond, a barrister who has represented the CLC in many of their most high-profile cases, is an ADF Allied Attorney (as is Andrea). Speakers from ADF are always present at the Wilberforce Academy, Christian Concern's annual youth leadership conference, which is loosely based on ADF's own Blackstone Legal Fellowship (BLF).[77] Indeed, I started my fieldwork internship alongside two American law students who were carrying out their BLF placements at the Christian Legal Centre. As noted above, this close relationship with ADF has led to accusations that Christian Concern is part of an emergent (and unwelcome) US-style 'Religious Right'.[78]

While Christian Concern is extremely high-profile, it is difficult to determine its level of support with accuracy. One measure used at the office during my time there was the number of people on its e-mailing list, which was then estimated at approximately 35,000. Those on this list receive Christian Concern's weekly news digest, 'Christian Weekly News', as well as occasional updates and prayer requests relating to ongoing cases and campaigns. Regardless of the exact figures, what is certain is that Christian Concern draws support from across the social, racial, and geographical spectrum. They receive spiritual and financial assistance from all four countries in the United Kingdom; from the leafy Home Counties and industrial cities; from conservative Anglicans, Baptists, charismatics, independent evangelicals, and Pentecostals; from Asian-, black-, and white-majority churches; from the students and young professionals who attend their annual youth conference to the retirees who tend to dominate their weekday demonstrations. They have Presbyterian supporters in Northern Ireland, Pentecostal supporters in central London, and Baptist supporters on the southwest coast. It was from among this fairly diverse constituency that I sought to find a second set of interlocutors, in the form of a conservative Protestant congregation.

A Lighthouse in London: Fieldwork at Christ Church

While preparing to undertake this project, I had become interested in the ways in which everyday acts infused with Christian meaning could take on the sort of media profile and legal significance common to the Christian-interest cases. For this reason, I was keen to complement my research at the legal coalface with fieldwork at a conservative church, where I could observe and discuss these everyday acts with those for whom they remained, well, everyday. This seemed to speak to a gap in the ethnographic literature, which, despite containing numerous accounts of doctrinally varied English Christianities and accounts of Christian engagement with the democratic process, the law, and identity politics,[79] offered little insight into the relationship between Christian activists and the conservative churches that might be thought of as their natural allies.

Given Christian Concern's multidenominational supporter base, I did not limit my search to any particular denomination. My only criterion was that the church members identified as Bible-believing Protestants who, like the CLC's clients, understand the Bible to advocate socially conservative positions on such contested issues as abortion, LGBTQ+ rights, and religious pluralism. Finding a willing church, however, proved more difficult than I had anticipated. Of the four I approached, three were wary of hosting a researcher.[80] (The fourth, by contrast, had already been the subject of an ethnographic study.) By December 2012, after almost six months at Christian Concern, I was no closer to finding a church base. Yet the more time I spent with lobbyists and lawyers, the more convinced I became that their strategic use of the law to remake the world in a religious register would be best contextualised by reference to the experiences of Christians who were not personally invested in legal activism, with the reflections of evangelicals 'on the ground' reinserting quotidian Christianity into what might otherwise become an account of political rhetoric and legal discourse. Further, I hoped that multiple field sites would result in comparison by default, highlighting both parallels and differences between the two groups.

Dual-sited fieldwork also appealed for theoretical reasons. Case studies have long been viewed as an essential methodology in legal anthropology, underscoring the idea that one will learn more about dispute resolution from its practice than its theory. Yet, as John Conley and William O'Barr note, cases also risk shifting attention away from 'routine compliance with law', highlighting 'conflict' over 'concord'.[81] In other words, although we may appreciate the honesty behind Malinowski's admission that it 'lies in the nature of scientific interest, which is but refined curiosity, that it turns more readily to the extraordinary and sensational than to the normal and matter-of-course',[82] it seemed equally important to attend to the concerns of those conservative

Christians whose confrontation with these sensational forms came not from personal experience, but from the morning papers or the evening news.

It is for this reason that I am grateful to Lucy, a Christian solicitor with close social ties to the Christian Legal Centre (albeit not a staff member herself). Lucy's interest in my project ultimately led me to her home church, which I refer to (pseudonymously) throughout the book as Christ Church. I first visited Christ Church on a Sunday evening in December 2012, after which Lucy and I had dinner at a nearby Indian restaurant. Over plates of mango and coconut chicken, we discussed the place of Christianity in national life. Lucy appreciated the opportunity to put into words concerns she'd long held, but had never systematically articulated. She later introduced me to her church friends, with whom I began to meet before Sunday services at a local cafe. I was soon doing fieldwork by default. Eventually, and having received permission from one of the Christ Church staff team—an affable trainee minister named James, who cheerily responded to my request by telling me to 'fill [my] boots'—this de facto field site became *de jure*.

Founded in the late nineteenth-century, Christ Church is a large, conservative evangelical Anglican church in Greater London.[83] It is what is sometimes called a 'lighthouse church'; its reputation for 'biblically sound', unswervingly conservative teaching means smaller evangelical churches look to it to lead the way on issues of doctrinal controversy. The vast majority of its approximately five hundred members are white British (although, as one might expect from cosmopolitan London, it has sizeable minorities from as far afield as Australia, Japan, South Africa, and the United States). It has a wealthy, well-heeled, and overwhelmingly middle-class congregation. (I use 'middle-class' in the British sense, wherein 'upper class' is reserved for the aristocracy. American readers should take 'middle-class' to range from comfortably well-off to elite.) Many church members work in medicine, law, finance, teaching, and Christian ministry. Most are educated to degree level, and it is assumed that a child graduating from the church youth group at age eighteen will attend university (and a prestigious one at that). The church's noticeably middle-class culture was something its congregants often referenced, both easily—Lucy, for example, joked that although she was 'not posh enough' to have grown up writing thank you cards, she had now adjusted to Christ Church's 'thank you card culture'— and uneasily, with many members worrying that conservative evangelicalism, despite its aspirations to the universal, was really a middle-class sport.

Although Christ Church is part of the established Church of England, this is by no means an easy relationship. Many congregants are affiliated to conservative Anglican movements critical of the Church's perceived liberalism, such as Reform, which was founded in 1993 to oppose the ordination of women priests, and the Global Anglican Futures Conference (GAFCON), which 'began in 2008 when moral compromise, doctrinal error and the collapse of biblical witness in parts of the Anglican communion had reached such a level that the leaders of the majority of the world's Anglicans felt it was necessary to take a united stand for truth'.[84] Theologically, they have more in common with independent conservative churches than they do with the liberal wing of the Church of England. It was sometimes implied that at some point in the not-so-distant future, they would be unable to remain Anglican in good conscience. Yet Christ Churchites are also quick to point out that, if they no longer agree with the theological obfuscation necessary to keep the C of E together, the onus to leave should not rest with them. After all, they argue, conservatives like themselves continue to affirm the Thirty-Nine Articles (the defining doctrines of the Church of England, which date back to the sixteenth-century English Reformation). It is *liberal* Anglicans, they suggest, who have abandoned the Church's historic tenets.

During my sixteen months at Christ Church, I attended morning and eve-ning services every Sunday; joined a women's Bible study group; attended the monthly prayer meeting; took an evangelistic course; volunteered on the cof-fee rota (every service is followed by tea and coffee, which is made by volun-teers in the church kitchen and served in the church lounge); and undertook one-on-one Bible studies with two Christian women (a nurse in her fifties and a lawyer in her twenties). I ate at the communal meal that follows the eve-ning service, sometimes helping the volunteer cooks in the kitchen (where my culinary ineptitude limited my role to that of sous chef). I also attended seasonal, annual, and one-off events: April's Annual General Meeting; the autumn weekend away; missionary suppers; December's evangelistic carol services. Indeed, it was only after spending a Saturday morning cleaning the church toilets as part of its annual Spring Clean that I began to think of myself as part of the community. Because many members live within easy reach of the church by foot, car, or bus, I moved within walking distance in April 2013. This greatly facilitated my church-based social life, enabling me more easily to attend Sunday lunches, to host and be hosted for dinner, and to meet friends for Saturday morning coffees and post-work drinks. In an effort to 'Christian-ise' my new home, I followed the lead of others at Christ Church by writing out Bible passages on Post-its and adorning my walls, wardrobes, and cupboard doors with 'the Word'.

I had initially assumed that my church-based data would be somewhat secondary, acting as a supplement to that gathered at Christian Concern. However, I soon found myself captivated by Christ Churchites' efforts not only to live faithful Christian lives, but to explain the values that motivated these efforts to those who would otherwise reduce their faith in God to an emotional crutch or intellectual failing.[85] The CLC's cases and campaigns proved a useful lens through which to investigate these struggles, as my church interlocutors' longing to see the nation evangelised means they are especially sensitive to debates over how their faith 'can and should' go public.[86] Ruth Braunstein, in a comparative study of liberal faith-based organisations and conservative Tea

Party groups in the United States, argues that these competing social movements model different 'democratic imaginaries' that shape their engagement
with public life.[87] Although the members of Christian Concern and Christ
Church share their social and theological conservatism, they display differing,
albeit intersecting, *legal* imaginaries. The book's account of these intersecting
imaginaries is, I believe, unique in putting the work of English evangelical
activists in direct conversation with the experiences of (one subsection of)
the wider evangelical community these activists hope to represent, offering an
ethnographic account of both the generation and reception of legal theology
in contemporary England.[88]

This conversation was facilitated by a surprising number of informal connections between my two field sites. In addition to Lucy, I learned that Andrew
Marsh, Christian Concern's campaigns director, was a friend of Luke, the Christ
Church minister. (Andrew had even visited him when Luke lived abroad as a
missionary.) During my fieldwork, both attended the second GAFCON conference in Nairobi (as did Andrea, Christian Concern's CEO, who spoke at the
event). Theologically, Christ Church is doctrinally identical to the conservative evangelical church where Andrea had worshipped in her twenties. Andrea
described her time at this church—another Anglican lighthouse, which I will
refer to as St George's—as being 'very formative'. It was here that she 'really
got real, strong, biblical foundations like never before'. Carol, a Christ Church
member with whom I undertook regular Bible studies, had also been at St
George's during this time. She remembered Andrea well, as did Hannah, a fellow
congregant who served with the Lawyers' Christian Fellowship (the organisation from which Andrea had initially run the Christian-interest cases). I
sometimes saw younger church members wearing merchandise connected to
Christian Concern's NOT ASHAMED brand, the logo of which is a cross in a
speech bubble (NOT ASHAMED is a Christian Concern initiative focused on
publicly articulating the Christian message, even in the face of public apathy).
Perhaps the most interesting link was provided by Kate and Jim, a Christ
Church couple who had been involved in one of the CLC's earliest cases, whose
experience I recount in chapter 5. These connections cemented my interest in
the congregation's nuanced, shifting evaluations of Christian Concern's brand
of public religion, a use of legal theology that remained somewhat foreign to
their middle-class, English sensibilities; yet one which their conservative theology meant they were unable to dismiss outright.

Book Outline

This book charts the contested place of public Christianity in contemporary
England through the lens of evangelical-spearheaded politico-legal activism. It argues that this activism is equally a response to and constitutive of
the changing role of Christianity in the life of the nation, in that, by framing

certain moral norms and ritual practices as specifically *Christian*, evangelical activists risk reifying their religious worlds as something increasingly set
apart from—and potentially irrelevant to—broader English culture. In other
words, the public accommodation of religion tends to turn on its acquiescence to secular classification. The tensions that emerge between my two sets
of interlocutors are, I suggest, expressive of evangelicals' discontent with the
law's ability to shape (their) Christianity, a faith that seeks to resist the normative constraints of a liberal order even as it remains trapped within this order's
conceptual frame. I build this argument through five ethnographic chapters,
the contents of which I outline below.

Chapter 1 explores my interlocutors' 'hostile world' thesis, which posits Christians as the increasingly countercultural inhabitants of a de-
Christianising, 'hostile' state. This view both unites and differentiates my two
field sites (and, indeed, many Christian communities worldwide).[89] While
both groups agree that Britain's 'Christian heritage'—a somewhat nebulous
concept, but one in which those aspects of socio-political life deemed positive
are thought to be the result of Christianity—is being dismantled or rejected,
their responses to this process differ. For the members of Christ Church, the
hostility they (expect to) face is thought to be inevitable. For the staff of Christian Concern, by contrast, ungodly legislation is met with what I call an urgent
theology of activism, in which Christians must 'stand for Truth' regardless of
either personal cost or practical outcome. This approach helps rationalise the
pursuit of the (sometimes unwinnable) legal cases that have propelled the
organisation to fame. In focusing on particular policy areas, however, this
urgent theology also risks circumscribing and relativising Christianity, suggesting that—as a minority interest requiring protection under rights-based
law—it is merely one identitarian option among others.

Chapter 2 builds on this in the context of English law's changing approach
to the regulation of religion. It uses two of the CLC's cases, *Chaplin v Royal
Devon and Exeter NHS Foundation Trust* [2010] and *Playfoot v Millais
School* [2007], to examine the ways in which theological categories are recognised (or misrecognised) in law. These cases involved a nurse and a schoolgirl
seeking exemptions from uniform policies that prevented their wearing a cross
necklace and a purity ring respectively. Both my activist and church-based
interlocutors understood *Chaplin* and *Playfoot* in terms of an archetypically
Protestant distinction between grace and law, albeit in different ways. For
those at the Christian Legal Centre, these cases functioned as proof of the
legal system's discrimination against Christians. By virtue of Reformed Christianity's antinomian approach to religious dress—that is, because Protestants
do not usually see religious dress as a *requirement*—the courts felt justified in
denying these claimants the 'right' to wear religious jewellery. The Christian
Legal Centre interpreted this as anti-Christian bias. For the members of Christ
Church, however, the cases were problematic precisely because they seemed

to imply that one *needed* to wear a cross to be a Christian, thereby conflating grace and law and misrepresenting the faith to outsiders. I use this theo-legal dispute to explore the ways in which English law constructs material religion as optional and inessential, such that cases aiming to protect the right to wear religious jewellery end up confirming the ease with which restrictions can be placed on it.

Chapter 3 zeroes in on one aspect of Britain's contemporary legal culture: the rise of rights-based discourse. It argues that by framing their cases as conflicts of rights, the CLC aims to undermine the universalism of human rights language. By constructing themselves as a marginalised counterpublic whose rights are frequently 'trumped', they hope to convince their fellow Britons that a society built upon the logic of competing rights cannot hope to deliver human flourishing. By contrast, only a society based on the foundational Truths of the Bible can achieve the utopian vision sought after by rights proponents. The chapter concludes that although the CLC has been successful in highlighting the inconsistency of human rights idealism, the use of rights-based claims to undermine a rights-based legal framework leaves them open to the charge that they are reinforcing the very system they hope to challenge.

Sticking with rights discourse, chapter 4 focuses on the way this language is deployed at Christ Church. Although Christianity and human rights are sometimes genealogically linked, I show that English law's replacement of the 'passive accommodation' of religion with the more robust 'prescriptive regulation' of a positive right to freedom of religion is experienced by some conservative Protestants as a *dilution* of their religious liberty.[90] Drawing on comparative Melanesian ethnography, I discuss the values of individualism and relationalism in global Christianities to argue that, for those at Christ Church, the perceived egocentrism of rights-based claims is thought to undermine the relationality necessary for a successful gospel encounter. For this reason, Christ Churchites encourage one another to forgo their rights for the sake of the gospel. This suggests that, even among those who embrace the interior, conscience-driven understanding of religion privileged by Euro-American law, there is little faith in the state's ability to protect religious liberty, with positive rights seen to privilege secular norms over Christian morality.

Moving from legal activism to political lobbying, chapter 5 explores my interlocutors' use of biblically-inflected speech in political debate. It begins by examining the arguments raised by conservative Christian activists in their campaign to prevent the passage of the Marriage (Same-Sex Couples) Act 2013. Introducing the concept of 'communicative doubt', I argue that there is a sense in which neither 'religious' nor 'secular' arguments are thought to be an appropriate means of conveying Biblical Truth to those who are not (yet) Christian, for what is needed is the intervention of a speaking God. I then explore this doubt as it manifested in the lives of two Christ Church members, Kate and Jim, who had been involved in one of the Christian Legal Centre's earliest cases. Five years on, they remained unsure of whether or not it communicated the Good News they'd hoped to share. These doubts, hesitations, and ambivalences speak to the contested place of public Christianity in contemporary England, and to the difficulties faced by those who insist that their faith must go public: the challenge of rendering Christianity legible not only to law and politics, but to the individual men and women who are subject to these worldly institutions.

Finally, the Conclusion returns to the Synod debate referenced above to draw together these threads, highlighting the almost paradoxical situation in which English evangelical Protestants feel themselves to live: one in which Christianity is valued as an aspect of heritage, but rejected as a living faith.

Ethical Considerations: A Note to Readers at Christ Church and Christian Concern

It is now almost clichéd to refer to conservative Protestants as being, in Harding's terms, anthropology's 'repugnant cultural others'.[91] Yet this does not change the fact that my research continues to be met with surprise or suspicion from friends and colleagues, who, during seminars and conferences, either challenge me for being too 'sympathetic' to my interlocutors, or phrase their questions in such a way as to ascertain whether I, too, accept the capital-T Truth claims they make. This is, perhaps, an occupational hazard of my sharing so many of my interlocutors' characteristics: as a white, university-educated, lapsed Irish Catholic, I have much in common with the (primarily) white, university-educated, practicing British Protestants with whom I was in dialogue.[92] Or perhaps, as Joel Robbins suggests in his account of anthropologists' difficulties with Christianity, it is because 'Christians . . . appear at once too similar to anthropologists to be worthy of study and too meaningfully different to be easily made sense of by the use of standard anthropological tools'.[93] This interplay of similarity and difference—the fact that both Christianity and anthropology make claims 'concerning the bases of knowledge or the importance of tolerance', but come to very different conclusions about them—renders the task of familiarising the exotic, and exoticising the familiar, particularly challenging.

Given the nature of some of my interlocutors' political beliefs (and the passion with which they publicly articulate them), there were instances in the field where I felt acutely uncomfortable on account of my proximity to those espousing very different ethical commitments to my own. And this 'problem of belief', as the anthropologist Matthew Engelke puts it, was equally discomfiting for those participating in my research.[94] As time went on, it became apparent that, to some Christian Concern staff, the fact that I had not been born again posed a serious impediment to my ability to understand their work. But surely ethnographers do not have to agree on the moral value of a belief, practice, or political position to appreciate that it is understood *as* a moral practice from another perspective or social world.[95] While I do not deny that my interlocutors and I approach many of the topics on which this book focuses from very different vantage points, I follow Michael Lambek in arguing that the anthropologist 'ought to be able to locate something in the sphere or domain of the moral, as having an ethical quality, without [themselves] thereby necessarily either placing a value judgment on it or, conversely, cautiously refusing to do so'.[96] As such, I do not seek to uncover, as Saba Mahmood once put it, a 'redeemable element' in politics that are not my own.[97] Nor do I aim to sensationalise or demonise a movement that some readers will already find unsettling.

I take this opportunity, then, to thank those I met at both Christian Concern and Christ Church, and to explicitly state that my purpose is neither to cast aspersions on nor to rescue our differences of opinion. (As scholar of religion Joram Tarusarira would say, albeit of a very different context, to humanise is not to endorse.[98]) Barring those instances where disagreements led to ethnographic insight, I do not focus on them in what follows. Writing of an approach to biblical studies that seeks neither to valorise nor demystify the Bible, scholar of religion Yvonne Sherwood suggests that '[t]o explore blasphemy and profanation is, by definition, to be interested in and invested in the sacred and, relatedly, questions of proximity and distance, fidelity and faith'.[99] It was impossible to undertake this research without this 'investment in the sacred', and I hope and trust that my interlocutors will take my findings in the spirit of 'proximity and distance, fidelity and faith' with which they were written.

CHAPTER ONE

Confronting a Hostile World

If the world hates you, know that it has hated me before it hated you.

—JOHN 15:18

Laura and the Lions' Den

One Saturday morning in mid-October, I travelled to Methodist Central Hall, Westminster, to attend the London Women's Convention, an annual Christian conference run by an evangelical women's group. I had been invited by Leah, a lawyer in her twenties, who was attending the conference with a number of friends from Christ Church. Built in the first decade of the twentieth century in the elaborate Viennese Baroque style, Methodist Central Hall is central London's largest conference venue. We arrived to find it packed with women casually dressed in jeans, sweaters, and boots, who ranged in age from teenaged students to the retired. Old friends greeted each other with warm embraces, and new friends were introduced: *X and I met at our school's Christian Union; Oh, then you must know So-and-so? We used to run a Christian camp together!* The auditorium buzzed with the laughter and conversation of the assembled crowd. All were looking forward to gaining a biblical foothold on this year's Convention theme: 'Live, Pray, Hope in a Hostile World'.

No sooner had Leah and I taken our seats than the programme began. After an introductory prayer acknowledging God's sovereignty over the nation, we stood to sing a number of up-tempo worship songs. Attendees raised their hands and danced where they stood. Others swayed gently to the music. All sang enthusiastically. We were in fine voice; the building reverberated with the sound of hundreds of women singing, our songs of praise reaching up to fill the hall's ornate domed ceiling.

The conference was organised around the Book of Daniel. A Jewish exile in pagan Babylon, Daniel is one of the great heroes of the Old Testament. In perhaps one of the most famous of the biblical narratives, Daniel's refusal to compromise his faith results in his being handed what ought to be a certain death sentence: a night in the lions' den. For centuries, his miraculous protection during this trial has been read as evidence that, even in the face of persecution, God will not abandon those who honour Him and keep His commandments. Laura, the Convention's main speaker, explained why she had chosen Daniel for this year's conference theme:

> I think we all know the Book of Daniel. Lots of people are teaching it at the moment, I think because it is becoming increasingly relevant for us in Britain, and we'll be thinking about that through the talks. [My husband and I get a weekly] email from Christian Concern, and week after week more and more stories are coming through of Christians who are in the firing line for their faith.[1] I think it's going to become more and more common for us, so I think the Book of Daniel really girds our lives. I think it gives us such a fantastic example of God's people living in a hostile world.

She defined the national context in which she spoke as one of 'escalating hostility' towards Christians and Christian values: 'the historic validity of scripture, Christ Himself, moral absolutes, Christian lifestyle: everything is under assault'.

From her position on the podium at Methodist Central Hall, Laura was physically surrounded by the trappings of what might be thought of, and what was often described, as a Christian country.[2] Central Hall is just a stone's throw away from the Houses of Parliament and Westminster Abbey, both tangible proof of the ways in which Christianity is 'literally incorporated', as Matthew Engelke puts it, into the physical and political architecture of the United Kingdom of Great Britain and Northern Ireland.[3] (Interestingly, it also plays a key role in Andrea's Christian testimony. Although she had fallen in love with Jesus as a small child at Sunday School, it was as a teenager at a mission event at Methodist Central Hall that Andrea pledged to spend her life serving Him.) What, then, did it mean for Laura to say that the Book of Daniel was 'increasingly relevant' for Christians in Britain, including the approximately two thousand women who would hear her preach over the course of the Convention?

This chapter introduces the ethnographic context in which my interlocutors live, focusing on the ways in which they, like other Christians before them, construct themselves as the inhabitants of a hostile world. It begins with a discussion of Christian Concern's culturally fundamentalist vision of Britain's religious heritage, in which perceived attacks on those cultural structures and assumptions that form 'the "givens" of life' result in apocalyptic warnings of a destabilised, disorderly, and increasingly bleak future.[4] I then turn to the members of Christ Church to explore how the hostile world thesis is received by conservative evangelicals who are not formally involved in religious lobbying or legal activism, calling attention to the contested nature of this narrative and the heterogeneous responses it evokes among those who identify as conservative Christians. While Christian Concern's public statements often stress their surprise at the rapidity with which, in the words of their website, the nation has 'turned her back on Jesus and embraced alternative ideas such as secular liberal humanism, moral relativism and sexual licence',[5] those at Christ Church tend to view this transformation as inevitable: in a fallen world, it is to be expected that true Christianity is unpopular. Because they understand the increasing hostility they (expect to) face as the norm for Christians, both historically and in the contemporary moment, it is the ostensibly Christian *past* which ought to be thought of as unusual.

This suggests a potential tension in Christian Concern's stated project. Given that Jesus warned those who followed Him that they would be reviled— 'because you are not of the world, but I chose you out of the world, therefore the world hates you' (John 15:19)—we might wonder what these activists seek to achieve in their public-facing work. This chapter's third section focuses on this apparent paradox to suggest that, for my activist interlocutors, success cannot be measured in terms of cases won or laws changed. Rather, their theology of activism rejects a focus on the results of cases and campaigns in favour of an emphasis on the immediate necessity of 'standing', regardless of the worldly outcome of this stand. By displacing attention from the long to the short term, I suggest that this rhetorical strategy offers a biblical justification for what Christian Concern's opponents would see as failures or defeats, even as it remains always open to the possibility of divine intervention and radical social change. This *urgent theology* can account for both worldly success and worldly failure, thereby accommodating the variety of theological positions represented by Christian Concern's staff and supporters.

Truth under Attack

Christian Concern presents Christianity as coming under attack on two fronts. First, Christian *principles* are seen to be under threat from 'permissive' legislation,[6] such as the Abortion Act 1967 (which, providing certain conditions are met, offers a defence to the crime of procuring a miscarriage), the Equality Act 2010 (which outlaws discrimination on the basis of 'protected characteristics', including gender and sexual orientation), and the Marriage (Same-Sex Couples) Act 2013 (which legalised marriage between partners of the same sex). This legislation is seen to be contrary to God's will. Second, Christian *people* are thought to be under attack from the various lobbies, interest groups, and employers who are opposed to the public expression of Christian principles and penalise those who attempt to 'live them out'. (What counts as excessively permissive legislation is, of course, a matter of debate, including among England's conservative Protestant community.)

Although both fronts bleed into each other, it is this distinction—between principles and people—that explains the difference between Christian Concern and the CLC. Christian Concern, as a lobby group, exists to campaign against laws that undermine God's design for human flourishing, whereas the CLC exists to defend those who, by refusing to compromise their biblical faith, have fallen foul of these laws. These cases are thought to be the logical result of the increasing number of holes in Britain's previously Christian social fabric, holes which have come about through intentional ripping—Acts of Parliament pushed through by intolerant secularists, say, or the result of a small but vociferous LGBTQ+ lobby—and through unintentional fraying, such as the general public's perceived religious illiteracy, or the increasing purchase of a multicultural relativism that posits Christianity as just one faith among many.

This was explained to me by Andrea, CEO of Christian Concern and the CLC, when we sat down for an interview on an unseasonably cold day in May 2013. The Marriage (Same-Sex Couples) Bill was then going through Parliament, and Christian Concern was at the forefront of the conservative Christian community's opposition to its passage (see chapter 5 for more details on this campaign). They had spent the first few months of 2013 organising prayer rallies outside the Houses of Parliament, sending regular prayer requests and updates to their 35,000-strong mailing list, and lobbying MPs to vote against the bill. As such, Andrea's schedule—which was full at the best of times—had been pushed to breaking point, and the bill was at the forefront of her mind. When I asked what she saw as Christian Concern's raison d'être, her answer included a reference to same-sex marriage:

> It's a campaign organisation which seeks to proclaim Christ in the public sphere, in law, media and politics, and particularly where Truth is under attack. And nothing could be more evident of that than this week, where we see the first building block for society, marriage, being undermined at the heart of our Parliamentary system.

By 'Truth' Andrea is referring to the tenets of reformed evangelicalism, a socially conservative theology that stresses the depravity of humankind, the necessity of trusting in Christ's substitutionary death for salvation, and the inerrancy of the Bible. Although every generation of Christians will be asked to defend biblical Truth—'I think at any moment in history, gospel Truth is under attack in a particular sphere'—the example that sprang most readily to Andrea's mind in the Spring of 2013 was the God-given institution of marriage, then 'under attack' from its proposed extension to gay and lesbian couples. This threat to marriage could not be seen in a vacuum. Rather, because the Bible is thought to provide a holistic approach to moral living, challenges to God's plan for marriage are linked to the many policy areas in which His 'blueprint' or 'good pattern' for society is under attack, including the sanctity of life, the exclusivity of Jesus Christ (that is, the belief that faith in Christ is the only way to achieve salvation), and freedom to proclaim the gospel.

Andrea believes that previous generations of Britons underwrote the UK's legal and parliamentary systems with what she sees as Christian values. She credits Britain's historic 'flourishing'—including the development of parliamentary democracy and the common law, and their exportation through the British Empire—to this Christian heritage, the result of God 'prospering' those who keep His commands. Such an understanding of the relationship between faith and law presumes the Bible and liberal democracy to be not just compatible, but genealogically linked, with Christianity having both civilising and liberalising effects.[7]

As with 'vernacular theology', which may not live up to the standards of academic theologians, this vernacular history ought to be taken as a cultural product rather than as a coherent historiography.[8] It is a reading that, perhaps of necessity, is somewhat messy and incomplete. The historic failure of the ostensibly Christian past to actually achieve universal human flourishing is accounted for by the inevitable presence of sin in every age. At the risk of caricature, for example, William Wilberforce's campaign against the slave trade is happily claimed as the fruit of his Christian faith, while those eighteenth-century Christians who looked to Scripture to justify the possession of human chattel are seen to have misunderstood the Bible, to have been caught up in sin, or to prove the distinction between professed and true Christian conversion. In this way, the potential (if always contested) justifications for violence, authoritarianism, and inequality present in the Bible are displaced onto Protestant England's religious Others, with England's 'traditional' or 'home' Scriptures largely purged of these disruptive associations.[9]

The majority of Christian Concern's staff agree that Britain's institutions of law, politics, and justice have been positively shaped by their Christian roots. Andrew, the group's campaigns director, felt that a country could self-consciously identify with 'the person of Jesus Christ' through its constitution and legal framework. Similarly, Maria, a CLC lawyer, explained that although 'some people would like us to forget that Britain does have a Judeo-Christian heritage', it was from this heritage that 'we've got all our freedoms', freedoms 'based on what God says and how that's been brought into society hundreds of years ago'. Carrie and Louise, who worked, respectively, in events management and finance, felt that the principles of the welfare state and the National Health Service (NHS)—of which Britons from across the political spectrum are, as a general rule, extremely proud—were also those of the Bible.[10]

Indeed, the only Christian Concern affiliate who was openly sceptical about this narrative, at least in conversation with me, was Jake, a British-Nigerian film maker who produces videos for the organisation. When asked whether Britain was, at least historically, a Christian nation, he explained that it was difficult to answer this question without 'sounding and being African, being black'. Christianity had been used, he felt, to achieve 'an agenda beyond Christianity', namely, imperialism: 'The Englishman wants to rule, and he will use anything he can.' He acknowledged that this was a surprising position for a Christian Concern staffer to take, but felt that a direct question required a direct answer. As a general rule, however, and despite some staff members having family ties to formerly colonised countries in Africa, the Caribbean, and South Asia, there was remarkably little discussion of the British Empire among my Christian Concern colleagues.

By contrast to Jake's account, Andrea sometimes spoke of Britain's Christianity-infused political and legal structures as having been 'copied' the world over. The distinction between 'copying' and colonial enforcement was not dwelt on, and I was sometimes surprised by how uncomplicated this heritage was taken to be. It seemed to encompass everything that continues to be seen as positive in British history and culture, while excluding those elements— such as racism, sexism, and classism—that, although baked into the structure of the British establishment, have recently come to be questioned. (It is worth noting that the fairly positive view of Britain's colonial past implied here is not unique to Christian activists. A 2014 poll carried out by YouGov, for example, found that 59 percent of respondents felt the British Empire was something to be 'proud' of, with only 19 percent thinking it was a source of shame. On the question of the Empire's legacy, almost half of respondents felt that countries colonised by Britain were 'better off' as a result.)[11]

If adherence to the Bible was what had allowed Britain to flourish, its contemporary rejection of the Word suggests that God will no longer 'prosper' the nation. Rather, He will allow it to suffer the consequence of its disobedience, including progressive immorality and social breakdown. This pessimistic message was often expressed in presentations to church groups and Christian organisations. One sunny Saturday morning in July 2012, for example, Andrea was the guest speaker at a north London Christian women's group. The meeting, which took place in the dining room of a local hotel, began with the assembled women sharing that culinary staple of the British Isles: a fry up, complete with bacon, sausages, scrambled eggs, toast, and tea. After breakfast, Andrea rose to speak. It was just a few weeks until London would host the 2012 Summer Olympics, and she began by saying that she loved her country and was looking forward to supporting Britain's athletes in their various sporting endeavours. Yet she stood before us with 'a heavy heart for our nation'. 'What made Great Britain great?' she asked rhetorically. Great Britain was great, she ventured, because it had been 'founded on Christ'. This was no longer the case. The results were 'bad laws' and the 'breakdown of families'.

Frequent references to the apocalyptic moral consequences of religious decline suggest a culturally fundamentalist relationship with this Christian past.[12] Writing of the defeat of the Equal Rights Amendment (ERA), a proposed amendment to the US Constitution that would have prohibited discrimination 'on account of sex', Donald Mathews and Jane De Hart define cultural fundamentalism in terms of a 'moral imagination' that rejects 'the flexibility of cultural forms', preferring instead to view these forms as natural and fixed.[13] Although cultural fundamentalism does not require 'a transcendent religious commitment', the fixity of contested norms—the immutability of distinct gender roles, for example—are often explained by reference to their having been ordained by God.[14] As Mathews and De Hart note, an absolute emphasis on traditional values as the key to a well-ordered society renders perceived diversions from these ahistorical norms anomalous, disruptive, even threatening; the very same sentiments expressed by those who worry that 'permissive' legislation has resulted in a hostile world for Christian principles and Christian people. As with those who warned that the adoption of the ERA would result in families torn apart, femininity destroyed, and the foundations of society fatally weakened, Christian Concern warns of the dire consequences of rejecting the eternal Truth of the Christian faith. As one staff member put it: 'I fear for what our children will inherit if this tide is not reversed.'

This framing of the world, which views historicist understandings of social change as an exercise in moral relativism, has resulted in Christian activists adopting a Janus-like temporal orientation. Many Christians operate within a temporality that posits their heavenly eternal destiny as being of more pressing concern than their mundane present. The Urapmin Baptists, among whom Joel Robbins carried out fieldwork, for example, are 'forever pitched forward', with their primary attention directed towards the future,[15] while Susan Harding has explored the ways in which American fundamentalist preachers encourage their congregations to view contemporary political events as 'signs' that point towards the fulfilment of biblical prophecy.[16] Noting this tendency towards the eschatological, the anthropologist Jane Guyer has suggested that contemporary evangelicals 'evacuate' the near future of meaning, focusing instead on the immediate and the long term (that is, today and the Second Coming). For Guyer, the evangelical near future is a 'hiatus' or 'gap', the intelligibility of which is 'in abeyance'.[17] Damian Thompson and Joseph Webster, meanwhile, have offered accounts of Christians in central London and coastal Scotland seeking out evidence that they are living in the End Times.[18]

Even as they look forward to the Second Coming, however, the members of Christian Concern also orient themselves in relation to the past. Their focus on the fact that society is, to quote Marilyn Strathern on the rhetoric of traditional values, '*going somewhere*' has led them to conclude that 'back to tradition may be the best way forward'.[19] They find the speed with which society is 'going somewhere' particularly troubling, for without intervention the logical end point of these legislative and cultural assaults is presumed to be nothing less than outright persecution. As Andrea once put it in an opinion piece for the *Law Society Gazette*, 'I believe Christians are seeing the beginnings of persecution in the UK because, as a nation, we have forgotten our history, our heritage and our Christian foundations.'[20] This prompts the sense of urgency evident in Christian Concern's public engagement, an urgency born of both a forward-looking desire to revitalise and of the pull of an imagined past. Such a past appears, from the outside, to be equal parts concrete and nebulous; an idea strongly felt, yet difficult to define.

The temporal qualification in the above quote—in which Andrea suggests that British Christians are seeing '*the beginnings*' of persecution—is significant. It is important to note that although many activists view themselves as living in a hostile world, they do not equate this to the situation facing Christians in, for example, North Korea, Somalia, or Iraq. The differences in scale and severity are readily acknowledged. Yet the two are seen to share, as it was once put it to me, a 'subtle continuity'. This is often missed in media accounts and editorials dismissive of Christian Concern's brand of activism. In an opinion piece decrying the persecution of Christians worldwide, for example, journalist Paul Vallely criticized those who used the language of persecution to describe such 'trivial' issues as 'receptionists being banned from wearing religious jewellery': 'Adopting the rhetoric of persecution on such matters obscures the very real persecution of Christians being killed or driven from their homes elsewhere in the globe.'[21] But as Andrew Marsh, Christian Concern's campaigns director, argued during a slot on the BBC's Sunday Morning Live programme, the two were comparable to early and late stage cancer. Yes, one was much more serious; but shouldn't the early stage disease be treated too, *before things got worse?* To Andrew's co-panellists on Sunday Morning Live, including the head of the British Humanist Association, this comparison was rejected as offensive to those Christians undergoing—for want of a better word—'real' persecution. But from the perspective of Christian Concern, real persecution doesn't emerge out of the ether. Rather, it starts with small acts of opposition: with losing one's job for wearing a Christian symbol; with the refusal to accommodate a conscientious objection.

This idea was brought out most strikingly during a conversation with Jake, the film producer introduced above. In addition to his work with Christian Concern, Jake is an activist in his own right. He runs campaigns to raise awareness of sectarian violence in central and northern Nigeria, where the church he had once pastored had been repeatedly, violently, and often fatally attacked by Muslim militants. A tall, broad man with a neat, clipped beard, Jake had a knack for disarming me with his candour. I once hesitantly asked him whether he 'really' thought the horrific things he had seen in Nigeria could happen in England. His answer was devastating in its conviction: 'I don't think it will happen. I *know* it will happen.' It was, he explained, only a matter of time. To those who doubted the possibility of escalation, he offered his experience in Nigeria. Prior to the attacks, a friend had warned him that, before too long, his community would be targeted. 'And I was like "forget it. I've been living here for many years. All my landlords have been Muslims. This is the most peaceful place. It would never happen." In less than a year, we were attacked.'

Jake was speaking specifically of the risk of what Christian Concern calls 'radical Islam'. What's important for our purposes, however, is the gradual intensification of the violence he described. He disproved the assertions of those opponents of Christian activism who supposed that, if Christians in the UK knew the 'reality' of persecution, they would not approve of the 'trivial' cases handled by the CLC. (A number of Christians from more liberal congregations told me they felt the organisation's rhetoric was disrespectful to those facing 'real' persecution.) After all, it was a reality he knew all too well. He had seen his neighbours cut down in the street. He could recount, in truly harrowing detail, the experience of weaving his car through the bodies of his fellow believers. He had seen his congregation murdered and turned into murderers. But it did not start that way. 'It started just with "oh, well, you can't have your church here, you know, you have to go down the road."' It had started with 'a little here, a little there'.

In this hostile world, my interlocutors feel obliged to fight back. But having been warned that they will always be persecuted for their faith, it is sometimes unclear what results they expect. Before considering their theology of activism, I now turn to the congregation of Christ Church in an effort to enhance our understanding of the nation's Christian past, its hostile present, and the meaning of persecution.

Unfair Things

Throughout my Christ Church tenure, I spent a great deal of time studying the Bible under the tutelage of Carol, a nurse in her fifties. Carol, who lives just minutes from the church, is a slim woman with curly, greying hair and a warm, ready smile. Although many members of the church community were generous with their time, trust, and knowledge, Carol was, perhaps, exceptionally charitable in this regard. We had first met at Christianity Explored, a five-week course for curious non-Christians interested in learning about the Christian faith, where Carol had been one of the course leaders (see chapter 2). Having taken an immediate interest in my project (and my salvation), she would often invite me to her flat to discuss life, the universe, and everything over a cup of tea and a specially selected Bible passage. A long-time member of a Christian nurses' association with a particular interest in students, she was used to conducting one-on-one Bible studies with people in my demographic, that is, women in their twenties. Different in form from either the formal, expository preaching the congregation received from the pulpit, or the more egalitarian, discussion-based ethos of my women's Bible study group (see chapter 4), Carol's well-honed one-on-one approach was almost Socratic in method, with each guided question—*What is the Apostle Paul writing about in these passages? What sort of evidence does he use? Why might this be surprising?*—placing me, gently but unequivocally, in the role of a novice under instruction. And although I certainly began as one, I like to think that Carol's unparalleled generosity was not in vain; I learnt as much theology sitting in her comfortable living room as I did in the church pews a few doors down.

One afternoon in the summer of 2013, I arrived at Carol's flat to find her casually dressed in tracksuit bottoms and a t-shirt, hard at work in her small kitchen. She was, as she often did, baking in honour of my visit. Today's treats were homemade chocolate biscuits sandwiched together with buttercream icing. Over the noise of an electric whisk beating together butter and cocoa powder, Carol told me that she had recently given a presentation on Psalm 23 to a group of Christian healthcare professionals. Psalm 23 is one of the best known, and best loved, psalms in the Bible, beginning with the famous words 'The Lord is my shepherd, I shall not want.' Although the older Christians in the audience had all known the verses, many of them by heart, it had seemed remarkably unfamiliar to the student nurses present. Carol had found this very surprising. She recalled it as 'the Psalm of my childhood', the stock Psalm of school assemblies. That her younger colleagues did not have this relationship with it was indicative, she reflected sadly, of the 'erosion' of Britain's Christian heritage.

The results of this 'erosion' were not limited to young nurses' inability to recite the Psalms. Having made our biscuits, we retired to Carol's living room to continue our conversation. Up until the 1950s, she explained, many British people had accepted the moral strictures laid out in the Bible. Most people, whether or not they had a personal relationship with Jesus Christ, '*were* living "moral lives", in inverted commas'. Now, however, the majority of people seemed to have decided that 'no, we don't give a stuff about Christianity', and there was increasing pressure on Christians not to speak about their beliefs. Some of the nursing students she worked with, for example, had even asked whether or not it was legal for them to share their faith with their patients. Given this explicitly anti-Christian climate, she thought that 'ultimately, it could easily be that I will know people who will be imprisoned for their faith'.

From my position in one of her comfortable leather armchairs, with the smell of freshly baked chocolate biscuits still wafting through the air and the sound of the birds chirping on her leafy, suburban street coming through the open windows, the thought of Carol or her co-congregants being imprisoned for their faith seemed a fairly remote possibility. Responding to my surprise, she explained that 'there are unfair things happening', particularly in secular workplaces. While most of the Christians being 'caught out' at work were 'caught on technicalities rather than "we don't like you because you're a Christian"', the real issue seemed to be that they had shown 'their faith' at work. As with the incremental process described by Jake at Christian Concern, the fact that 'unfair things' were already happening was taken as evidence that things would, most likely, get worse.

Carol was not alone in this belief. A similar theme emerged during a conversation with James, a Christ Church curate (assistant minister), over a coffee one wintery afternoon. A tall, slim man who is always keen to share a joke, James is much loved by the church family. His voice bubbles with energy, enthusiasm, and good humour. As we discussed the Christian discrimination cases, however, he became more serious. Pausing to sip a decaf cappuccino, he told me that although he didn't take a particular interest in the cases, he read about them when they surfaced in the press. In a matter-of-fact tone, he suggested that they would become more common in future. Societal changes meant that Christians were increasingly likely to rub up against the laws of the land, 'and I'm sure some of us will go to prison within the next few years for being Christians'. James linked the likelihood of his incarceration to wider society becoming 'less and less' Christian.[22] In this Christian ontology, identity, belief, and practice are infrangible, such that those going to prison 'for being Christians' would be doing so because they could not separate a belief from its implementation.

These musings on future persecution highlight the tension in what Winnifred Fallers Sullivan calls 'legal' religion, or the law's imagining of religiosity. By affirming the protection of religious belief while limiting the right to 'manifest' those beliefs, European human rights law posits a distinction between conviction and action. This distinction is wholly at odds with the desires of those seeking to cultivate and express what the anthropologist James Laidlaw, using philosopher Bernard Williams' terminology, frames as a 'moral incapacity' to disobey divine commands.[23] Andrea, for example, would often say that the courts' interpretation of equality law meant that Christians 'could not' be registrars or sex therapists, as the law now required them to treat gay or lesbian couples as morally equivalent to heterosexual couples. The language of (in)ability—'could not'—rather than personal preference—'would not'—is of critical importance here. As we shall see throughout this book, it is the law's refusal to appreciate the force of this incapacity that causes the CLC and its clients such difficulty—an issue that is particularly ironic in light of the fact that, by defining religion in belief-centric terms, this legal religion owes a genealogical debt to Reformed Christianity.[24] Indeed, disputes over the meaning of religious liberty often play a critical role in the construction of legally recognisable religion through their marking of certain practices as anathema to the public good, notions which, as Sarah Barringer Gordon puts it of the US context, often appear to be both secular and 'indelibly Protestant'.[25]

But whereas Andrea expressed surprise at the speed with which the law had been severed from its ostensibly Christian roots, stating in an opinion piece in the *Daily Mail* tabloid newspaper that 'I never imagined that my skills as a lawyer would be used to defend Christians for following their faith in 21st Century Britain',[26] the members of Christ Church expressed no such surprise. Indeed, they seemed almost resigned. Carol, after explaining that imprisonment might be the logical end point of a scenario in which Christians were already losing their jobs, suggested that reformed evangelicals were 'coming out of a period that's probably been *ab*normal for Christians, and the norm is for people to not like us'. James, for his part, stated that it was 'no surprise' that Bible-believing, conservative Christians were in the minority in Britain: Throughout the Bible, Christians have always been a small number.' For those at Christ Church, the preferred response to this hostility was to continue to evangelise, readying oneself for the coming trials while pointing others towards God.

Leah, the lawyer with whom I attended the London Women's Convention, expressed a similar view. A petite brunette, Leah is a committed member of the church. In addition to co-leading a students' and young graduates' Bible study group, she is a member of a prayer triplet (a three-person accountability and prayer request group) and is a regular fixture at the communal meal served after the Sunday evening service. Leah tries to live for Christ during her every waking moment. (While exercising at the local swimming pool, for example, she goes through the alphabet praying for her colleagues, friends, and family: one letter, one name, one lap's worth of prayers.) Apart from losing some non-Christian friends at school, Leah hadn't experienced any hostility on account of her religion. Rather than putting this down to the inoffensiveness of her faith, her cheerful disposition, or her good relationships with friends and co-workers, though, she framed it in terms of a personal failing. Perhaps, she ventured, the reason she hadn't received much flak was because she was not being 'distinctive' or 'bold enough', at least not yet: 'The Bible warns us on numerous occasions, there will be persecution and there will be trouble. You see it now, you know, people who are losing their jobs because they stand up for what they believe in.' As such, Leah claimed she wouldn't be surprised to face opposition in the future. If anything, she felt it might be a sign 'that I was going in the right direction. Obviously it wouldn't be pleasant, but I would think, "Yeah, this is what we've been warned in the Bible that we probably will experience."'

Of course, it is important not to overstate my interlocutors' concern with the threat of persecution, nor to dehistoricise their understanding of Christian Britain. It was sometimes pointed out to me that the eighteenth-century England of the Wesley brothers was even less 'godly' than the England of our current day. Further, references to the imminence of state-backed persecution were often tempered by the recognition that, when compared with the situation facing contemporary martyrs, the members of Christ Church were living in an age of unparalleled religious liberty. For example, during a session with my women's Bible study group, Catherine, the group's amateur church historian, remarked that she would not be surprised if evangelical ministers began to be arrested under hate speech legislation. Perhaps, she mused, it would happen within the decade. Kristen, who had recently joined the church, said these arrests were already happening. She offered as proof the case of Tony Miano, a CLC client who had been arrested in southwest London after members of the public complained about his street preaching. Catherine agreed: 'We're getting to a stage where biblical Christianity will be ghettoised.' Yet when it came time to close the study with a prayer, the group prayed in thanks that Christians in Britain could practice their faith freely, while so many others risked life and limb simply by attending church.

All this points to the somewhat liminal experience, from an emic or internal perspective, of identifying as a conservative evangelical Anglican: ongoing membership of the established Church of England, but a feeling of marginality within it. Perhaps this is the inevitable result of Christianity's emphasis on sacrifice and martyrdom, which encourages believers to identify with ancient Jewish and early Christian victims of persecution. Christian Smith's account of American evangelicals as both 'embattled and thriving', for example, suggests that many such Christians draw parallels between themselves and the persecuted early church,[27] while Anna Strhan's ethnography of a conservative Anglican community in London confirms that Christianity's alleged marginality is emphasised even among members of legally established churches (and even when the congregation, as in this case, is exceptionally privileged in terms of social class).[28]

Regardless of its theological underpinning, many members of Christ Church expressed a belief that the freedom currently extended to British evangelicals was, as Carol put it, '*ab*normal' for (true) Christians. As one church member explained from the pulpit while leading prayers on the International Day of Prayer for the Persecuted Church, the persecution facing Christians abroad should not come as a surprise, for the Bible tells us that 'anyone desiring to live a godly life will be persecuted'. These biblical references to persecution raise questions as to the rationale behind the work of Christian Concern and the CLC. If God's Word predicts persecution, what could political lobbying and legal activism actually achieve? Rather than expressing surprise that Christians in twenty-first century Britain needed legal defence, one could just as easily argue—as Carol, Leah, and James seemed to suggest—that this was exactly the sort of situation that Christian Concern ought to have expected.

In fact, this *was* how many of the activists I met understood the responses they sometimes received from non-Christians. To take but one example, in the summer of 2012 I attended a small demonstration organised by the Core Issues Trust (CIT), an 'ex-gay' ministry that aims to help those who are unhappily 'same-sex attracted' develop their heterosexual potential. The demonstration was held outside the British Library, in London's busy King's Cross. The Library was hosting a conference run by Stonewall, the UK's premier

LGBTQ+ rights charity, on how to combat homophobic bullying in schools. From CIT's perspective, Stonewall's anti-bullying platform was merely an attempt to 'normalise' homosexuality, and they were protesting for this reason. Throughout the demonstration, those wearing the Trust's distinctive red t-shirts, which bore the slogan GAY FEELINGS CAN CHANGE, were subject to abuse from passersby, many of whom found this message abhorrent. As a fieldworker and Christian Concern intern (albeit one who had declined to wear the T-shirt), I was also on the receiving end of this hostility. I had never before had a stranger tell me that I was 'disgusting' and 'should be ashamed' of myself. I found it a distressing experience, one which required a number of deep, steadying breaths and repeated reminders of the importance of participant observation in anthropology's methodological toolbox. In marked contrast to my reaction, however, when I asked one of the demonstrators how she felt the protest had gone, she explained that Christians rejoice when they are persecuted. She was not surprised that she had heard 'nasty words' from their opponents. Even the Apostle Paul, she reminded me, had once persecuted those who professed Christ; she hoped that those who had tried to 'bully' them might one day have a similar conversion experience.

While this may seem like a pat response to a researcher's question, it is one that highlights the rhetorical value of framing difficult circumstances as par for the course. Indeed, Andrea herself expressed the inevitability of persecution in conversations with Christian Concern's supporters (although she is less likely to reference it in conversations with outsiders and the press, with whom, as we have already seen, she stresses her surprise at the situation facing her fellow believers). In her 2013 Christmas message, which was sent to Christian Concern's supporters by email, she said:

> We at Christian Concern and all of you, our supporters, are simply not ashamed of [Jesus], not ashamed of everything that He stands for, even though . . . it's often very difficult to speak of Him, to speak of the Truth that He proclaims, to speak for everything that is good. I sometimes ask myself why, how can it be so hard? But if He Himself was born to die a death where He faced a false trial, where His very own religious leaders rejected Him, then why are we to be surprised?

Further, there is some support for this perspective in the CLC's track record. At least during my time with the organisation, it was rare for CLC lawyers to win a case.[29] (At the time of writing, their primary successes—at least in those cases that are publicly reported—have involved street preachers arrested for breaching the peace.) Nor have they been successful in limiting abortion access or preventing legislation recognising LGBTQ+ rights.

When coupled with their portrayal of themselves as the guardians of Britain's recently Christian past, this low success rate might lend itself to an analysis of Christian campaigners as reactionaries engaged in largely ineffective efforts to reverse social change. Social psychologist Peter Herriot's account of conservative movements within the Church of England, for example, refers to these movements as 'reactionary': 'seeking to recapture an earlier golden era in contrast to today's godless secularism'.[30] Similarly, Callum Brown's postscript to *The Death of Christian Britain* speaks of the 'new vigour' of conservative Christian activists in terms of a 'backlash' against their faith's 'increasing irrelevance'.[31] For Brown, these campaigners have responded to his titular death by 'trying to roll back the reforms of the 1960s'; a task, he suggests, that their 'absence of significant popular membership' has rendered particularly difficult to achieve (and with which he has little sympathy).

Yet the work of Christian Concern is more than defensive or reactionary. Their campaigns and cases, whether or not they are framed in the negative language of the 'anti-', are also run with an eye to the positive. These initiatives are not only critiques of the status quo, but trailers for an alternative vision of human flourishing that emphasises the transcendent Truth of the Bible. Prompted in equal measure by an aversion to sin, a desire to combat perceived injustice, and a passion to spread the gospel, they seek nothing less than the transformation of the nation. Their cultural fundamentalism expresses a longing for what is both a formerly and future Christian nation. That they are both conservative and radical underpins the following section, which aims to complicate the notion of success underlying Christian activism.

An Ezekiel Season

Christian Concern's working week is book-ended by two staff gatherings: Monday morning prayers and Friday evening drinks. Monday prayers, which are equal parts staff meeting and Bible study, are usually held in the office's main boardroom. The boardroom is a bright, airy space. Looking out of its large windows, one can enjoy the Edwardian and Georgian architecture of Marylebone's Wimpole Street, perhaps allowing oneself the indulgence of imagining the worlds inhabited by some of the street's famous former residents: the London of poet Elizabeth Barrett Browning, say, or *Pygmalion*'s Professor Henry Higgins. Staff members drift into the room in ones and twos, taking their seats around the boardroom's central table and helping themselves to the tea, coffee, grapes, and biscuits that have been brought up by Grace, Andrea's personal assistant. The meeting begins with the reading of a Bible passage and a reflection on that passage, usually—but not exclusively—delivered by Pastor Ade Omooba, one of Christian Concern's co-founders. This is followed by a discussion about the previous and coming weeks, which may include debriefing sessions on recent events and speaking engagements, updates on a particular fundraising initiative or campaign, and a focus on upcoming deadlines, conferences, and cases. Prayer requests, which can relate to matters both personal and professional, are then taken. The meeting ends after a time of prayer, during which, heads bowed towards the large table around which they are gathered, those present pray aloud in response to the requests they have just heard: *Thank You, Lord, for every penny this organisation receives, and let us be good stewards of it; may Your design for marriage be upheld in this nation; please comfort X, whose father died last week.*

One week in October, the prayer meeting began with a reading from Joshua 6, which recounts the fall of Jericho. In this Old Testament narrative, Joshua, a military hero, brings down the city of Jericho by following unusual instructions from God. Jumping from one Old Testament hero to another, Pastor Ade, who was leading the study, declared that Britain was in an 'Ezekiel season'. The prophet Ezekiel was sent by God to warn the Israelites that, unless they turned from their rebellious, sinful ways, they would be destroyed. Ade pointed out that although God told Ezekiel that the Israelites would not listen to him, He also told him that 'you need to go and talk to them anyway' to warn them they were heading for crisis. Christian Concern, he suggested, was in a similar position. 'That's why it feels like an Ezekiel season. We're speaking to those who don't listen, but we need to proclaim and believe in our vision.' Encouraging us to both pray and act on this vision of Christian revival—'prayer without action will not work, action without prayer will not work'—Pastor Ade closed the study by reminding us of the necessity of speaking out, regardless of its outcome: 'This nation needs us, it needs more of us.'

A few weeks later, the prayer meeting focused on the meaning of victory. Our Bible reading had come from Acts 5:17–42, in which the Sanhedrin, or counsel of Jewish elders, orders Jesus' disciples to be flogged for preaching the gospel. In spite of the flogging, the apostles rejoice 'that they were counted worthy to suffer dishonour for the name [of Jesus]' (Acts 5:41). Ade pointed out that although the apostles had not been killed for their preaching, they had still been found guilty by the Sanhedrin. 'That doesn't sound like victory.' Yet they had rejoiced. 'So I pause and ask myself, what does victory look like?' Victory, he continued, had to be defined in relation to Truth. It was for this reason that the apostles had rejoiced in their pain, for although they were imprisoned, tried, and found guilty, their commitment to speaking the Truth rendered them victorious in God's eyes. Similarly, Christian Concern's 'true victory' lay in standing for Truth, not success in the courts. After all, 'even if we win, the best the courts can do is endorse the Truth. They don't define it.' Rather than becoming frustrated with losses in the courts, Ade encouraged us to remember that 'our victory is in standing, whether in court or in the public square'.

Encouragements to stand for Truth in a hostile world are typical of the weekly prayer meeting. Bible studies often likened Britain to the rebellious nation of Israel, home to an obstinate people who had hardened their hearts to the Truth. Conservative Christian activists, by contrast, were painted as prophetic voices in the wilderness, destined to be unwelcome in their hometowns.

Highlighting the urgency of the nation's 'needs', they stressed that Christian Concern's stand was a necessary, compassionate, and loving response to a nation spiralling into disarray. Further, by offering biblical justifications for the frequent frustrations suffered by Christian Concern in their public work, Pastor Ade's studies reminded his listeners that God's economy was not their own. That their campaigns and cases did not yield worldly victories did not mean that they had been unsuccessful. A subtle lesson in the humility with which the divine ought to be approached, they channelled a very different model of functionality or rationality than that associated with secular, bureaucratic law, in which it is a 'means to an end'.[32] By contrast, Ade emphasised the importance of following God even in the face of adversity or mockery, and even when the results weren't forthcoming; for just as Joshua had been called to circle the walls of Jericho, and as Ezekiel had been called to preach to those who rejected him, so Christian Concern was called to speak Truth to a rebellious nation.

This definition of 'true victory' is markedly different from that assumed by Brown in the quote above, in which success is thought to be measured by Christian activists' ability to 'roll back the reforms of the 1960s'. By contrast, Ade locates victory not in ends, but in means. As Andrea once told me, 'Do you not take a case because you're going to lose? No!' You take a case, she explained, because it's the right thing to do; because justice demands that the Truth be spoken; and because someone has to defend those who speak it. Indeed, it is not even that Christian activists are victorious *in spite* of their failing to win legislative change or court approval. Rather, it is the very act of standing that constitutes their success. The fact that Parliament and the courts refuse to 'endorse' the Truth places Christian Concern in an ancient, prophetic narrative in which their victory is assured not only in the present moment, but in the future, when the Truth will—as it inevitably must—win out. Within this Ezekiel season, God's Word is both always already true and always coming true, and Christian activists—like Old Testament prophets and New Testament apostles—are simultaneously, in Harding's words, 'temporary victims and the ultimate heroes of history'.[33]

One way of looking at the frequency with which Christian Concern staff and clients remind each other that 'true victory' lies in 'standing' rather than winning would be to suggest that their losses in the courts are not only personally frustrating, but demand theological justification. After all, in addition to its references to the inevitability of persecution, the Bible also states that 'for those who love God all things work together for good' (Romans 8:28). But this does not render these explanations insincere, any more than it renders their occasional successes theologically obscure. Biblical and historical precedent (and for those at Christian Concern, the two are one and the same) can account for both wins as losses. Just as God will sometimes give a nation up to its sins, as the Apostle Paul wrote in Romans 1, He will sometimes intervene and reverse this judgement, as He did in the time of the Judges. Or, indeed, as He did in eighteenth- and nineteenth-century Britain, which my interlocutors occasionally point to as a time when the faith of evangelical politicians had a lasting impact on the nation. Regardless of whether God chooses to intervene, the hostile world inhabited by the staff of Christian Concern and the CLC is one they are called to pray for, evangelise, and call to repentance: 'This nation needs us, it needs more of us.'

To say that the world must be engaged regardless of outcome, though, is not to render outcome unimportant. Rather, it is to recognise that the vernacular theology on which this engagement is based is both pragmatic and urgent, such that the necessity of offering an immediate response may take precedence over a theologically airtight explanation of the long-term impact of this involvement. This is important because of the diversity of theological positions represented by Christian Concern's staff and supporters. Theology, and particularly eschatology, may influence a Christian's approach to social reform. Historian David Bebbington, for example, suggests that the evangelical activism of the eighteenth century, including that of William Wilberforce, was made possible by the rise of postmillennial theology, which posits that the Second Coming of Christ will follow a thousand-year period of peace (the millennium).[34] Within this theology, godly men and women were encouraged to work towards the millennium by preaching the gospel and enabling the gradual improvement of society—an idea that gelled well with both Enlightenment ideals of progress and evangelical reform movements.

Postmillennialism can be contrasted with premillennialism, in which, because Jesus will return to earth before the millennium of peace, human history is thought to become increasingly bleak until the Second Coming ushers in a time of Tribulation. Harding describes conservative American Baptists' retreat from 'fundamentalist exile' in terms of a theological shift in this premillennial perspective. By positing the existence of a 'pre-Tribulation tribulation', religious leaders like Jerry Falwell and Tim LaHaye suggested that, in spite of the ultimately regressive trajectory of human history, Bible-believing Christians in the 1980s should engage in moral reform so as to positively impact the nation before its final demise. While the story of humanity was ultimately one of decline, the 1970s and 1980s represented a window of opportunity for such Christians to insert themselves into the biblical narrative, winning souls for God's Kingdom in the moments before the very *last* of the last days. It was this opening up of the end times that rendered their political activism—which previously would have amounted to polishing brass on a sinking ship—a legitimate, nay, *necessary* use of time and resources.[35]

Christian Concern's activist rationale has much in common with the Baptists studied by Harding, particularly in terms of the presumed relationship between evangelism and religious freedom. As I argue in chapter 5, my interlocutors present their work as enabling the continued spread of the gospel, which would otherwise be threatened by, for example, the regulation of offensive speech. This bears a conceptual debt to Jerry Falwell's 'signature innovation' in 1980s Bible prophecy, in which he suggested that conservative Christians must mobilise politically to safeguard the freedoms of speech and assembly that enabled them to evangelise in the first place. In other words, 'in order to do the only thing Bible prophecy prescribed [Christians] to do in the end-times, namely, spread the gospel to the four corners of the world, Christians must do more than that'.[36]

Yet unlike the Christian Right of the 1980s, which was composed, Harding writes, of those who were deeply invested in or influenced by Bible prophecy, and for whom the ultimate trajectory of human history remained one of depravity and deterioration, the range of eschatological opinion at Christian Concern requires a theological justification that can accommodate both long-term success *and* long-term decline. After all, although eschatology was rarely discussed at the Christian Concern offices (indeed, the staff couldn't say for sure where their colleagues stood on the end times), diversity did exist. For example, while Maria's work in discrimination law seemed to have confirmed a pessimistic view of human history, in which the nation appeared to be on an inevitable downward slide, John, a postmillennial Calvinist who worked in finance and data entry, described himself as being pessimistic in the short term only: Europe was in a religious slump at present, but he expected the world to be largely Christianised by the time of Christ's return.[37] John thought the Second Coming would not be for many centuries. He would sometimes tease (in his words, 'troll') Maria about this, for she insisted that Christ could return at any moment. No doubt an equally great range of opinion exists among Christian Concern's supporters, who encompass not only optimistic postmillennialists like John, but pessimistic premillennialists and amillennialists (and those who have simply never given the matter much thought).

I suggest that it is the urgent theology outlined above that enables the members of these diverse Christian communities to continue to view Christian Concern's work as essential, biblical, and mandated by God. This theology emphasises both the necessity of Christian intervention in a hostile world and God's absolute power to alter a nation's destiny. By rejecting the profane logic that measures achievement in courtroom wins, instead defining victory as the act of standing, it taps into a prophetic biblical tradition that reinterprets worldly failure as spiritual success. Yet this foregrounding of engagement-in-the-moment always leaves open the possibility of divine intervention, however unlikely it might currently appear. God has wrought miracles before. He can certainly do so again. That Britain is a hostile world now, then, does not mean it will stay that way forever; *but even if it does*, working to counter this hostility is never in vain. In this imagining, even failed prophets are symbols of hope, evidence of a faithful God reaching out to a faithless people.

As such, Christian activists simultaneously inhabit two latent forms, embodying both the prophetic voice that is destined to be maligned, and the successful moral campaigner, whose work may forever change the face of the nation. They are the prophet Ezekiel; they are also William Wilberforce. It is this latency, this pessimistic-optimism, that accounts for the equally radical and restorative elements of the cultural fundamentalism discussed above, in which activists seek a nation that both was and will be Christian. As Andrea once put it: 'Are we a nation in the process of turning our back on Jesus Christ? One thousand percent yes. Am I hoping that we'll turn back still? Yes.'

Conclusion: Chameleons and China Shops

'Beloved, do not be surprised at the fiery trial when it comes upon you to test you, as though something strange were happening to you' (1 Peter 4:12). So wrote the Apostle Peter to the suffering Christians of Asia Minor, reminding the fledgling church of the inevitability of persecution and the joy of suffering for Christ's sake. Christianity's 'full-fledged ideology of martyrdom'—including various theologies relating to the martyrdom of God Himself—underpins the message of thriving under threat that evangelicals embrace.[38] The danger of the lions' den is ever present, just as the Bible warns it will be; but Christians are enabled, through prayer and grace, to persevere.

If the hostility my interlocutors expect to face links them to Daniel's trials in pagan Babylon, it also connects their nation to the rebellious people of Israel. Like Israel, Britain had been chosen and blessed by God. Despite its small size, Andrea told me, it had commanded 'the respect of the world', creating 'systems that have been stable and democratic and free, not coercive, truly free'. But as with its Old Testament forebear, Britain had chosen to reject this privileged relationship with the divine; the very same relationship without which, as she saw it, its stability, democracy, and freedom could never have emerged: 'And over and over again in the Bible we see that where nations trust in God, the God of the Bible, they flourish, and when they turn their back on Him they become unstable.' Indeed, the very foundations of society seemed to have been fatally compromised, as the structures of which it was composed— 'the "givens" of life', in Mathews and De Hart's terminology—increasingly came under attack. Men called evil good and good evil, and the nation hurtled towards catastrophe.

Of course, not all Christians accept the hostile world thesis, and disagreement exists within denominations as much as it does between them. Many deny what one speaker at the Church of England's General Synod called 'the growing mythology of slights apparently done to Christians', instead highlighting Christianity's privileged place in national life. For these Christians, believers cannot piggyback on heritage or history (a history they acknowledge to have involved both justice and injustice) but must prove the relevance of their faith post-Christendom.[39] Even among those who agree that 'unfair things are happening' to Christians, as many members of Christ Church do, there is a range of opinion on how one ought to respond to this hostility. Distinguishing those situations where one ought to turn the other cheek, as Christ did on the cross, from those where one ought to insist on one's rights, as the Apostle Paul did when threatened with flogging, is a constant struggle. Indeed, it is the contested nature of this question that forms the ethnographic core of the following chapters.

With this in mind, it is useful to return to Laura, the speaker at the London Women's Convention. The bulk of the Convention's programme was devoted to Laura's three blocks of 'teaching', that is, Bible-based talks offering practical advice for Christian living. Laura proved an engaging speaker, peppering her talks with anecdotes drawn from her own imperfect efforts to live, pray, and hope in a hostile world. Reflecting on how best to live in such a world, she asked her audience to consider three 'wrong responses' to this challenge. The first was to become a 'hermit': 'The hermit is a Christian who retreats into a Christian ghetto. The only people they meet with and hang out with are Christian people', such that they are never called upon to 'defend God's glory'. The second was to become a 'chameleon', a 'secret believer' who 'shuts up, blends in, and avoids speaking out because it's just too uncomfortable'. Finally, she announced to peals of laughter, 'there is the bull in a china shop'. This sort of Christian 'endeavours to defend God's glory, confronting the culture head on, but actually in the process they're rude, arrogant, contentious, and actually dishonouring in the way they try and defend the Truth'.

None of these three caricatures, Laura reminded us, reflected a positive vision of Christian living; but all those present, she suspected, could identify with at least one. By contrast, the right way to live in a hostile world was to be found in the words of the Apostle Peter. The text of 1 Peter 2:10–12 flashed up on a projector screen at the back of the hall. Laura read the verses aloud, emphasising a single word:

> Once you were not a people, but now you are the people of God; once you had not received mercy, but now you have received mercy. Dear friends, I urge you, as foreigners and exiles, to abstain from sinful desires, which wage war against your soul. Live *such* good lives among the pagans that, though they may accuse you of doing wrong, they may see your good deeds and glorify God on the day He visits.

This was how Daniel had lived in pagan Babylon, and this was how Christians were called to live in the here and now.

Whether or not they attended the Convention, members of both my field sites were, in their different ways, seeking to live as Laura (and the Apostle Peter) advised. Yet they also struggled with the temptation to be hermits, chameleons, or bulls. A Christ Church apprentice named Chris, for example, risked sliding into hermitage when he explained that—unlike the visiting anthropologist!—he hadn't brought a non-Christian friend to the church's much promoted Open Day, something the minister had been encouraging the congregation to do for a number of weeks. His excuse, he sheepishly explained, was that he didn't really know any non-Christians. After all, he worked in a church; *where would he meet them?* For others, the temptation was not to be a hermit, but a chameleon. Many church members echoed Leah's fear, recounted above, that they were not 'bold' or 'distinctive' enough in their faith. Of course, such a charge could never be levelled at Andrea, who, after taking a 'Leading from Your Strengths—Ministry Insights' (LFYS) personality test (a Christian version of the Myers-Briggs test), jokingly announced to the office that she had scored 'ten out of ten for aggressiveness' in her decision-making style. (The survey opposed 'aggressive' with 'reflective', as opposed to gentle.) Being a chameleon was something she had, in Williams' and Laidlaw's terms, developed a moral incapacity to achieve.[40] Yet she also knew that her urgent, prophetic style risked her being dismissed as the proverbial bull: a particular risk, perhaps, for an evangelical woman in a leadership position.

Keeping these three tendencies in check is a struggle for those seeking to discharge their duties to both God and the unsaved. Christian Concern certainly sees its ministry as evangelistic, particularly in terms of the relationship between legal activism and the freedom to preach the gospel. Pastor Ade once prayed that they would 'continue to be an evangelistic, soul-winning organisation'. He even suggested that this commitment to evangelism was the reason they faced such hostility in their public-facing work: 'That's why we're under attack, because we're evangelistic and the devil doesn't like that.' But while Christian Concern does hope to be 'a soul-winning organisation', it is equally a prophetic voice. It speaks Truth to those who do not want to hear it. And it sometimes seemed to speak particularly loudly on those controversial subjects where the views of conservative Christians are, as I experienced at the Core Issues Trust protest, thought especially abhorrent by their non-Christian neighbours.

The members of Christ Church tend towards the same conservative positions on these issues as those at Christian Concern. Many were pleased, at least in an abstract sense, that a biblical perspective on such issues as sexuality, abortion, and free speech found its way into public debate through the work of Christian organisations. In practice, however, some worried that the perceived aggressiveness or offensiveness of prophetic speech—its potential bullishness—risked unsettling their own evangelistic efforts. For those who had decided that the appropriate response to a hostile world was one of individual witness through words and deeds, Christian Concern's frequent calls to national repentance could appear evangelistically ineffective. One woman, for example, told me she truly admired Andrea's commitment. She had previously worshipped at Andrea's church and had family members who were involved in Christian Concern campaigns. Yet there were moments when she felt that viewing society as a battleground was counterproductive. However much she disagreed with abortion, for example, 'society's *clearly* decided where it wants to go on this . . . It's not going to change anything. Why not focus efforts on actually talking to people about Jesus?'

These words hint at the central difficulty facing Christian activists: that by focusing on cases and campaigns related to a circumscribed set of policy interests, it is those contested issues—rather than talk of Jesus—that come to stand for Christianity itself. This tendency may well be exacerbated by the law's propensity to reify the identities it regulates. By pushing theological categories through the legal mill, lobbying and litigation contribute to a public understanding of Christianity as primarily defined by its stance on LGBTQ+ rights, abortion, and Sabbath observance.

Of course, from the perspective of those working at Christian Concern, speaking of 'God's good pattern' for human flourishing *is* talking to people about Jesus. Lest I be accused of obfuscation as regards the many similarities between my two sets of interlocutors—it was a source of some amusement among my Christian Concern colleagues when the results of my own LFYS personality test suggested a tendency to 'avoid accountability by overstating the complexity of the situation'[41]—it is important to remember that they are united in their commitment to spreading gospel Truth. Indeed, they acknowledge this shared commitment even when their opinions on evangelistic strategies diverge. The differences of approach that the following chapters document are primarily those: differences of approach, not conviction. But for evangelicals who take seriously the task of bringing glory to God in an unwelcoming world, determining the *right* approach—negotiating between belligerence and blending in—is a loaded question, one that is confronted daily in their interactions with those who remain 'of' this hostile world. My LFYS test results notwithstanding, it is a sense of the complexity of these negotiations that the following pages hope to convey, beginning in chapter 2 with an account of my interlocutors' application of theological categories to legal activism.

Grace and Law

*Do not think that I have come to abolish the Law or the Prophets; I have
not come to abolish them but to fulfil them.*

—MATTHEW 5:17

Evangelical Spelling

'M-E-R-?'

James, Christ Church's ever cheerful curate, was holding an impromptu
spelling bee. It was a cool, fresh evening in April, and I was one of sixteen
guests at the first session of Christianity Explored, an informal course for curious non-Christians interested in finding out more about Jesus. Christ Church
runs the course a number of times a year. Held over five consecutive Monday evenings, each session begins with the course attendees sharing a glass
of wine, beer, or juice and a home-cooked meal in the church lounge. After
the meal, a Christ Church staff member gives a short talk about one aspect
of the Christian faith (such as the person of Jesus Christ, sin, or the importance of the cross). This is followed by a half hour of discussion and question
time, during which the guests can ask any questions they might have about
Christianity.[1]

On this particular evening, I was sitting at a table with seven others, four
of whom were members of Christ Church, and three of whom, like myself,
would have been classed as 'exploring'. Of the three other explorers, two—Joe
and Susan—had been invited by friends who were already church members,
and one, Rose, had come along after hearing the course plugged during a Sunday service she'd happened to attend. The evening's talk having been given,
and our dinner—chicken in a mushroom sauce, which had been cooked by
volunteers from the congregation—having been served, we were now ready
to settle into the discussion portion of the evening. James, who was chairing

the conversation at our table, was trying to explain what he saw as Christianity's defining characteristic. All religions, he told us, are based on words which begin with the same three letters: 'M-E-R'. In every other religion, the word is—he spelled it out—'M-E-R-I-T'. Muslims and Catholics,[2] for example, believe that they will get to heaven by performing meritorious actions. They die hoping against hope that these good deeds will outweigh a lifetime's worth of sin. Other religions, then, ask people to try to 'climb a ladder up to God'. In Christianity, however, the word is: 'M-E-R-?' 'Mercy?' offered Rose. Joe, Susan and I murmured approvingly in her direction; Rose was fast becoming the course's star pupil. James beamed at her: 'Thanks for coming, Rose!'

James' spelling test was one of the many times I heard my evangelical friends pose an absolute distinction between (evangelical Protestant) Christianity, which they understand to be grounded in God's mercy, and its religious competitors, the salvific logic of which they understand to be based upon merit. Founded on the Reformation doctrine of salvation by faith alone, this theology posits human beings as unable to earn their way to God through the performance of religious ritual or the purchasing of indulgences. Humankind's absolute depravity means that the 'debt' of sin cannot be 'paid for' by one's own actions. The slate can only be wiped clean by Jesus' redemptive death on the cross, which allows God to forgive and treat as sinless those who trust in His Son. In this understanding, Christians live under 'grace'—the unconditional and undeserved gift of forgiveness and salvation—as opposed to 'law', that is, the strict moral, civil, and juridical code of Old Testament Judaism, the inevitable breaking of which required the Israelites, both individually and corporately, to make regular atoning sacrifices.

Evangelicals understand the death of Jesus to have been a 'once and for all' sacrifice that fulfilled the Old Testament law. As such, they see themselves as having a level of freedom unparalleled in other religions, for they do not have to keep prescriptive laws relating to rules of dress (such as headscarves or turbans); dietary restrictions (kosher or halal food); charitable obligations (good works or *zakat*); and ritual responsibilities, such as Catholic confession or Islam's daily prayers. (It is worth pointing out that these caricatured renderings of, say, Catholicism and Judaism would be unrecognisable to many Catholics and Jews.)

But if salvation is dependent on the gift of grace, and does not depend on the performance of (or refusal to perform) meritorious (or sinful) works, then what did the clients of the Christian Legal Centre mean when they argued that their right to freedom of religion had been violated by employers who asked them to perform (or cease their performance of) certain actions? If Christianity was not, as I was often told, about 'following rules' or 'keeping laws', then why did these clients argue that it was impermissible for them to perform a civil partnership, work on a Sunday, or remove a Christian symbol? As I came to understand the distinction between grace and law, I began to notice the ways in which this rhetorical device was deployed in discussions of the cases taken by the CLC, both by the members of Christ Church and by the CLC staff themselves.

In this chapter, I focus on the categories of grace and law as they were applied to two CLC cases, *Chaplin v Royal Devon & Exeter NHS Foundation Trust* and *Playfoot v Millais School Governing Body*. These cases, which concerned restrictions on the wearing of a nurse's crucifix necklace and a schoolgirl's purity ring (which symbolises the wearer's commitment to chastity before marriage), were the subject of grace/law discussions not only among my interlocutors, but in the courts. In different ways, Christianity's—for want of a better word—lawlessness rendered *Chaplin* and *Playfoot* problematic for all parties involved. From the perspective of the staff of the CLC, Christianity was treated unfairly by the English courts precisely because it was not a law-based religion. Its lack of formal dress code allowed the opposing counsel to argue that the wearing of religious attire was not a 'generally recognised practice' of the Christian faith, and therefore undeserving of legal protection. From the perspective of the members of Christ Church, however, the cases were problematic because they risked painting Christianity as a religion that 'required' the wearing of religious symbols. By positing the removal of a cross or purity ring as a violation of the Christian faith, they could be read as suggesting that these items were, in fact, *necessary* for salvation. Drawing a distinction between interior conviction and exterior symbols, Christ Churchites critiqued the religious jewellery cases on the basis that 'wearing a cross doesn't make you a Christian'.

Writing of the curious lack of attention traditionally paid to the concept of 'grace' in anthropology, Julian Pitt-Rivers asks: 'surely the anthropology of religion can no more ignore Western theology than the anthropology of law can ignore Western jurisprudence?'[3] Taking up this call, this chapter seeks to (re)insert theological reflection into anthropological analyses of the court by applying the doctrine of grace to the *Chaplin* and *Playfoot* cases. In talking about theology, I do not necessarily mean the 'theological prehistory', as Fenella Cannell might put it, of British law.[4] Rather, I mean my interlocutors' explicit commentary on the relationship between litigation and conversion: what if a particular case led to non-Christians misunderstanding the nature of salvation? What if it reduced Christianity to a set of rules, rites, and rituals rather than an overarching relationship with the divine? Moving from the soteriological to the sociological, what if 'juridifying' these everyday practices (fastening a chain around one's neck, slipping a ring onto one's finger) pressed them into the legally manageable category of *religion*? So conceived, these actions become an optional, voluntary add-on to personality and culture, a value to be measured against competing considerations—and, almost invariably, declared of lesser weight.

Merit and Mercy

Louis Armstrong sings *What a Wonderful World* as bombs fall on a Vietnamese village. American troops trundle through the jungle while civilians are rounded up and shot. Journalists and protestors are beaten. A toddler runs from a burning building. A bloody flip flop lies abandoned in the street.

It was the second week of Christianity Explored, and James had opened the evening's talk by dimming the lights and projecting a clip from the 1987 film *Good Morning Vietnam* onto a screen at the back of the church lounge. The clip began with a shot of the actor Robin Williams, who plays a Vietnam-based DJ for the US Armed Forces Radio Service, dedicating *What a Wonderful World* to the US soldiers stationed there. While Satchmo sings of the beauty of 'trees of green/red roses too', the camera cuts from Williams' DJ booth to a montage of carnage and violence.

When the two-minute video clip had finished, James, semi-casual in a pink and white checked shirt, turned up the lights and began to speak. 'Louis Armstrong is right', he said. 'It's a wonderful world.' And yet, as the video showed, there's an awful lot of bad in it. We seem 'hell bent' on destroying one another. 'What has happened to this wonderful world that we live in?' The answer, he suggested, ought to be familiar to us, because it's a condition—'a spiritual heart disease'—common to us all. 'The Bible has a word for this universal condition, and we all know what it is. It's sin.'

As James' talk that evening highlighted, conservative evangelical theology posits the natural orientation of all people, saved and unsaved, as one of 'sin', which evangelicals understand as rebellion against God. Although God made the world good—indeed, Genesis 1:31 declares it 'very good'—it was soon corrupted by man's desire for self-mastery. Sin enters the world through the actions of Adam and Eve, who disobeyed God by eating of the tree of the knowledge of good and evil.[5] This initial disobedience is representative of humankind's Original Sin, summarised in the Church of England's Thirty-Nine Articles (its defining doctrinal statements) as 'the fault and corruption which is found in the nature of every person who is naturally descended from Adam'.[6] In this understanding, to be a 'sinner' is not just to perform immoral actions. Rather, sin is an ontological state: 'In his own nature he is predisposed to evil. . . . In every person born into this world there is found this predisposition which rightly deserves God's anger and condemnation'.[7] That spring evening, the usually upbeat James soberly warned us that the result of this 'proud declaration of autonomy away from God' was that all men and women—including those sitting in this very room—were burdened with a 'debt' of sin they could never repay. This debt would, by default, result in their—in our—spending eternity in what Jesus refers to as 'the unquenchable fire' (Mark 9:43).

Yet God has found a way to dispense both justice and mercy to the irredeemably sinful inhabitants of His once wonderful world. He has decreed that the punishment due every sinner can fall in one of two places: on the individual sinner in hell, or on the body of His Son, Jesus Christ. Jesus, the only human being ever to have lived without sin, offered Himself up as a 'once and for all' atoning sacrifice, thereby fulfilling the sacrificial law of the Old Testament and rendering unnecessary its legalistic system of atonement. During what my informants referred to as the great 'transaction' of the cross, Jesus takes on the sinner's sin, and the sinner takes on Jesus' glory. It is at this moment that the Holy Spirit comes to dwell in the believer, thereby enabling them, through a process of sanctification, to become more and more like Jesus—that is, less and less sinful—with each passing day.

The distinction between salvation by law and salvation by grace is critical in the construction of Christian believers as individuals who are assured of their fate after death. By accepting that they cannot save themselves and must trust in Jesus' sacrifice on the cross as the only suitable atonement for their sins, Christians no longer have to worry that the weight of a lifetime of sin will tip the scales on Judgment Day. As such, it can be an attractive doctrine to those who are religious 'seekers', such as Rose, Joe, and Susan. Indeed, Bebbington argues that the doctrine of justification by faith alone was 'the motor of expansion' of the English evangelical revival of the mid-eighteenth-century.[8] But this grace is important throughout the Christian life, not only at the moment of conversion. This is because Christians ought to live lives motivated by the gratitude they feel for the grace they have received.

This approach was typified by Diana, a primary school teacher in her thirties. One Sunday afternoon in January, Diana and I met at a café near the church before attending the evening service together. As I was still relatively new to what evangelicals refer to as 'Christian things', I asked Diana if she could explain to me how Christianity impacted her life. Sipping a cup of mint tea, she explained that she tried to live 'as a response to what has been done for me': 'Christianity isn't about following laws, it's not about following rules, it's about realising what has been done for you and then living a life motivated in gratitude of that.' Diana's desire to live in 'response' to 'what has been done' for her reflects a view of herself as innately sinful, and thus in need of something to be 'done'. Throughout our conversation, she positioned Jesus' atoning death, the death which had bought her salvation, as an act deserving of eternal gratitude. When I asked her if she had ever made sacrifices for her faith, she suggested that although she had probably lost 'status' in the eyes of some of her non-Christian friends and colleagues—she had been patronised by those who interpreted her faith as a 'crutch' to lean on, and she sometimes wondered if her non-Christian friends reduced her 'to the status of a child' because she had never had a sexual relationship (Diana, who is single, believes in abstinence before marriage)—she understood herself more in terms of privilege than of sacrifice. After all, 'what could I possibly sacrifice compared to what's been done for me?'

Given this desire to inculcate a sense of gratitude, the members of Christ Church are wary of treating the religious activities they undertake—including their daily 'quiet time' (a time of individual Bible reading and prayer), their presence at the monthly prayer meeting, and their various 'serving' commitments, such as teaching Sunday School, cooking for Christianity Explored, or running a Christian summer camp—in a legalistic manner, that is, as duties to be performed rather than services gratefully offered. They are keen that others see them as recipients of grace rather than doers of law, and they worry that the greatest misunderstanding their non-Christian friends have as regards their faith is the idea that salvation can be achieved through being kind, charitable, or living a good life rather than through trusting in Christ alone. As Leah, a solicitor, put it: 'One of the things I hate is if someone just says, "Oh, Leah, she's really nice."' As an inherently sinful being, she simply couldn't accept this description of herself. More importantly, however, she didn't want non-Christians to link the idea of 'niceness' to her faith: 'I don't want you to think I'm "nice". I want you to think Jesus is amazing, and the way to salvation.'

One way in which Christ Churchites seek to show others that 'Jesus is amazing' is to live in what Luke, the minister, once referred to as a 'grace-fuelled' manner. As noted above, the spiritual transaction of the cross involves not only the imputation of Jesus' righteousness onto the now redeemed sinner, but the indwelling of the Holy Spirit within that sinner. As James once explained, 'God's grace never leaves us where it finds us.' Rather, it begins a process of internal transformation that ought to be noticeable to outsiders.

For some converts, and particularly those who had not been raised in evangelical homes, the difference made by the Spirit's indwelling was immediately obvious. Bethany, the minister's wife, became a Christian at the age of fifteen. A slim woman with thick auburn hair and a ready smile, we got to know each other through a women's Bible study group. Brought up in a Catholic home, Bethany had first become interested in Protestant Christianity when an evangelical friend invited her along to her church's youth group. She was then attending an all-girls school, and as the teenage 'party scene' kicked in, she began to question the friendships she'd long cherished: 'Why does this person who I've been friends with for ten years suddenly have a greater loyalty to some boy she met two weeks ago?' She had been immediately impressed by the Christian friendships she saw between the boys and girls at the youth group, which were radically different from the relationships she had seen between her non-Christian friends. It was on a countryside retreat organised by the group that she accepted Jesus and received the gift of grace: 'I remember praying a prayer, sitting on a big bale of hay, and really very immediately feeling quite a change.' She sensed 'the indwelling of the Holy Spirit' as she prayed, and knew she would never be the same again.

For Bethany, then, it was the visible outworking of grace that first sparked her interest in evangelicalism, because she saw the Holy Spirit working in her new evangelical friends. She then experienced this grace subjectively when she accepted Jesus and felt a sense of the 'indwelling' of the Holy Spirit. For others, the sanctification process sparked by the Holy Spirit's indwelling might be less dramatic. During one of our regular Bible studies, Carol, a nurse, told me of a colleague who had recently become a Christian. Kitty was short-tempered, had a poor bedside manner, and was often late to work. Her behaviour frustrated her colleagues, one of whom told Carol that if Kitty could behave this way and still be a Christian, clearly Christianity wasn't good for much. Carol had responded by asking her colleague what Kitty had been like *before* she became a Christian. Wasn't it true that she had been even more short-tempered, even less polite, and even less punctual? Her colleague had had to admit that yes, this was true; Kitty was bad now, but she had been worse before.

The point of the above is that although it is faith, sparked by God's grace, that saves the Christian, the result of this grace—the sanctifying work of the indwelt Holy Spirit—ought to be visible to what Luke referred to as the watching world. Christians, I was often told, are people who are *in Christ*, just as the Spirit is in them. Their Christlikeness ought to be both noticeable and attractive to non-Christians, who will then wonder how it was possible that anyone could be so kind, gentle, and content. By demonstrating the power of the Spirit to change one for the better, living 'in response' to the grace one has received is a form of evangelism. Grace-filled people ought to be gracious people, and it is this which must be kept in mind as we consider the impact of cases like *Chaplin* and *Playfoot*.

Dear Prime Minister

One morning in July 2012, I attended a training session for the staff and volunteers who would be representing Christian Concern at a number of Christian festivals taking place over the summer.[9] Christian Concern would be 'exhibiting' at three such festivals, each of which targeted a slightly different demographic: the Keswick Convention, which is aimed at older, evangelical Christians; New Wine, which is family-oriented; and Soul Survivor, a broader, more eclectic festival aimed at Christians in their teens and twenties, which spans the theological spectrum from conservative evangelical to charismatic Catholic. The interactive workshop, which was held in the office's large boardroom, had been organised by the Christian Concern events team, then comprised of Annabelle, an energetic twenty-year-old who had met Andrea through the youth group Andrea's children attended, and Carrie, a marketing graduate who had previously worked for a number of Christian organisations, including the African and Caribbean Evangelical Alliance.

The training session was held just months before two of the CLC's cases (those of Gary McFarlane, a relationship counsellor who lost his job after voicing a possible conscientious objection to offering psycho-sexual therapy to same-sex couples, and Shirley Chaplin, who was removed from frontline nursing after refusing to take off the crucifix necklace she had worn since her confirmation) went before the European Court. One of the goals of the session was to help the volunteers become familiar with the CLC's literature, much of which related to Gary and Shirley's cases. Carrie stressed how important it was to know this literature well: 'Next to your Bible, this info pack should be beside your bed. You should know it inside out.' Being involved in these cutting-edge cases, Carrie told us, was Christian Concern's 'USP', or unique selling point, and this was what might inspire festival attendees to start supporting their ministry financially or spiritually. Andrea, who had popped in to see how the session was going, agreed. We had been discussing how to encourage festival-goers to sign up to the Christian Concern mailing list (Carrie, ever the market-ing graduate, had spent the morning repeating the mantra 'data, data, data!'), and Andrea told us to stress the importance of the European cases, which many festival-goers would have read about in the papers or seen on the news.

Annabelle then asked Andrea if she could give the trainees any advice on how to respond to difficult questions about the cases. The four cases going to Europe (in addition to those of Gary McFarlane and Shirley Chaplin, the Court would also hear the cases of Lillian Ladele, a London registrar who had resigned after being refused an exemption from registering civil unions between same-sex partners, and Nadia Eweida, a British Airways check-in clerk who had breached BA's uniform policy by refusing to remove a cross necklace) had been the focus of a great deal of media attention as they pro-gressed through the courts. While much of this was supportive of the Christian claimants—particularly the two cross cases, and particularly in the conserva-tive press—some was critical. What should we say, Annabelle asked, to people who ask: 'Wasn't nurse Chaplin told to take off her cross because of health and safety?' Andrea responded with her customary passion, advising us to explain that visibility, not health and safety, was the real reason behind the ban:

> The thing is, health and safety was never an issue at the start of Shir-ley's case. Her case was about visibility, not safety. We have emails to show it was about visibility. Then a few weeks into the case, they started to talk about health and safety, so we tried to mitigate those issues. She didn't want to take off the chain, but we offered that she could wear a magnetic clasp, so that, if a patient pulled it, it would fall away easily, but that wasn't accepted. . . . All this while letting Muslim women wear hijabs pinned with a brooch![10]

Andrea's response hints at the competing discourses surrounding Shir-ley's case, which included not just the visibility of Christian symbols in public spaces, but multiculturalism, the alleged privileging of non-Christian religions, and the supposed excesses of Britain's 'health and safety' culture. The case had arisen in 2007 when the Royal Devon and Exeter NHS Foundation Trust, the hospital trust for which Shirley worked as a geriatrics nurse, amended their uniform policy to prevent the wearing of dangling jewellery, including all necklaces.[11] Shirley had worn her crucifix throughout her nursing career without incident. She saw it as a manifestation of her faith and was unwilling to remove it. After a number of failed attempts at compromise, she was moved to a non-clinical role, but sought to return to frontline nursing. Relying on the Employment Equality (Religion or Belief) Regulations 2003, which incorporate Article 9 of the European Convention, she complained of both direct and indirect discrimination, and a violation of her right to freedom of religion. An Employment Tribunal found against her on all counts, stating that there was no evidence that the policy had been applied in a discriminatory fashion,[12] that she could not prove herself to be part of a plurality of persons disadvantaged by the policy (indirect discrimination will only be found where multiple 'persons' are disadvantaged on account of belief), and that, even if discrimination had been found, this would have been justified by the hospital's pursuit of health and safety.

Shirley's case followed in the wake of the very public dispute between British Airways (BA) and Nadia Eweida. Ms Eweida, a Coptic Christian, had alleged that she was discriminated against by BA's uniform policy, which forbade the wearing of visible jewellery unless it was a 'mandatory' requirement of the employee's faith. Having lost her case at an Employment Tribunal, an Employment Appeal Tribunal, and the Court of Appeal, she appealed to the European Court of Human Rights, where her case was later joined with Shirley's, Gary McFarlane's, and Lillian Ladele's. Although the reasoning behind the various rulings need not concern us here,[13] the *Eweida* decision was frustrating to Shirley's legal team because of the tribunal's frequent references to Ms Eweida's desire to wear a cross being a 'personal choice', not a practice of religion:

> [No practicing Christian], including the claimant, gave evidence that they considered visible display of the cross to be a requirement of the Christian faith. . . . [The] decision to wear the cross visibly was a personal choice, not a requirement of scripture or of the Christian religion.[14]

This was repeated in *Chaplin*: 'The evidence we have is that there is no mandatory requirement of the Christian faith that a Christian should wear a crucifix. . . . It is, as we understand it, a matter of personal choice.'[15]

A similar point had been made in one of the CLC's earliest cases, that of Lydia Playfoot. Ms Playfoot, who was just sixteen when her case came before the High Court, argued that her school, which forbade the wearing of jewellery, had violated her right to freedom of religion by preventing her from wearing a purity ring.[16] Much like the British Airways' uniform policy objected to by Ms Eweida, the school made exceptions for those who believed their religion required them to wear certain items, such as Sikh *kara* bracelets. The Court found against her, stating that Ms Playfoot 'was under no obligation, by reason of her belief, to wear the ring; nor does she suggest that she was so obliged'.[17]

These judgments give some indication of English law's '"legal" religion', that is, religion as it is conceptualised and regulated by the courts. Writing of legal religion in the United States, Winnifred Fallers Sullivan notes that although popular conceptions of religious freedom emphasise the right of the individual to, in the words of one judge, '"have whatever beliefs we choose to have,"' the actual protections offered by the Constitution's First Amendment tend to be limited to religious observances with institutional backing.[18] This somewhat paradoxical situation results from the practical application of America's ideology of religious freedom, in which the privileging of a 'small p' protestant understanding of religion (in which religion is approached as a set of private, voluntary, individually held beliefs) sits alongside the law's authority to determine the legitimacy of these beliefs. Given that judges must separate the sufficiently from the insufficiently religious, it is, perhaps, inevitable that they defer to the authority of religious professionals and sacred texts in their deliberations, albeit supplemented with 'what they learned in Sunday School or their college world religions course'.[19] After all, to declare every idiosyncratic act worthy of First Amendment protection would be to institute a religious free for all. America's ostensibly 'free' religion, then, remains what Sullivan terms an 'unsolved problem', the result of efforts to disestablish religion while simultaneously working to confine it to citizens' private lives.[20]

A similar approach to religious legitimacy is clearly at work in the judgments quoted above, with the 'personal choice' to wear a religious symbol dismissed as insufficiently religious to engage the protections of Article 9 of the UK's Human Rights Act (and the European Convention, on which this legislation is based). While this emphasis on institutional support is somewhat surprising in the American context, where religion is, in theory, 'radically disestablished',[21] it is, perhaps, less so in Britain. Indeed, it may be that England's history of church establishment led the courts to adopt this particularly legalistic, authority-based approach. Sullivan writes that American courts, by regarding disestablished Protestantism as the paradigm of true religion, are ill-equipped to deal with those who *regret* this disestablishment.[22] Here we see that English law, at least under its recently domesticated human rights regime, appears equally resistant to those who think establishment, by failing to make good on the promise of privilege it implies, *no longer goes far enough.*

From the perspective of the CLC, England's legal religion discriminated against Christians by protecting symbols linked to religions of law while excluding those related to religions of grace. The case law, however, paints a slightly different picture. Regardless of the religion in question, the courts have been largely unwilling to protect the right to wear religious symbols. Claimants seeking to establish that a violation of their religious freedom has occurred must show not only that the act in question is 'religious', but that its restriction was unjustified. Many cases that clear the first hurdle fall at the second. In other words, the fact that an act is deemed to fall within the scope of Article 9—that is, that it is recognised as being 'religious'—is no guarantee that its restriction will be deemed illegitimate.

The case of Shabina Begum is instructive here.[23] Ms Begum, a schoolgirl from Luton, felt that her high school uniform was insufficiently modest to meet her obligations as a Muslim. (The conservative press presented Ms Begum as a pawn of the Tablighi Jamaat, a piety movement encouraging a strict interpretation of Islam, which some commentators—including those at Christian Concern—view as extremist.[24]) When the school refused to allow her to attend classes in a *jilbab* (a long, loose outer covering), she sued under the Human Rights Act, arguing that both her right to freedom of religion and her right to an education had been infringed. After a highly publicised legal battle, she ultimately lost her case: Article 9 was engaged, the Law Lords argued, but it had not been violated. Similar cases have received similar judgments.[25] Indeed, in a rare victory for a schoolgirl seeking to wear a religious symbol (in this instance, a *kara* bracelet), the case was won under race discrimination law, not the right to freedom of religion.[26] In practice, then, Article 9's legal religion is just as protestant-inflected as the First Amendment: the right to *believe* may be absolute, but the right to *manifest* belief is heavily curtailed.[27]

For those involved in *Eweida*, *Chaplin*, and *Playfoot*, however, the fact that the policies complained of featured an inbuilt imbalance—in which 'mandatory' symbols were treated as exceptional—was seen to penalise Christianity on account of its grace-based freedom. Further, the Conservative-led coalition government's approach to the cross cases was felt to be both disingenuous and inconsistent. In the months leading up to the hearing, Christian Concern started a postcard campaign to highlight this inconsistency. They encouraged their supporters to send three postcards about the case, one to then Prime Minister David Cameron, one to their local Member of Parliament, and one to a member of the House of Lords. Under a banner title—WHAT DOES THE GOVERNMENT REALLY BELIEVE ABOUT SHIRLEY'S CROSS?—the postcard was divided into two halves. On the left hand side was an extract from the government's submission to the European Court, which read:

> In neither case is there any suggestion that the wearing of a visible cross or Crucifix was a generally recognised form of practicing the Christian faith. . . . Where the individual in question is free to resign and seek employment elsewhere or practice their religion unfettered

outside their employment, that is sufficient to guarantee their Article 9 rights in domestic law. . . .

On the right were remarks made by David Cameron in response to a question he had been asked at Prime Minister's Question Time:

I fully support the right of people to wear religious symbols at work; I think it is a vital religious freedom. If it turns out that the law has the intention [of banning the cross] as has come out in this case, we will change the law and make it clear that people can wear religious emblems at work.

The back of the postcards read:

Dear Prime Minister,

Whilst I welcome your declaration in the House of Commons (11th July 2012) of your support for the wearing of the cross I am concerned that this stands in sharp contrast to the Government's official submission to the court. Shirley Chaplin had worn her confirmation cross for nearly thirty years in frontline nursing before being told to remove it, despite the fact that accommodation was made for those of other religions. Her case will be heard at the European Court of Human Rights on 4th September. In spite of your statement, the UK Government is opposing her.

Please ensure that the Government changes its position and supports Shirley's freedom to wear the cross.

With Shirley's case fast approaching, the postcard initiative was strongly pushed at the summer festivals. It had the double benefit, Annabelle thought, of raising awareness of the case and allowing Christian Concern's supporters to feel that they 'owned' a political campaign. Throughout the summer months, festival volunteers would return to the Christian Concern offices with their suitcases heavy with signed postcards, for which Christian Concern paid the postage and dispatched in staggered bundles.

One morning in August, I arrived at the office to find Annabelle sitting on the floor surrounded by Christian Concern merchandise and literature brought back from the festivals, and working her way through what looked like hundreds of Shirley postcards. Joining her on the floor, I began to help sift through the cards to find those which had been partially left blank. (Because many of the people signing the cards didn't know the name of their Member of Parliament, the staff had to work this out based on their address details. We spent many August mornings Googling postcodes to find out which MPs served Christian Concern's new supporters.) As the morning advanced, so too did the piles of literature, mailing list sign-up sheets,

Coalition for Marriage petitions (see chapter 5), and Shirley postcards piling up around us.

That afternoon, we were joined by Louise. Louise usually worked in Christian Concern's finance department, but had spent the past few weeks exhibiting at the Keswick and New Wine festivals. A mother of three, Louise was used to light chaos, but even she was taken aback by the devastation we had wrought in a formerly tidy office. As she helped us return the reception area to a state of normalcy, she explained that the Shirley postcards had been particularly useful in engaging the festival-goers she'd met, because they 'show how insane the government's position is. I can't believe they're saying wearing a cross isn't a practice of the Christian faith.' Louise and I had had conversations about theology before, and, keen to demonstrate what I had learnt, I challenged her: 'but it's not, really, is it?' After all, I said, Christianity isn't practiced through wearing a symbol, but through maintaining a relationship with God. 'Well,' she replied, 'you can't say that the cross doesn't have significance.' It wasn't the same as 'any piece of jewellery': 'Some people say, "People wear crosses as fashion items", and that's true, but just because some people wear scarves as fashion items it doesn't mean that burqas have no religious significance.' Pausing to reflect, she articulated the issue in grace/law, or faith/works, terms: 'They've jumped on the fact that it's salvation by faith rather than works.' Highlighting the inherent imbalance in a policy which protected only religious requirements, she concluded: 'if there's a no jewellery policy, it needs to be across the board. You can't have exceptions for some faiths but not Christians.' In other words, it wasn't the uniform policy that was unacceptable to her. It was the fact that it did not seem to extend to religions of law.

Louise's position was echoed, in part, by Shirley herself. In September 2012, I accompanied Shirley and a team from the CLC to the European Court of Human Rights in Strasbourg. Shirley, then in her late fifties, combined a quiet reflectiveness with a surprising sense of humour. She had taken her case not because she wanted to get involved in a legal challenge—on the contrary, she had found the whole process very stressful, disliked doing media appearances, and joked that Maria, her CLC solicitor, might have to step in and do her interviews if she just happened 'to wake up with a very sore throat tomorrow'—but because she felt a duty to stand up for her faith. Indeed, by the time her case was heard at the European Court, Shirley had come to believe that it was no longer about her as an individual; rather, she saw it as speaking to much broader questions of religious freedom and Christian witness.

The day before the hearing, Shirley, Maria, and I decided to explore Strasbourg on foot. As we walked over one of the city's medieval stone bridges, the conversation turned to Shirley's case. Noting the apparent contradiction in David Cameron's position, which seemed to differ from that of the government's legal submissions, Shirley asked: 'But how can some religious symbols be protected as rights, like Sikh turbans, but not crosses?' Playing devil's advocate, I pointed out that the government posited a distinction between mandatory and optional religious dress. Shirley and Maria argued that this was both unfair and difficult to enforce. After all, Maria said, it would be extraordinary if only mandatory religious practices were protected. Echoing Sullivan's critique, Maria wondered how, exactly, the Court would propose to determine them.

As it happened, Maria and Shirley were right. The European Court rejected the UK government's submissions on the cross cases, stating that a manifestation of religion could be protected so long as there was a 'sufficiently close and direct nexus between the act and the underlying belief'. A belief in Jesus' death and resurrection more than met this requirement. As British Airways did not have a weighty legitimate aim in the restriction of Ms Eweida's right to wear a cross, she won her case. However, the hospital's legitimate aim, the protection of health and safety, meant that although the Court found an *interference* with Shirley's Article 9 rights, they did not find a violation. This was a profound disappointment for both Shirley and her legal team. As she told the BBC at the time, 'I've worn it without incident, I've nursed a very wide range of patients, I've been bitten, I've been scratched, I've had computers thrown at me, but no-one has ever, ever grabbed my crucifix. To say it's a health and safety risk, I really don't agree with that at all.'[28]

External Signs

Despite sharing much theological ground with the various conservative Christianities expressed by the staff of the CLC, the members of Christ Church had a different, and significantly less supportive, take on *Chaplin* and *Playfoot*. The discomfort they felt about the jewellery cases was brought home to me through a number of conversations with Hannah, a charity lawyer in her thirties, who had been worshipping at Christ Church for seven years. I was repeatedly directed to Hannah throughout my time at Christ Church—'*You're interested in Christians and the law? Oh, you must meet Hannah!*'—and, in August 2013, we met for lunch at the Salvation Army's central London headquarters.

Located between St Paul's Cathedral and the Millennium Bridge, the SA HQ is a large, glass-fronted building, the transparent walls of which are adorned with quotes from the Bible. As we sipped coffee in the building's basement café, Hannah explained that she knew of Andrea through her work at the Lawyers' Christian Fellowship (LCF), where Andrea had been a Public Policy Officer before she left to found the CLC. (Hannah is an active member of the LCF.) While Hannah was supportive of Christian-interest cases focusing on the tension between religious freedom and LGBTQ+ equality, she worried that some litigation had resulted in negative outcomes for the individuals involved. In these cases, she thought, mediation might have led to a better solution for the claimant.

Shirley's was one such case. Given that the law was always likely to find in favour of the hospital—health and safety, after all, was a serious consideration—surely Shirley's lawyers should have encouraged her to accept one of the compromises offered, such as wearing her cross on her identity badge and only removing it when undertaking close clinical work?[29] Besides, Hannah mused, 'It's not a requirement of Christian faith.' It surprised her that the Christian Legal Centre had invested so much in the cross case, which didn't seem critical to questions of Christian freedom. She even worried that it risked 'misleading' the public, because it made 'a really big issue' out of something she considered fairly incidental.

This was echoed by Jenny, a friend of Hannah's from the Lawyers' Christian Fellowship. She had met her husband, also a lawyer, through the LCF, and was heavily pregnant with her second child when we met at a café in October 2013. As we queued to order our drinks, I explained that the case that had first interested me in Christian activism was that of Lydia Playfoot, the schoolgirl who had been prevented from wearing a purity ring with her school uniform. Jenny remembered having been 'saddened' by the case. This was not, however, because of the alleged violation of Ms Playfoot's rights. Rather, it was down to the way it had been pursued. Her former church minister, she explained, had lived in the area where Ms Playfoot had gone to school, and had built up a 'brilliant relationship' with the school in question over a number of years. He had regularly been invited to contribute to Religious Education classes and had hosted assemblies at Easter and Christmas. With the support of the administration, he had had many opportunities to explain the gospel to the students. After Ms Playfoot's case, however, this relationship was terminated. Although this minister had not been involved in the case, he was no longer invited back to hold assemblies or teach RE lessons. As far as she knew, no other Christians were either. Jenny felt this was a great shame, particularly because wearing a purity ring had 'no impact' on one's ability to follow Jesus: 'There's no suggestion at all anywhere in the Bible that anybody needs to wear anything like that.' In taking the case, Jenny argued, '[The activists were] totally oblivious to the damage they caused in Christian relationships that had been built up over a number of years to fight a battle that was lost and has, in my view, absolutely no impact on the Christian faith.'

Jenny was equally dismissive of the cross cases: 'Jesus certainly never wore a cross, and none of His followers did, and so I don't see why we need to get worked up about external signs which have never been part of our faith.' When I asked whether Christians were treated less favourably than members of other religions, she responded by explaining the difference between Christianity and other traditions in terms of law and grace: 'It is a fundamental part of Islam and Sikhism to carry certain things and to cover certain parts of your body up, because they're not free under grace like we are.' For that reason, she continued, 'I genuinely think there is a difference.'

Hannah and Jenny seemed to be making two points. First, both women appropriated the language of the English courts, arguing that wearing a cross or purity ring was not a requirement of Christian faith, nor did it have any impact on one's ability to practice it. As Jenny pithily observed, 'It wasn't as though Lydia's school was saying, "You have to sleep around to come to this school," you know.' She differentiated the kind of injury or harm done to someone whose faith required them to wear a religious symbol from that experienced by the claimants in *Playfoot*, *Chaplin*, and *Eweida*. In Hannah's opinion, the wearing of a cross was 'incidental' and unworthy of serious debate. The fact that it had gone to Europe was, she thought, 'bizarre' and disproportionate. In a case like Shirley's (and it's important to remember that Hannah did not feel this way about all of the Christian discrimination cases, but only about those where she deemed the subject matter trivial), she wondered whether Christian Concern's agenda had led them to pursue a path that was not necessarily the most helpful for the claimant involved. This analysis suggests an acceptance of the small-p protestant approach to religion noted above, in which embodied, material, sensory religion appears less '"true"'—in Hannah's words, more 'incidental'—than religion in its interiorised, conscience-centric form.

Second, they worried that the pursuit of these cases might have a negative impact on gospel witness. Hannah wondered, for example, whether focusing on religious symbols might mislead the public, who could end up thinking that this 'incidental' issue was critical to Christianity. As with the understanding that religion is primarily a matter of interior belief, this reflects an anxiety often associated with (although not exclusive to) Reformed Christianity, in which the (mis)attribution of agency to objects may prove a stumbling block to salvation.[30]

Remember that many Christ Churchites worry that the greatest misunderstanding of their faith is that it is about law rather than grace. They fear that, in a context marked by both increasing religious pluralism and rising religious illiteracy, the unsaved might think that evangelical Christianity is interchangeable with any other faith; that it is about externals rather than internals; that it concerns rules and rituals rather than a relationship with a Saviour God. With cases like *Chaplin* and *Playfoot* seeming to suggest that Christians were as concerned with symbolic trinkets as they were with saving grace, how could potential converts understand what was different about Christianity, that is, its emphasis on faith, not works? One way to ensure that outsiders understand this difference, of course, is to preach the gospel. Yet Jenny's tale of her former minister posited a direct link between the *Playfoot* case and the termination of gospel preaching at Lydia Playfoot's school. The friendly relationship between local Christians and the school administrators had taken years to build up, but it had been quickly destroyed by what Jenny saw as the legal team's unwillingness to compromise (an unwillingness, it should be noted, that those at the Christian Legal Centre would contest).

As Christian lawyers, Hannah and Jenny had a more detailed understanding of the CLC's cases than most of the people I met through Christ Church. Yet they were not the only ones who questioned the jewellery cases. Almost every Christ Churchite with whom I discussed these cases made reference to the fact that 'Christians don't *need* to wear a cross.' Further, some congregants worried that by asserting their rights in the courts, rather than demonstrating a Christlike, forgiving attitude to their employers, those involved in these cases might be failing to adequately express their gratitude for the grace they had received. We will explore this idea in greater depth in chapter 4, which focuses on the use of rights-based language at Christ Church. For now, however, I will merely highlight that some congregants thought a better approach would be to do your job *so* well and be *so* conscientious, caring, and loving in your attitude to others—in other words, to live such a grace-fuelled life—that your colleagues couldn't help but notice the grace of God working within you. As with the Christian teens who had had such a strong impact on Bethany, letting your colleagues see the work of the Holy Spirit in you was thought to be a better advertisement for Christianity than a piece of jewellery or a litigious attitude.[31]

This was the opinion of Carol, the former nurse with whom I had regular Bible studies. Carol was a keen advocate of sharing your faith in the workplace, and thought it was a great shame that the state was, as she understood it, clamping down on Christian medics who wanted to tell their patients about Jesus. However, she was also concerned that the gospel be communicated in a loving, gracious way. With a wry smile, she explained that telling a patient she went to church on Sunday was one thing; refusing to give them a sponge bath until they professed faith was quite another. She questioned whether the cross cases had a positive gospel impact. Yes, she acknowledged, wearing a cross was a way of signalling your beliefs, but what mattered more was your behaviour: 'It's the way that you conduct yourself, how you care for people, how you speak, how you work.' It was through demonstrating grace in these everyday acts that a non-Christian might notice your distinctiveness, leading to conversations about faith coming up 'quite naturally, because of your good lives'.

Concern about the impact of the cross cases is not limited to conservative evangelicals. Those from different traditions, including liberal Anglican speakers at the Synod debate discussed in the Introduction, also suggested that the insistence on wearing a cross might damage one's efforts at evangelism. Speaking at Synod, the Venerable Jan McFarlane, the archdeacon of Norwich, said:

> If there are uniform rules banning the wearing of jewellery, then why should Christians be exempt? I am not wearing a cross today. It does not make me any less of a Christian. In fact I could argue that it may

even have the opposite effect; it could mean that I am not actively putting off somebody who may otherwise be frightened of talking to me,
for fear that I may be pushing religion down their throat.

Although both identify as Anglican, Archdeacon McFarlane is theologically distant from conservative evangelicals like Carol. (Jan McFarlane is one
of the first women archdeacons in the Church of England, while the members of Christ Church sometimes wondered if the inclusion of women in the
episcopate would force them to break with the established church.) For our
purposes, however, what is interesting is not that Archdeacon McFarlane and
many members of the congregation of Christ Church agree about the cross
cases, but that the members of Christ Church do *not* agree with the staff of the
CLC, with whom, theologically, they share much more common ground. After
all, they do not oppose all of the Centre's cases. Many are sympathetic to claimants with a conscientious objection to service provision for LGBTQ+ persons,
including registrars unwilling to perform civil partnerships. Many supported
at least two of the four cases that went to Europe, those of registrar Lillian
Ladele and relationships counsellor Gary McFarlane. Yet they dismissed the
cross cases on the basis of a soteriological principle: that salvation is 'received'
rather than 'achieved'; and that wearing a cross doesn't make you a Christian.

Conclusion: Legal Iconoclasm

On September 4, 2012, Shirley and I sat in the public gallery of the European Court of Human Rights to hear Paul Diamond, barrister for the CLC,
and James Eadie, counsel for the United Kingdom, present their arguments
to the seven judges who would decide Shirley's case. After their submissions,
I asked Shirley how it had felt to have her name bandied about in court. It
was strange, she said, to hear the events she'd lived through discussed from
an outsider's perspective: 'I suppose there's their version, there's my version,
and there's the truth.' As Shirley recognised, the way a case is understood is
inevitably shaped by the technology of law, including its transmission and dis-
semination through law reports, newspapers, and online media. The words
written in a legal judgment or spoken at an international court may bear little
relation to the experience of the person to whom they refer, and the actual
reasoning behind a court's decision may not feature in public discussions of
the case. Legal technicalities may, intentionally or otherwise, end up being
'misread' by the reporters covering high-profile disputes, leading outsiders to
lose confidence in the legal system's ability to dispense justice.[32]

Regardless of the potential difference between the hospital's version, Shirley's version, and 'the truth', her case came to be understood in very different ways by my two sets of interlocutors. For both, however, law and grace
were important discursive categories. For the staff of the CLC, it was seen

as proof that Christian symbols were policed in a way in which the material culture of other religions was not. Christianity's lack of Scriptural dress code— barring what one evangelical woman described to me, in earthy language, as 'not dressing as a slut'—meant that Shirley was repeatedly faced with claims that wearing a religious symbol was not a practice of Christianity, and did not, therefore, merit protection under rights-based law. By the lights of England's legal religion, Protestant Christians seemed to be being penalised because Jesus, in fulfilling the law, had freed them from it.

As noted above, the European Court overruled this approach. The Court found that the wearing of a cross *did* qualify for protection under the European Convention—that is, it did constitute a 'manifestation' of religion—but that this manifestation could be prevented in the interests of health and safety without violating a claimant's Article 9 rights. It was for this reason that Nadia Eweida, the airline check-in clerk, won her case, whereas Shirley lost hers. Yet those at the CLC never accepted this distinction. Even after the Court's ruling, they maintained that the issue was one of visibility, not health and safety.

In May 2013, four months after the judgment had been released, I went to Wimpole Street to conduct an interview with a CLC client. While I waited for my interviewee, I chatted with Louise, the festival exhibitor who had found the Shirley postcards so useful in revealing the disingenuousness of the government's position. Around her neck was a gold cross. I had never known Louise to wear a cross, and asked if it was something she had recently started doing. She explained that she had worn a cross when she was younger, but when her children were little, one of them had grabbed it and pulled, breaking the chain. 'Once you have kids', she laughed, 'you learn that you can't wear anything they can grab.' How funny, I said; isn't that the argument that the hospital made about Shirley's cross? Hadn't they been worried that it might be pulled by a disturbed or confused patient? Well, Louise said, no one was hurt when my cross broke. Besides, Shirley had offered to wear hers on a magnetic chain, which meant it would have come away easily if pulled. And one more thing, she said, smiling: 'Just because a bee might fly in, it doesn't mean you should never open the window.'

Those at Christ Church saw things differently. If the claimants in *Eweida*, *Chaplin*, and *Playfoot* had wanted to manifest their faith, they thought, it made more sense for them to live 'grace-fuelled' lives than to fight a legal battle over something trivial. It is, perhaps, unsurprising that the members of Christ Church were dismissive of the potential religious significance of crosses and rings. As Reformed Protestants, they are part of an iconoclastic tradition with a suspicion of religious objects, a tradition much—and, as Birgit Meyer reminds us, perhaps excessively—invoked in Protestant discourse and discussions thereof.[33] Glossing John Calvin's *Institutes of the Christian Religion*, for example, Luke's sermons often argued that the human heart was 'a factory of idols'. This semiotic ideology, or governing narrative of how signs, language, and objects function (or ought to function) in the world, implies a firm boundary between subject and object.[34]

I would occasionally hear hints of this in discussions of the cases. Mark, for example, after repeating what I had begun to think of as an evangelical mantra—'as a Christian, you don't *need* to wear a cross'—stated: 'and you certainly don't want people to idolise the cross. We often make an idol of it.' Mark had grown up in a Catholic home and had become an evangelical at university. Given his religious genealogy, he was, perhaps, particularly attuned to accusations of idolatry, and was keen that I—a fellow cradle Catholic—understood the difference between the salvific possibilities of internal conviction and the window dressing of ritual symbols. (As Webb Keane notes of Dutch Calvinist missionaries in Indonesia, both ancestor worshippers and Roman Catholics were thought to 'confuse or conflate exterior and interior'.[35]) To that extent, debates over crosses and purity rings are just one example of the tension inherent in a semiotic ideology in which belief ought to be distinct from material practice, but in which the goal of 'purification'—defined, in Latourian terms, as the effort to distinguish human from nonhuman, or subject from object—cannot ever be fully realised.[36]

On the whole, however, physical religious objects were not the sort of idols that most troubled my Christ Church interlocutors. Although concerned with idolatry, they didn't think its temptations would come to them in the form of the Catholic material culture that had so upset their iconoclastic forebears, those English Reformers who, as Eamon Duffy puts it, 'smashed the statues, whitewashed the churches and denounced the Pope and the Mass'.[37] Their dismissal of the jewellery cases was framed in terms of their being unnecessary or misleading, but not spiritually dangerous to those wearing religious symbols. Christ Churchites are significantly more worried about the idolatrous fetishisation of achievement, financial security, and the pursuit of 'happiness' over 'holiness' than they are about mistakenly attributing moral agency to statues, icons, or jewellery.

By contrast, at least one staff member at the CLC, Maria, *was* wary of the attribution of moral agency to religious objects. On the day after Shirley's hearing, Maria, Shirley, and I visited the Cathedral of Our Lady of Strasbourg. An immense sandstone building, the Cathedral is an ornate merging of Romanesque and Gothic architecture. Its pink exterior swarms with gargoyles and flying buttresses, while its interior houses tapestries, stained glass, ornate baptismal fonts, and statues of the saints. It is, to put it mildly, a Calvinist nightmare, and Maria, who attends a Reformed Evangelical Baptist church, was sceptical of its spiritual legitimacy. Knowing that Maria was wary of idolatry (she had recently returned from a church mission trip to Sri Lanka, where she had been particularly disturbed by a local taxi-driver who had stopped at a small shrine to touch what she called an 'idol'), I asked what she thought of the decor. Surveying a large cross upon which an almost unblemished Jesus hung as though sleeping, she told me that it didn't reflect the biblical narrative: first, Jesus looked far too white to have been born in Palestine; and second, the Bible says He was beaten so badly that His face was unrecognisable. The Bible, she told me, says that no one can imagine God, and yet the human tendency is to anthropomorphise Him. 'That's why my church doesn't have any pictures or statues in it', she explained. 'What, not even a crucifix?' I asked. She smiled: 'Not even.'

Maria, then, was exactly the sort of Christian who might have been most suspicious of Shirley's cross. Yet she had been involved in Shirley's case almost from the beginning, and fervently supported her in it. By portraying the case in terms of the legal system's apparent privileging of religions of law over religions of grace, the staff of the CLC were able to reconcile their handling of a case that, for many conservative Protestants, might have worked to trouble these very distinctions. Instead of a potential idol—the kind that Maria's church would not display on its walls—Shirley's cross became a matter of principle. By stressing that the case was about the discrepancy in the treatment of religious objects, the CLC could simultaneously argue that Christians were saved through faith and did not 'need' to wear crosses or purity rings, but that restrictions on their ability to do so were a violation of their religious freedom. Thus, they could distance Christianity from what were seen to be more legalistic religions while also seeking to partake in the privileges apparently afforded them.

As noted above, many evangelicals reject what Luke called the 'modern myth' that all religions are similar. They strongly differentiate Christianity's grace-based narrative from their law-based (and highly caricatured) renderings of other traditions. Yet the desire to draw others to Christ through living 'good lives' does not greatly differ from the strategies of other religious groups that seek converts or reverts. Reform movements in Islam, for example, also emphasise personal faith and piety, detailed knowledge of the scriptures, and becoming 'born again',[38] and as one reader of Keane's work on Protestantism and modernity astutely quipped, 'We are *all* Protestants now.'[39] In this context, it is interesting to compare Shirley's desire to visibly wear a cross with the reasons given by members of other religions for their adoption of religious dress.

In her study of Somali Muslim women in London, Giulia Liberatore found that young Muslims saw their conduct as a means of endearing their faith to others. On one occasion, Liberatore attended a lecture by a Sheikh who spoke about how Muslims should 'avoid creating barriers' between themselves and non-Muslims.[40] Instead, European Muslims were encouraged to demonstrate their faith through their manners. Following the talk, Layla, one of Liberatore's interlocutors, said, 'I think he's completely right about being a Muslim through manners–through the person you are, not through a uniform. That's the universal aspect of Islam, it's what unites all cultures.' Layla felt that doing *da'wa*, or raising awareness of Islam, was best achieved through good character. Although she wore a headscarf, she hoped that her friends and co-workers would see past it to her inner sense of modesty, focusing 'less on her exterior appearance, and more on her virtues' and temperament.[41]

Layla's belief that modesty was better demonstrated by manners than dress bears some similarity to Hannah, Jenny, and Carol's belief that Christians ought to be recognisable through their grace-fuelled demeanour, not their religious jewellery. However, this was not the only approach to religious dress that Liberatore found in the field. While Layla hoped that non-Muslims would recognise her good moral character almost in spite of the fact that she wore *hijab*, her friend Ikraan believed that her external dress could cement her internal convictions. When she decided to wear the *jilbab*—the same long, loose outer garment that Shabina Begum had been denied permission to wear by Denbigh High School—Ikraan explained her decision, in part, in terms of her external clothing strengthening her faith.[42] The objectification of modesty in the *jilbab* would, she thought, result in increased religious self-discipline as she went about her everyday life.

Although I am not sure she would appreciate the comparison (particularly as she felt that headscarves were given preferential treatment over crosses at her hospital trust), there is a sense in which Shirley's rationale mirrors Ikraan's. She had no doubt that it was her faith in Jesus, and not the cross around her neck, that ensured her salvation. However, she also understood her crucifix as enabling her to keep her external actions consistent with this internal faith. Her crucifix created a sense of accountability: 'If others know I am a Christian because they see the cross on my necklace, I tend to focus more on my actions and words to keep them as consistent as possible with the requirements of my Christian faith.' In this sense, then, her use of a physical object—the kind of object which has long troubled Reformed Christianity's semiotic ideology—allowed her to pursue that most Protestant of religious aims: sincerity, or the alignment of belief, speech, and character.[43] Her cross was an anchor by which both she and others could locate her belief, and her commitment to it was based on her desire to keep her actions consistent with the grace she had received.

As a result of its juridification, though, Shirley's cross took on a number of alternative meanings. Whereas she saw it as a marker of divine grace, it was treated by some of her fellow believers as its opposite, a 'trivial' item that risked 'misleading' the non-Christian public about the nature of salvation. Soteriology, of course, was likely less of a concern for the Employment Tribunal that heard her case. Although the Tribunal accepted what the ruling records as the 'sincerity of her religious beliefs', they called into question the religiosity of the item itself, reading it as a 'personal choice' rather than a generally recognised 'practice' of the Christian faith. It was only at the European Court that her desire to visibly wear a cross was finally accepted as a 'manifestation' of religion.

Yet this recognition did not lead to its protection. Rather, it worked to draw the cross into a regulatory regime that allows signatories to the Convention to limit would-be religious practitioners so long as they are in pursuit of a 'legitimate aim'—one of which, of course, is health and safety. As such, the effect of its recognition by the Strasbourg judges was simply to confirm that *religion*—in this instance and in many others—was, in the end, inessential; of lesser weight (and greater risk) than the competing claims of insurance policies and institutional bureaucracy. Opening a hospital window might result in a bee sting, but the benefits of fresh air outweigh this risk. When it came to Shirley's cross, however, it seemed the law could find no such mitigation.

CHAPTER THREE

Broken Cisterns

And God said, 'Let there be rights; and there were rights.'

—GENESIS 1:3, ADAPTED BY YVONNE SHERWOOD[1]

Polonius' Poor Advice

Conway Hall, the headquarters of the UK's oldest established freethought organisation, might seem an unusual institution to host a speaker from Christian Concern. Nevertheless, it was to this bastion of secular humanism that I accompanied Carrie, the Christian Concern events manager, one evening in September 2012.[2] We were there to watch a debate in which Andrea would discuss 'Freedom of Speech, Anti-abortion Protestors and Women: Rights and Limits'. The debate, which had been organised by the British Pregnancy Advisory Service (BPAS), Britain's largest abortion provider, had proved exceptionally timely; while Andrea went over her debate notes, the Christian Legal Centre team was busily polishing their arguments for the following morning, when they would represent two such anti-abortion protestors in criminal court. Andy Stephenson and Kathryn Sloane, members of pro-life group Abort67, had been arrested under the Public Order Act after displaying large, graphic images of aborted foetuses outside one of BPAS's Brighton clinics. Their upcoming trial threw into sharp relief the issues to be discussed, reminding the three-hundred-person audience that although this particular debate was academic, the growth of groups like Abort67 meant it was being played out up and down the country with increasing frequency. Indeed, the subject of the debate—the rights and limits of people like Andy and Kathryn, who sought, in their words, not to protest abortion but to 'expose' it—would soon be determined by law.

Having arrived with plenty of time to spare, Carrie and I took a quick tour of the venue. Conway Hall's main auditorium resembles a cross between a small theatre and an old-fashioned school assembly hall. Its wooden floors, wall panels, and stage are ringed by an angular wooden balcony. Above the stage, topping its wooden framing, is Polonius' oft-quoted dictum: TO THINE OWN SELF BE TRUE.[3] As we surveyed the room, Carrie wondered aloud about the quote. Having determined that it did not come from the Bible, she announced it to be 'a very humanist statement'. I asked what she meant; weren't Christians to be true to themselves? The issue, she explained, was that asserting that one ought to be true to oneself begged the question: 'who *are* you?' Extending her index fingers and curling her middle, ring, and little fingers into her palms, she pointed two finger guns at me. 'A mass murderer can say they're being true to themselves, and then: bang bang!'

Carrie's finger gun example was intended as a joke, but her rejection of Polonius' maxim indexes very real concerns about the contested nature of goodness, morality, and capital 't' Truth. Indeed, it cuts to the heart of this chapter, which focuses on evangelical activists' understanding of the legal system's move towards a culture of rights. The staff of the CLC understand rights-based claims to rely on an atomistic logic that prioritises the perceived needs and wants of the individual over the pursuit of society's common good. More than this, though, they worry that the human rights project elevates the fallen morality of created men and women over the limitless wisdom of their Creator God. By pursuing human happiness and wellbeing in this life as its ultimate goal, the doctrine of human rights is seen to recklessly disregard the possibility of an eternal future, rejecting biblical commands as an unacceptable restriction on human autonomy. As such, the British legal system's embrace of the logic of rights was seen to pander to the worst excesses of those who took Polonius at his word: it encouraged depraved humans to be true to their fallen selves, permitting rather than restricting sinful behaviour.

Despite these concerns, the CLC often couches its arguments in the language of rights, including Articles 9 and 10 of the European Convention (as articulated in the Human Rights Act 1998 and other domestic instruments), which protect the rights to freedom of thought, conscience, religion, and expression. This is, in part, the necessary result of the British legal system's transition from recognising negative civil liberties to enforcing positive human rights. As Andrea once put it, 'You can only operate with the laws that you've currently got.' But the CLC seems to use the language of human rights even when alternative, and perhaps less risky, legal strategies are available to them, suggesting that they pursue rights-based claims for reasons that go beyond the necessity of operating within 'the laws that you've currently got'.[4]

This chapter argues that the CLC continues to pursue its cases under human rights law precisely because it wants to point out the flaws that a rights-based legal system embodies. Although they sometimes posit the human rights project's high valuation of the human as a secularised version of Christian thinking, they find its current expression in English law both undesirable and unworkable. Unlike (their understanding of) evangelical Christianity, which is thought to pursue the good of all, the human rights project is accused of prioritising the individual's desires over the building up of common values, focusing instead on personal entitlements and denying one's obligations to the community. In this way, the staff of the CLC find themselves in agreement with postliberal theologian Stanley Hauerwas, who argued some years ago that contemporary politics relies on the language of rights 'not because we have a vision of the good community, but because we do not'.[5]

The use of rights-based language is part of an attempt to both undermine human rights doctrine and to encourage others to embrace a biblical alternative. Focusing on two of the CLC's cases, *Johns v Derby City Council* and *R v Stephenson & Sloane*, this chapter shows how the CLC instrumentalises the language of rights to establish conservative Christians as the members of a self-identified counterpublic, highlighting their subordinate status as a means of marking themselves off from an allegedly dominant political elite. This counterpublic discourse seeks to awaken its hearers to the logical inconsistencies of a doctrine that posits people as the bearers of universal rights while simultaneously restricting the freedoms of those who disagree with what the Centre terms the 'prevailing politically correct orthodoxy'.[6] As such, although it would not be true to state that the Centre takes rights-based cases with the intention of losing them, there is a benefit to their frequent losses. Losses can be presented as proof that the human rights framework does not work on its own terms, as it cannot reconcile the apparently mutually exclusive claims of, for example, the rights to both religious freedom and non-discrimination.

In terms of my interlocutors' evangelical theology, then, the British legal system's embrace of rights discourse is taken as further proof of its renunciation of God and its elevation of the fallen individual; but from the pragmatic perspective of lawyers seeking to challenge public opinion, its use is both a necessary compromise and a chance to reveal its internal inconsistency. Taking this critique seriously, and contra those theorists who frame rights as an inevitable tool of state violence, I suggest that the CLC provides evidence of the ways in which rights can be instrumentalised to challenge the state to confront its own contradictions. Yet a critique that relies on the tools of the object under criticism will always have complicated outcomes, including the possibility of becoming entangled in the very legal framework it hopes to undermine.

On Human Rights

Despite the Universal Declaration of Human Right's confident assertion that human rights are the 'highest aspiration' of the people of the world, there is little philosophical or practical consensus as to the ultimate foundations of international human rights law. One oft-voiced explanation for the historic emergence of the belief that men (and, occasionally, women) are endowed with certain rights by virtue of their humanity frames it as the fruit of centuries of 'Western philosophical and theological thought', with an emphasis on Christian theology as a precursor to theories of natural rights.[7] In the words of Reformed theologian Nicholas Wolterstorff, modern notions of rights derive from the Bible's 'pervasive . . . insistence that human beings occupy a special place among earthlings in God's eye', as well as their resulting moral obligations to others made in God's image.[8] While Wolterstorff is an advocate of what he terms 'inherent rights', his theologically-inclined understanding of their origin is not limited to those who embrace the human rights project. Talal Asad's critical take on liberal accounts of rights, for example, also argues that these ostensibly universal values have 'specifically Christian roots', the result of Latin Christendom's understanding of natural law.[9]

If Asad and Wolterstorff link Christian theology to the emergence of inherent rights as thinkable ideals, recent historical scholarship has shown a more pragmatic side to this relationship. In their challenges to the foundation myth of the post-war rights revolution, in which the origins of the Universal Declaration and European Convention are to be found in collective disgust at the atrocities of the Holocaust, historians Marco Duranti and Samuel Moyn suggest that the codification of rights in law owes more to conservative Christian (and particularly Catholic) anxieties surrounding secularism, socialism, and individualism than to recognition of the horrors of genocide.[10] Thomist philosopher Jacques Maritain, for example, played a significant role in promoting universal rights as a bulwark against atheistic Marxism, while French Catholics determined to ensure parental control over religious education advocated for the codification of human rights on this basis. Post-war conservatives believed that a supranational European court was more likely to promote (Catholic) 'Christian values' than secular national governments, with human rights the vehicle through which they might 'reconstitute a Christian Europe'.[11] These Christianising aspirations, however, did not come to pass. As Udi Greenberg notes, neither the European Convention nor its attendant court was able to transform the legal order. Cognisant of its 'flimsy legitimacy', the European Court of Human Rights often deferred to those it was supposed to police: 'Everybody recognised that "Europe" could not overturn the decisions of national parliaments, and the court regularly parroted the words of nation states.'[12]

It is precisely this relationship between state-backed norms and human rights law that my activist interlocutors find frustrating. They reject the association of justice with the rule of law when that law, in their eyes, permits sinful behaviour in the name of rights. Yet they also complicate the narrative that sees rights discourse as Christianity's secular successor. By contrast to this genealogy, my interlocutors stress an assumed distance between what they frame as Christian Britain's tradition of tolerance and the contemporary application of human rights law. (While the literature cited above links the rise of human rights to a range of Christian traditions, including Catholicism, readers should understand the following references to 'Christianity' and 'Christian values' as emic terms, used by my interlocutors to index conservative Protestant theology.) Andrea, for example, believes that civil liberties such as freedom of speech, worship, and association are Christian in origin, and she associates the alleged dismantling of Britain's Christian framework with the corresponding erosion of these liberties. She understands the European Convention to have been 'infused' with Christian values. However, she also worries that the 'Christian backdrop', in her words, that lies behind human rights' 'recognition of human dignity' has been 'hijacked by an equality and diversity type approach'. This has undermined the law's structural unity, as the secularisation of contemporary rights discourse means the state does not recognise the Bible as a higher power to which to appeal when applying the law.[13]

During a presentation at a conference called 'Setting Love in Order: Protecting the Freedoms to Believe, to Exist and to Change When Homosexual Feelings Are Unwanted', Andrea spoke of the 'confusion of rights language' that had resulted from this failure to define and pursue the common good. The conference had been organised by the Core Issues Trust, an organisation that offers counselling to those struggling with what it terms 'unwanted same-sex attraction'. (Core Issues' founder and director, Mike Davidson, identifies as ex-gay.) Andrea was one of a number of speakers to address the sixty or so delegates, who came from a range of religious and political backgrounds. While the majority of attendees were conservative Protestants advocating (or offering) ex-gay therapy, the group also included at least one Catholic convert (an American ex-gay activist), a liberal Anglican working to increase the acceptance of LGBTQ+ Christians within the Church of England, and a politician campaigning to ban the kind of therapy offered by the Core Issues Trust. Indeed, the politician, Labour's Geraint Davies, was one of the speakers. Declaring himself the equivalent of 'a vegetarian opening a meat market', he explained his desire to ban this 'unregulated and dangerous' form of treatment.[14] He hoped that the Counsellors and Psychotherapists (Regulation) Bill, a private members' bill on which he was working, would prevent 'gay to straight conversion' and lead to a world in which LGBTQ+ identities were celebrated: 'In terms of human rights, people have a right to express themselves and be free.'

Andrea, of course, had a very different take on rights. She argued that Britain's constitutional freedoms, which she dated to the 1215 Magna Carta, were undone by laws such as that put forward by Mr Davies:

> Note that the Magna Carta is not really framed in the language of 'rights' . . . And human rights, of course, are actually very confusing, because actually what we need as a society, and what the Magna Carta set down in constitutional terms, was an idea of the common good,

of what is good, [which was] founded deeply in the precepts and the principles that are rooted in the Bible, in Christianity.

The embrace of rights, she explained, had led to a situation where 'there are competing rights and no idea of what the common good is, with Bible-believing Christians punished as a result'.

Why, then, does the Christian Legal Centre continue to mount challenges framed in the language of rights? Their complicated relationship with rights was summed up by Andrew Marsh, the group's campaigns director, at a presentation he gave at a Baptist church in September 2012. His talk, titled 'The Marginalisation of Christianity in Britain Today', focused on Britain's recent departure, as he saw it, from Christian values. After his presentation, the floor was opened up to questions or comments. Most of those present appeared to be over the age of sixty,[15] and one of the first comments came from a retired social worker. He told us that in the council where he had previously worked, a room had been made available for a Muslim colleague to pray in, but no such concessions had been made for Christians. Andrew responded by suggesting that this differential treatment was not uncommon. However, he then stated that the decision to seek to enforce one's rights in such a situation was complex. This was because Christians:

> Don't want to be quick to assert our rights, because . . . it doesn't tend to lead to a cohesive society. But I think in some of these cases we need to recognise that and to highlight it, because it shows really that the current approach isn't working. It's not even working on its own terms, where it preaches fairness but actually doesn't seem to reflect that in practice.

This answer draws attention to the instrumental potential of human rights law, not primarily in terms of its ability to right a wrong or wring justice from inequity—to insist upon the equal treatment of Christian and Muslim employees, for example—but to flag up injustice as evidence of the conceptual bankruptcy of a framework that 'preaches fairness but actually doesn't seem to reflect that in practice'.

Andrew encouraged this small pocket of the Kingdom to go against their Christian disinclination to 'cry discrimination' by highlighting the benefit of using rights-based language to reveal its own inconsistencies. Like Asad, he recognised that human rights law can be deployed as part of the state's attempt at civilising minority groups, those who reject the norms of their (often colonial) state authorities. But by contrast to Asad's account, which reifies rights as instruments of 'the most powerful nation-states',[16] Andrew suggested that rights discourse could be used to reveal and challenge the fickle nature of those same state-backed socio-legal norms. It is this strategy that the following section explores.

Rights and Rhetoric

Conway Hall fell silent as Andrea, the evening's second speaker, took to the lectern. Her presentation followed that of Ann Furedi, BPAS' chief executive, who had argued that although she found no words to be 'unsayable' and no images 'unshowable', the right to freedom of speech was 'not some kind of charter that allows you to say anything you want, at any time you want, in any place you want'. After thanking the debate organisers for her invitation to speak, Andrea said:

> I was . . . heartened when Ann Furedi said that nothing should be unsayable and no image unshowable, because in a sense I wanted to go to the very heart of what has caused this debate this evening, of why we're here this evening on the eve of the trial of Andy Stephenson and Kathryn Sloane in Brighton Magistrates' Court, charged under the Public Order Act. . . . So, what are the abortion images that Abort67, that Kathryn Sloane and Andy Stephenson are showing? Let's look at them now, shall we?

She pressed play. Vague murmurings of disapproval—at Andrea from the pro-choice side, at the act of abortion itself from the pro-life side—swept the room as a screen mounted on the stage began to play a video of a surgical abortion to the three-hundred-person audience. The video clip, which lasted about a minute and a half, was bloody and graphic. Footsteps at the back of the hall indicated someone leaving the room for its duration. When the clip had finished, Andrea used the screen to show some of the still images used by Andy and Kathryn in their anti-abortion protests, one of which showed dismembered foetal remains, including a foot, on top of coins.[17] Indicating the images, she continued: 'Ann Furedi talks of the right of autonomy for the woman, of the right of choice. But what about the right of that seven week embryo? The right of that little foot?'

Andrea's decision to spend a portion of her allocated speaking time standing in silence while the audience watched the removal of a dismembered foetus from an anonymous woman's vagina proves a useful starting point for an exploration of the use of rights-based language to undermine a rights-based framework. Of the four speakers (two of whom identified as pro-choice and two of whom identified as pro-life), Andrea's was the only presentation later accused of deviating from the topic of the debate; whatever her intentions, her video was taken as an attempt to condemn abortion itself rather than as a springboard for a discussion of the rights and limits of pro-life protestors. However, from Andrea's perspective, she had shown the images in an attempt to 'bring integrity' to a debate that, by focusing on the rights of (born) women and ignoring those of their (pre-born) babies, she felt to be 'intellectually dishonest'.[18] Her video sought to show that the evening's emphasis on rights was representative of the pro-choice constituency's unwillingness to engage with the real issues at stake.

Attempts to reveal the underlying deceit of rights discourse are not limited to public debates. In fact, accusations of intellectual dishonesty are implicit in many of the arguments put forward by the CLC in their cases, which aim to show that Britain's alleged commitment to protecting its Christian citizens' right to religious freedom manifests as little more than lip service. This section charts the CLC's efforts to reveal this intellectual dishonesty through the case of *Johns v Derby City Council,* which came before the High Court in November 2010,[19] and the Abort67 case, which was argued in Brighton Magistrates' Court in September 2012. These cases are prime examples of the way in which the CLC mobilises rights discourse to construct conservative Christians as a marginalised counterpublic whose interests are quashed by those of others.

As the circumstances in which the *Johns* case arose are quite unusual, I summarise them here in some detail. In 2007, Eunice and Owen Johns, Jamaican-born Derby residents and members of the Church of the God of Prophecy, applied to Derbyshire Council for approval as short-term foster carers. This was a position they had previously held without complaint. In the intervening years, however, the regulations governing fostering had changed. In accordance with the Council's fostering guidelines, the application process for prospective foster carers now required them to comment on their ability to support a child who was unsure of their sexuality or identified as lesbian, gay, or bisexual. According to the social worker who interviewed them, both Eunice and Owen stated that homosexuality was 'against God's laws and morals'. When asked how he would support a child who was lesbian or gay, Mr Johns told the interviewer that he would 'gently turn them round'. [20]

This left the Council staff in something of a bind. On the one hand, they felt unable to approve foster carers whose views seemed to breach the requirements of the National Minimum Standards for Fostering Services. On the other hand, they were equally bound by the Equality Act 2006, which prohibits discrimination on the basis of religion. The application stalled, and the Johns, represented by the CLC, instituted judicial review proceedings against the Council. As no decision had actually been made on the Johns' suitability as foster parents, both parties agreed to make a joint application for declaratory relief, asking the High Court to provide an answer to the following question:

> How is the Local Authority as a Fostering Agency required to balance the obligations owed under the Equality Act 2006 (not to directly or indirectly discriminate on the grounds of religion or belief), the obligations under the Equality Act (Sexual Orientation) Regulations 2007 (not to discriminate directly or indirectly based on sexual orientation), the Human Rights Act 1998, the National Minimum Standards for Fostering Services and Derby City Council's Fostering Policy when

deciding whether to approve prospective foster carers as carers for its looked-after children. Within that balancing exercise does the Local Authority have a duty to treat the welfare of such looked-after children as its paramount consideration?[21]

The question's reference to the Council's having to perform a 'balancing exercise' reflected the by then well-established trope that the duty not to discriminate on grounds of religion or belief and the duty not to discriminate on grounds of sexual orientation were diametrically opposed. The impact of the Equality Act (Sexual Orientation) Regulations 2007 on adoption and fostering agencies with a religious ethos had taken on an almost iconic status as an example of the tension produced by a system that sought to reconcile both the right to freedom of religion and the right to non-discrimination, an issue deemed especially inflammatory in relation to the welfare of looked-after children. For many conservative commentators, particularly (but not exclusively) those who identified as Christian, the requirement that LGBTQ+ and heterosexual couples be treated as legally equivalent by religious adoption agencies and foster parents was understood as an example of religious rights being trumped, with the duty to 'balance' competing rights seen as proof that the relationship between sexual orientation, religion, and the law was actually in a state of *im*balance.[22]

Indeed, the apparently irreconcilable conflict between these two competing rights was stressed in the CLC's submissions to the High Court. Barrister Paul Diamond, in his submissions for the CLC, asserted that LGBTQ+ rights were 'beginning to be seen as a threat to religious liberty'. He argued that to prioritise the right to non-discrimination over the right to freedom of religion was to issue 'a blanket denial on all prospective Christian foster parents in the United Kingdom', in that it provided local councils with an 'irrebutable presumption that no Christian (or faith adherent) can provide a suitable home to a child in need of a temporary placement'. This would force Christians *'into the closet'*. He was concerned not only to point out the conflict of rights that had been codified by the various statutory instruments identifying both religion and sexual orientation as protected characteristics, but to use this to paint Christians as a marginalised group at risk of *'second-class'* citizen status. [23] In other words, it was not just that individual rights could come into conflict with each other; it was that this would inevitably result in one right being deemed more important, and thus more deserving of protection, than another.

The judges who heard the case, Lord Justice Munby and Mr Justice Beatson, were unimpressed with what they later described as Paul Diamond's 'extravagant rhetoric'. Critiquing his submissions as a 'travesty of the reality', and claiming that parts of his argument were simply 'utterly unarguable',[24] they dismissed the question put before them as too vague to answer. Their strongly worded judgment was interpreted as a stinging rebuke to the parties involved, and, in particular, to Diamond himself. Nor were Justices Munby and Beatson alone in their opinion of the case. Legal commentator and journalist Joshua Rozenberg, for example, wrote that the case proved the paradox that 'it is never a good idea for an advocate to be committed to his or her cause', further stating that Christian campaign groups 'should avoid using tendentious arguments in support of claims which are unwinnable'.[25] Even fellow Christians, from both liberal and conservative church backgrounds, wondered what the CLC had hoped to achieve with the case. One conservative evangelical barrister told me that taking *Johns* had been a strategically unwise decision, while a report by the cross-party group Christians in Parliament criticised the CLC's reporting of the judgment as misleading.[26] More unforgiving still was Anglican bishop Alan Wilson, who argued that 'the customary paranoia of rightwing newspaper op-eds sounds silly in court'.[27]

Yet in spite of these less than positive responses from the legal and religious establishment, there is a sense in which *Johns* can be seen as a success. Although the judges declined to rule on the Council's non-decision and refused to give leave to pursue judicial review, they did state:

> While as between the protected rights concerning religion and sexual orientation there is no hierarchy of rights, there may, as this case shows, be a tension between equality provisions concerning religious discrimination and those concerning sexual orientation. Where this is so, Standard 7 of the National Minimum Standards for Fostering and the Statutory Guidance indicate that it must be taken into account and in this limited sense the equality provisions concerning sexual orientation should take precedence.[28]

From the perspective of those who had argued the case, this statement proved what they had been saying all along: that in a rights-based society which protects discrete, conflicting rights, some rights would take precedence over others.

Following the case, the CLC set about exposing the intellectual dishonesty of a judgment which could deny the existence of a 'hierarchy of rights' while simultaneously indicating that, in some cases at least, provisions relating to sexuality 'should take precedence'. In an opinion piece titled 'Permanent Exclusion and the Johns', published on the Christian Concern website, it was the above section of the judgment that allowed Andrea to write:

> I hope that the highlighting of the issue in the press will shatter the misconception that the Equality Act means equality for all. Some are very much more equal than others. We are currently living in 'Animal Farm' days; 'All animals are equal, *but some animals are more equal than others.*'[29]

By pitting two protected rights against each other, it seemed the CLC had called the human rights project's bluff. Although no order had actually been made by the court (as the judges pointed out, they were unwilling to rule on a hypothetical decision that Derby City Council had not yet made), the CLC could present the case as evidence that the context-negation of human rights advocates, in which all rights are presented as being innately held and of equal worth, was mere—and perhaps even *extravagant*—rhetoric. Some rights would always prove more violable than others. The only question was which value system would be used to decide between them. As the article went on to say, 'Judges and politicians want to restrict participation in public life to those who subscribe to their values, yet their values appear to be little more than whatever the prevailing politically correct orthodoxy is; fleeting, malleable and unsustainable.' From this perspective, *Johns* was not a case lost. It was an argument vindicated. It showed that the human rights framework did not work on its own terms. It was proof that it 'preaches fairness but actually doesn't seem to reflect that in practice'.

In the CLC's legal submissions and Andrea's article, conservative Christians are both objectively presented as being and subjectively encouraged to identify as marginalised. As the scholar of aesthetics Rita Felski has argued (in the very different context of feminist publics), references to perceived oppression can encourage 'the development of a self-consciously oppositional identity' in relation to what is taken to be an otherwise marginalising public sphere, indicating one's membership in a particular kind of public.[30] Literary critic Michael Warner defines a 'public' as a social form brought into being through circulating discourse, a conglomeration of strangers that exists '*by virtue of being addressed*'.[31] The ideology of the bourgeois public sphere requires this address to be grounded in rational-critical discourse, the convincingly disembodied reason of anonymous written texts and their unknown audience of readers. In this imagining, the public is thought 'to require persuasion rather than poesis'.[32] Some publics, however, are defined through their opposition to the ideological dominance of discourse that presents itself as representing *the* public. These counterpublics are constituted not only through rational-critical dialogue, but through their appeal to alternative forms of address and engagement, such as the passionate Quranic language of the Egyptian reformist preachers studied by the anthropologist Charles Hirschkind[33] or the critique of heteronormativity offered by the comportment of the lesbians and gay men featured in Warner's analysis. It is such a counterpublic that the legal arguments and opinion pieces cited above invoke, constituting, as they do, a form of discourse in which conservative Christians are understood to be defined by their marginal relationship to the dominant public sphere.

Indeed, in the CLC's court submissions in the *Johns* case, Christians are more than simply marginal. They are the victims of an intolerant and ethically bankrupt state using 'its coercive powers to de-legitimise Christian belief'.[34] In this portrayal, Christians suffer the kind of assault on personal integrity that philosopher Axel Honneth describes in terms of structural exclusion, an exclusion premised upon the belief that the injured party lacks 'the same degree of moral accountability as other members of society'.[35] Their perceived lack of moral accountability is evident in the assertion that the Council viewed Christians as second-class citizens unfit to foster vulnerable children. As we have already seen, these assertions were dismissed by the High Court as unable to satisfy the evidentiary requirements of the law. But by rejecting the norms of dominant public discourse, opting instead to express themselves in forms alien to the preferred rational-critical language of the public sphere in general and the legal system in particular—submitting, instead, claims couched in 'extravagant rhetoric', legally questionable assertions, and even emotionally arresting videos and images—the textual and photographic record of the CLC's cases, publications, and public pronouncements constitute a body of discourse that simultaneously draws upon and brings into being their counterpublic status. That this discourse is excluded from the court sheds light on the ideology of a legal system that defines religious 'passion', in Asad's terms, as 'inimical to reason', thereby subjecting it to restraint by secular authorities.[36] Cases like *Johns* reveal that in law, as in religion, evidentiary claims are a function of power, with certain kinds of proofs and truth claims—and particularly those couched in the words 'I believe'—quite literally ruled out of court.[37]

To be sure, to be a member of a conservative Christian counterpublic in twenty-first-century Britain is to adopt a subaltern, marginal, or minority identity by choice, at least in part.[38] (It is worth remembering that a number of claimants in high-profile Christian-interest cases come from migrant and/or racial or ethnic minority backgrounds. This includes Eunice and Owen Johns, who had moved to England from Jamaica as teenagers. Although not addressed in the judgment, it is possible that the couple's race or national origin had an impact on their reception by the Council and the Court.) The assumed social stigma attached to conservative Christian visions of gender or sexuality is taken on knowingly, particularly given Jesus' warnings about the inevitability of persecution: 'If they persecuted me, they will also persecute you' (John 15:20). Yet the CLC's counterpublic discourse is more than just the expression of a subculture. This is because, as with any public discourse, counterpublic speech requires the speaker to open their words up to what Warner terms 'indefinite others'.[39] Feminist counterpublics, for example, generate a gender-specific identity grounded in women's solidarity while also seeking to convince non-feminists of the validity of their grievances.[40] It is precisely by speaking into this space of unknown discursive circulation that Christian activists hope to convince wider society of the validity of their understanding of the good, even as they simultaneously construct themselves as a marginalised group that exists in opposition to dominant publics.

Can we conclude, then, that the CLC makes what Rozenberg calls 'tendentious arguments' while pursuing 'unwinnable' claims because it actually hopes to lose these cases, thereby vindicating a narrative of marginalisation? Such an analysis is, I believe, unsatisfactory. Although they often *anticipate* loss in the courts, and although they view success primarily in terms of pleasing God (as opposed to courtroom victories), the staff and clients of the CLC believe in both the moral and legal force of their arguments. The fact that God's economy trumps a judge's ruling does not mean that this ruling is unimportant. Wins are celebrated and losses mourned, not only because they have a real impact on clients whom the staff has come to know and respect but because they represent months of hard work and hours of fervent prayer. As such, it would be misleading to suggest that rights-based cases are taken with loss as their goal.

But although it would be inaccurate to say that the CLC takes its cases with the intention of losing them, it must be recognised that there can be a conceptual benefit to these losses. This is because they allow the CLC's staff and supporters to argue that the current approach to rights *does not work on its own terms*. It is hoped that publicising this through the legal system will achieve three interlocking aims. First, it reveals the intellectual dishonesty of the rights-based system, which ought to spark conversations about its lack of foundation or guiding principle. Second, it gives non-Christians a chance to hear a Christian alternative to, for example, dominant understandings of sexuality and gender. Third, it cultivates indignation and encourages other conservative Christians to join them in seeking to put Christ at the heart of the nation. (As the anthropologist Ronald Niezen has argued, cultivated indignation may be 'the central source of energy in movements of political and legal reform'.[41]) From this perspective, the potential discomfort a client might feel when they 'cry discrimination' can be justified as part of a broader strategy in which a legal case offers opportunities to articulate an evangelical alternative to the status quo. Legal activism, then, represents a two-pronged reform strategy: first, reveal the problems with the current system; second, offer a Christian solution.

Further, the portrayal of conservative Christians as the members of a maligned counterpublic means that the Centre's staff and clients can present their cases as evidence of the law's failure to practice what it preaches even when these cases actually result in victory for the Christians involved, when an alternative reading would suggest that the law had balanced potentially conflicting rights in their favour. It is in relation to this phenomenon that we return to the case of Andy and Kathryn, the Abort67 members who had been arrested under the Public Order Act for displaying graphic abortion images.[42]

Founded in 2008, Abort67 is the brainchild of Andy Stephenson, a small, bespectacled man with dark, wispy hair and a permanent five o'clock shadow.

A West Sussex resident, Andy formed the group after seeing pictures of aborted foetuses shortly after viewing ultrasound images of his own unborn daughter. Abort67 is the UK branch of the Center for Bio-Ethical Reform (CBR), a US-based pro-life campaign group, from which they receive advice, resources, and the graphic pictures used in their demonstrations. Named after the Abortion Act 1967, which provides a defence, under certain conditions, to the crime of procuring a miscarriage under the Offences Against the Person Act 1861, Abort67 presents itself as a public education project that 'exposes' abortion.[43] Andy believes that legislative change is dependent upon changing public opinion, and it is for this reason that he displays his banner images, some of which are over eight feet in length, outside abortion clinics, colleges, universities, and government buildings: 'Every time we take these pictures out, people's minds are changed about what abortion is.'

Although anti-abortion sentiment has existed in the UK since the passing of the 1967 Act (and, of course, before), by the late 1990s the existence of a largely pro-choice electorate meant that medical ethicist and lawyer Sally Sheldon could write that 'those who continue to kick against [the status quo]—be they pro- or anti-choice activists—are cast as marginal extremists', with attempts to export the more 'violent' tactics of American organisations such as Operation Rescue deemed 'largely unsuccessful'.[44] By the time of Andy and Kathryn's trial, however, this account was out of date. Abort67's confrontational approach—the group prioritises 'unborn lives' over 'born feelings'—and its explicit link to the California-based CBR had led to its being associated with attempts to (re)politicise the issue of abortion in a way reminiscent of the United States' abortion culture wars, with increasingly polarised rhetoric mobilised by both pro-choice and pro-life advocates as a result.[45] Andy and Kathryn's June 2011 arrests were seen as part of this increasing tension.

The case was heard in one of Brighton Magistrates' Court's modest courtrooms. It was a far cry from the gleaming glass and steel of the European Court of Human Rights, where the CLC had argued the cases of Shirley Chaplin and Gary McFarlane just weeks earlier. Courtroom number two's public gallery consists of two rows of wooden benches upholstered in leather the colour of pea soup, the former occupants of which have scrawled messages in the soft wooden railing separating the gallery from the courtroom proper. Sitting amidst the ghosts of previous spectators—'Carina + Beth woz ere 03,' 'Dawn H. 21.9.91'—I watched the CLC team use the language of rights to reinforce the conservative counterpublic in a different way than they had done in *Johns*. While *Johns* had suggested that the right to freedom of religion was trumped by the rights of sexual minorities, this case argued that the right to free speech did not seem to apply to Christian groups, while other organisations—such as animal rights and pro-Palestine activists—were apparently given free rein to use graphic images in their protests.

The assertion that Christians were treated less favourably than others when it came to enforcing their rights was made particularly forcefully by Paul Diamond during his cross-examination of one of the arresting police constables (PCs), whom I will call PC Thompson. He suggested that PC Thompson had made the decision to remove the banner based not on the criteria of the Public Order Act, which requires the expression under consideration to be insulting, abusive, or threatening, and to have caused harassment, alarm, or distress as a result, but on the basis of her own personal dislike of the image. There's nothing more frightening, he told the judge, than the 'personal predilection' of a police officer arbitrarily determining the limits of free speech. Having apparently lost none of the rhetorical flair for which he was chastened in *Johns*, he suggested that PC Thompson had acted as though she were in 'Putin's Russia'.[46] Had other groups been harassed in the way that Abort67 had been? Had the graphic images used by pro-Palestine campaigners been subjected to the same level of scrutiny as the graphic images used by anti-abortion activists? Producing an A4 image of the mutilated bodies of Palestinian children, which had apparently been used at a rally opposing Israeli occupation, he placed the photograph into PC Thompson's hands. As she began to cry, the judge called a short recess.

Nor were photographs of these broken bodies the only images submitted as evidence in the Abort67 trial. Throughout the case, the CLC argued that Abort67's pictures were no more graphic than many of the images exposed to the general public through newspapers, television news reports, and government campaigns. Indeed, Andy had compiled some of these graphic, bloody, and otherwise disturbing images into a book, a copy of which was given to the judge. The defence went through the images one by one: a front-page newspaper article about the death of Muammar Gaddafi illustrated with a picture of his corpse; a *Time* magazine cover depicting a woman whose nose and ears had been cut off by the Taliban; images of cancerous lungs and diseased hearts taken from government-sponsored anti-smoking campaigns. This evidence suggested that it was not *all* graphic or bloody images that were policed. It was only graphic or bloody images that threatened what Andrea's article had called 'the prevailing politically correct orthodoxy'.

These visual submissions both challenged the otherwise staid discourse of the court and seemed to confirm that Abort67 existed, at least partially, outside of this normative order. Indeed, it is precisely because they are seen to challenge the pro-choice majority that Abort67 seeks to display their images. During questioning, Andy explained that although he knew the images were disturbing, they were part of an opinion-changing strategy that had been used by social reformers since at least the eighteenth century. Citing the graphic images used by evangelicals William Wilberforce and Thomas Clarkson in their campaign against the slave trade, he argued that Abort67 was consciously following in the footsteps of a long line of social campaigners who had now lost their subaltern status. In the case of slavery, the opinion of a maligned minority, which had upset and disturbed the Britons of the day with their graphic portrayal of the unconscionability of the slave trade, had now become the opinion of the public at large.

Unlike most of the Christian Legal Centre's cases (at least during my time in the field), this one ended in a win: both Andy and Kathryn were acquitted. Here, then, we see the pragmatic benefit of legal theology, in which secular legal structures are used towards Christian ends. Activists like Andy and Kathryn feel justified in standing on their rights because it is through doing so that they can, in biblical terms, 'Cry aloud; do not hold back; lift up your voice like a trumpet; declare to my people their transgression, to the house of Jacob their sins' (Isaiah 58:1). In this sense, they are following in the footsteps not only of Wilberforce, but of the Apostle Paul, who used his rights as a Roman citizen to enable his preaching (Acts 22:22–28). These historical comparisons help cement the narrative of marginalisation that brings into being the Centre's counterpublic status. While other readings of their victory might suggest that the law, in this case at least, *did* work on its own terms—that if the police had been wrong to arrest Andy and Kathryn, the courts had rectified this injustice by finding them not guilty—the references to eighteenth-century social reformers allied Abort67 with an historic counterpublic, confirming their understanding of themselves as maligned but righteous crusaders who had been unfairly detained for speaking Christian Truth to power.

Finally, by invoking a counterpublic that had now lost its minority status, the case offered a concrete example of the ways in which the views of a counterpublic could become those of society at large. For many of the evangelical activists I met during my fieldwork, reformers like William Wilberforce and Thomas Clarkson have an iconic status as Christians whose faith inspired them to change society for the better, even when their reformist causes made them unpopular, even reviled, in their day.[47] Louise, one of Christian Concern's finance officers, told me that Wilberforce is such an important figure in evangelical activism because he is proof that no matter how deeply integrated an evil is into the political, economic, and social system of the day, sustained activism by godly men and women can eventually end its practice: *no matter how bleak things appear, God can always turn them around.* This understanding of the abolition of the transatlantic slave trade is, of course, almost offensively white-washed; for all I heard about the importance of Wilberforce and Clarkson during my time with evangelical activists, I never heard mention of the role of revolts led by enslaved persons against their enslavers, nor these uprisings' impact on the political economy of slavery. However, the near apotheosis of Wilberforce is important precisely because of what he is thought to say about the relationship between an unpopular position and that of the dominant public. His invocation both highlighted the virtue of Andy and Kathryn's actions and revealed the inequity of the legal framework that had opposed them. All this in spite of the fact that, in this case at least, their right to protest had actually been upheld.

The ethnographic record shows that conservative Christian activists are not the only members of human rights cultures who regard rights discourse with a dose of scepticism. Tobias Kelly, for example, claims that 'doubt' is omnipresent at the United Nations in Geneva,[48] while Annelise Riles writes that many of the elite academics, bureaucrats, and human rights activists with whom she carried out research display 'a profound and sophisticated scepticism about various aspects of the human rights regime—its theoretical claims, its institutional practices, and its archetypal subjectivities'.[49] And yet, this does not stop them from 'doing' human rights in its various guises: teaching academic courses on rights; serving as expert witnesses; training others in human rights technologies; producing human rights documents.

What is one to make of this apparent contradiction? In Riles' analysis, human rights must be understood as an area of legal knowledge in which the dominant understanding of the law, particularly among the US-trained lawyers and activists among whom she worked, is a technocratic, instrumentalist one: 'The phrase "law is a means to an end" or "law is an instrument" appears hundreds of times in the canonical texts of modern US jurisprudence.' Given that they must adopt this instrumentalist approach in their day jobs as lawyers, legal academics, and bureaucrats, her informants' critique of the claims of so-called human rights 'true believers' are ultimately ineffective, as they are made by those whose own daily lives lead them to see such critique as 'leisurely nonaction, as opposed to professional, up-to-the-minute instrumental action'. In other words, their critique of legal tools was easily transformed into 'a tool of legal critique'.[50]

Riles' analysis suggests that it is particularly difficult to challenge the human rights project using the tools of elite critical lawyers, bureaucrats, and scholars: 'critique and irony'. But how does this challenge fare when mounted by a very different set of critical lawyers, with very different conceptual problems with the project of human rights? Although one reading of the CLC's use of human rights language might see it as mere accommodation to the 'cunning', to use the anthropologist Mayanthi Fernando's term, of secular reason,[51] these test cases can also be seen to contribute to a meaningful critique of rights-based legislation. *Johns*, for example, upset the norms of privacy and publicity that regulate sexuality and religion in Britain, revealing that the domestication and privatisation of both faith and sex—characteristics which the bourgeois public sphere might want to see bracketed during the public use of one's reason—works to bolster the exclusionary practices of public space. As with studies of queer and feminist counterpublics, which suggest that patriarchal heteronormativity is perpetuated through the refusal to recognise that the personal is political, cases that pit these ostensibly private rights against each other show them to have an inevitably public component in which some rights—and, therefore, the groups to which those rights adhere—can be portrayed as 'more equal than others'.

In raising the possibility of rights-based critique, I do not mean to downplay the power of the state. Critical scholars are undoubtedly correct to highlight the fact that, as Asad puts it, an 'unresolved tension [remains] between the invocation of "universal humanity" and the power of political authorities charged with maintaining the law'.[52] In his analysis, rights become 'floating signifiers' to be attached and detached according to the needs of powerful states and capitalist expansion, with particularly devastating effects on the (often non-Western, non-Christian) people to whom state violence is eventually displaced.[53] As José Casanova suggests in his response to Asad, this is a 'stark picture of the secular, liberal democracy, and the human rights regime, all blurred into an undifferentiated totality of Western modernity'.[54]

But the fact that rights discourse can be marshalled to fortify state power does not mean that this outcome is inevitable. Historian Tisa Wenger's recent study of American 'religious freedom talk', for example, argues that the First Amendment played an instrumental role in justifying US imperialism at the turn of the twentieth century.[55] The rhetoric of religious liberty worked primarily to define the nation as white, Protestant, and secular. Yet it was also put to use by marginalised communities and individuals who rejected (or were rejected from) those categories. Indeed, as her example of an interpreter for the Board of Indian Affairs who refused to report the Arapaho's continued performance of the (banned) Ghost Dance shows, even employees of the state used First Amendment logic to subvert dominant racial-religious hierarchies. In the interpreter's words, 'It is their religion, and they have a right to it.'[56] Similarly, legal scholar Anna Su has argued that although the language of free religion is a double-edged sword, it contains emancipatory potential, providing linguistic resources for both the dominant and the dominated.[57]

Su and Wenger both focus on groups whose relationship with the United States' government is defined by subjugation and oppression, whether these communities live on the mainland or are the victims of American imperialism. As such, they occupy a very different structural position to the counterpublic Christians discussed here, some of whom are members of the cultural elite. Where the comparison is useful, though, is in pointing out that rights discourse need not always legitimise the norms of the state. As with the examples discussed by Su and Wenger, cases like *Johns* show a religious tradition confronting secular law, challenging it to face the ideological biases that mandate the separation of public law and private morality.[58] The legal establishment's rubbishing of *Johns* notwithstanding, the fact that it was heard at all suggests that it is the context-negation of human rights theory, and not—or at least not only—the overwrought language of Christian activists that contains 'extravagant rhetoric'.

Conclusion: Rootless Rights

Does it matter that there may be no universal foundation for human rights? For those who believe these rights to have their origins in the intellectual legacy of Christianity, it just might. Wolterstorff, for example, suggests that secularisation could result in a lessening in the moral force of rights-based theories of justice, as the widespread adoption of a non-theological anthropology might lead to a dereliction of the duties we owe one another as the loved creations of a loving, relational God. Contra rights critics, Wolterstorff argues that inherent rights are not individualistic or selfish per se—indeed, he understands rights, as duties owed in relationship, to have an inbuilt sociality—but become so only through their misuse.[59] Were we to forget their divine sociality, rights might indeed find themselves at risk, with their secular advocates as foolish as children who, in philosopher Louis Pojman's words, 'see beautiful flowers, grab them, break them at their stems, and try to transplant them without their roots'.[60]

For the staff of the CLC, there is some truth in this assessment. If the European Convention's recognition of human dignity is thought to flow from Europe's Christian heritage (however loosely defined), then one might suspect that the lessening of the moral force of Christianity could result in the lessening of the moral weight attached to human rights. However, this narrative is complicated by the way these 'broken flowers' are understood to have been replanted in secular soil. In a reworking of Wolterstorff's suggestion that a societal decrease in belief in the biblical God might go hand in hand with a general decrease in those who agitate for justice on the basis of inherent rights, Andrea and her team seem to see the human rights project as representing, if not enabling, Britain's increasing rejection of what they deem to be biblical values. In this way, the European Convention on Human Rights is simultaneously posited as the result of Europe's somewhat ill-defined Christian heritage—an instrument infused with 'Christian values'—*and* a sign of its departure from these biblical beliefs.

Indeed, some might go further still. As Andrea put it in a presentation given to a church group in 2009, Britain's embrace of the human rights project not only challenged biblical beliefs, but eroded the protections they ought to enjoy in law:

> I was called to the Bar in 1988, and it is astonishing to see how [Britain's Christian foundations] have been eroded that rapidly. And what is the core philosophy at the heart of the law that has eroded those freedoms? It is the philosophy of human rights. The philosophy of human rights is founded on humanist principles, the idea that human conduct should be based on natural knowledge, and not upon supernatural knowledge, and that human welfare in this world is the proper end to all thought and action.[61]

Here, then, we return to the issue highlighted by Carrie at the beginning of this chapter, the question of Truth (and who defines it). In the above quotation, the legal system's embrace of rights shows Britain to have entered a world in which the limited knowledge of the created is prioritised over and above the limitless wisdom of the Creator, where fleeting pleasures are chosen over lasting glory. In this world, rights are representative of the rejection of Jesus Christ and all that flows from Him—goodness, joy, and stability—and the priority this rejection attaches to individualism, selfishness, and the empty gratification of the here and now. In biblical terms, the embrace of a rights-based legal system shows Britain to have committed the 'two evils' of Jeremiah 2:13: it has forsaken God, 'the fountain of living waters, and hewed out cisterns for [itself], broken cisterns that can hold no water'.

I once asked Andrew, Christian Concern's campaigns director, whether or not their use of human rights law amounted to 'having your cake and eating it too'. He responded by reminding me that having a law to which one could not appeal was tantamount to having no law at all (confirming, as Andrea had done, that one must work within the limits of the legal framework). But there was more to it than that. As he went on to explain, 'there's something in rights', even when one is trying to prompt people to critically rethink them. After all, despite their criticism of human rights legislation, the staff and clients of the CLC believe that all people have innate rights as a result of their being made in the image of God. They worry, however, that society has embraced a rights-based system without understanding the origin of these rights or the responsibilities that might accompany them. Rather than grounding them in a notion of the common good based on the teachings of the Bible, rights had become individual, fragmented, and mutually exclusive.

It is for this very reason that the Centre instrumentalises the language of rights in their legal arguments. Constructing rights as if they were, as legal scholar Carl Stychin puts it, a 'zero sum game'[62] is part of Christian Concern's mission to show that only a society built upon the Truths of the Bible is capable of delivering what many secular proponents of human rights might identify as underlying their own vision of a flourishing society: the pursuit of the common good, grounded in a recognition of human dignity. As such, and whether an individual case is won or lost, counterpublic language always works to supply the Centre with further evidence of conservative Christians' marginality, thus proving, from their perspective, that a rights-based society fails to practice the equality of rights it preaches.

Ambiguity, however, remains. Warner suggests that counterpublics are inevitably 'damaged forms of publicness', distorted by virtue of their relationship of subordination to dominant public discourse.[63] The idea of a 'damaged' form of publicity has some purchase here. The problem with using rights to undermine rights is that, in the end, it is rights talk—and not God talk—that takes centre stage. When Christian activists respond in kind to the rights-based agenda they hope to counter, they might end up reinforcing the structures they wish to contest. The Abort67 case, for example, ensured that Andy and Kathryn's right to 'expose' abortion was upheld. But it also risked them being seen to have bought into the individualist, atomistic culture they sought to challenge. To quote the anthropologist Sally Engle Merry, 'resonance is a costly choice'.[64]

To return to the counterpublics of gender and sexuality mentioned above, one might see in the CLC's use of human rights language the same problems that some feminists and queer theorists have with campaigns that seek to 'normalise' queer lifeways: that by adopting the terminology and structures of already existing institutions, particularly those which are already problematic, the possibility of radically restructuring human relationships was either lost or made more difficult to articulate.[65] Rather than expanding the possibility of living Christianly in every aspect of one's life, litigating in pursuit of religious freedom could well be seen to circumscribe it. By emphasising a presumed link between 'Christianity' and a narrow range of socio-political positions, these positions were made to seem increasingly distant from the concerns of England's (primarily non-practicing) majority, the preserve of a sectarian group seeking to enforce their rights against others (or, worse still, to prevent others from exercising theirs). As such, although I have argued that the CLC uses rights claims to demonstrate the fragmenting impact of a rights-based system, others—including, as we will see in the following chapter, some members of Christ Church—might see in them the difficulty experienced by Riles' elite rights critics, who, though seeking to challenge the structures of individualistic rights-based discourse, ultimately reproduced it.

While recognising the risk of individualism inherent in rights-based claims, however, this chapter must conclude by stressing that the CLC's concern with human rights remains a collective one. In the end, what matters most to my activist interlocutors is not the language of the European Convention but the universal applicability of divine Truth. Carrie, the Christian Concern events manager who found Conway Hall's interior decor to be somewhat lacking, offers a useful reflection on this issue. The concept of Truth was of great importance to Carrie, who had attended charismatic evangelical West Indian–majority churches since the age of five. It was at church that she first learned that her strange nocturnal encounters—the especially vivid nightmares, the creatures she saw moving in her room—were the result of demonic activity, and it was only through her relationship with Jesus that she was able to recognise and overcome these demonic forces. A decade later, it was her Christian faith that enabled her to identify and resist the subtle nudging of the devil when he encouraged her, as she sat on the bus to school, to stray from God's path. This prompted Carrie, then a teenager whose faith had become 'a nominal thing', to recommit herself to Jesus, declaring: 'I'm going to follow You, Lord, I'm not going to treat this as a nominal thing. I can't afford to.'

From Carrie's perspective, then, the world contains right and wrong, Truth and falsity, God's Word and the devil's promptings, and it is essential that both individuals and nation-states are able to distinguish between the two. A philosophy that elevated the individual fulfilment of created men and women over the divine law of their Creator fails to do this, and it is ultimately its perceived rejection of Christian Truth that undergirds Carrie's opposition to the human rights project. Sitting on a crowded train on our way home from the BPAS debate, Carrie and I continued chatting about the implications of Abort67's protests. Competing rights, however, were not how she framed the issue. Wistfully, she turned to me and said: 'Wouldn't it be wonderful if we lived in a world where no one had abortions? We've gone away from God's original plan, and we've created our own understanding of right and wrong. And that's scary.'

CHAPTER FOUR

Getting Rights 'Right'

Nevertheless, we have not made use of this right, but we endure anything rather than put an obstacle in the way of the gospel of Christ.

—1 CORINTHIANS 9:11–12

A Right to Rights

'Do Christians have rights?'[1]

So asked Luke, the Christ Church minister, as he stood to preach one Sunday morning. London was in the last throes of a heat wave, and the Victorian church building was uncomfortably warm. Despite the best efforts of a whirring air conditioner, the congregation—particularly those, like me, who had walked to church—was unusually restless. We had spent the first half of the service fanning ourselves with the hymnals and prayer books stacked in the pews, occasionally ducking out to grab a glass of water from the small kitchen in the church lounge. As always, however, when the minister rose to preach, the congregation gave him their full attention. Pew Bibles were opened, and pens and notebooks were fished out of bags and pockets. (Anthropologists are not the only visitors to Bible-believing churches who fill notebook after notebook with sermon notes. On any given Sunday, about a quarter to a third of those sitting in Christ Church's pews jot things down during the service.) Standing at the pulpit in a suit and tie, his open Bible in his hand, Luke continued:

> Do Christians have rights? Many of us would instinctively answer 'yes' to that question. After all, in our ever more litigious society, everyone else seems to have rights. Women's rights, gay rights, animal rights, children's rights, students' rights, and so we could go on. . . . But some Christians would say we don't have any rights. I mean, that's the whole point, isn't it? When we become Christians, we give up our rights to rights. . . . So, which is it? Do Christians have rights or no rights?

As Luke's sermon hook indicates, one need not be an evangelical lawyer to be the kind of Christian who is concerned with the meaning and applicability of rights. Nor were discussions of rights limited to Sunday sermons or exhortations from the church minister. In fact, the kinds of rights they could or should rely on were the subject of many conversations among the Christ Church laity,[2] who see themselves as the inhabitants of a rapidly de-Christianising country and fully expect their civil liberties, which are understood to be Christian in origin, to be eroded as a result.

Yet this threat to civil liberty, this apparent dilution of 'freedom of—', was rarely discussed in the language of Britain's human rights framework. By contrast to an ideology of rights in which individual, positive entitlements are enforced against an overbearing state, the members of Christ Church tended to speak of rights with an element of consequentialism, evaluating their use in terms of their perceived impact on the spread of the gospel. For those who are always hoping to welcome others into the Kingdom, the claim to rights—so often critiqued as evidence of the West's focus on the individual as 'the centre of the moral universe'[3]—was usually discussed relationally.

Much like the human rights project, Christianity (and particularly the kind of evangelical Protestantism practiced by those at Christ Church) is often understood in terms of its presumed individualism. Ernst Troeltsch, for example, writes that Protestantism posits God's grace as 'seeking out the individual'.[4] Louis Dumont, meanwhile, traces the affinity between Christianity and individualism to well before the Reformation, suggesting that the early church was a key contributor to the emergence of the 'essentially non-social moral being' as the carrier of modern society's 'paramount values' (although he notes that this early 'outworldly' individualism took many centuries to develop into its contemporary 'inworldly' form).[5] And as we saw in the previous chapter, the grounding of human rights in bounded individuals is sometimes seen to have its roots in Christian thinking (broadly construed), even if the rights deemed to flow from being created in God's image have been inconsistently applied to those outside of Christendom.[6]

As such, one might imagine that the 'individualisms' of rights discourse and evangelical Protestantism make easy bedfellows. But although evangelicals tend to view salvation itself as individual, the practice of evangelicalism (and, of course, many other Christian traditions) remains profoundly relational. As Joseph Webster notes, this relationality is both 'vertical' (human-divine) and 'horizontal' (between persons),[7] as those who have been born again are particularly concerned with the salvation of their 'not yet' Christian friends, family, and colleagues, whom they have a duty to evangelise. These obligations colour their understanding of the rights-based claims handled by groups like the Christian Legal Centre.

This chapter posits my Christ Church interlocutors' response to rights discourse as a reflection of both local theological concerns and changing church-state relations. Scholars of law and religion have long argued that state regulation simultaneously shapes and is shaped by religious expressions, traditions, and ideologies. Yet, as Isaac Weiner has argued in the context of the United States, in the absence of grievances filed or cases taken, it is difficult to measure the law's impact on everyday religious experience.[8] This chapter uses sermons, Bible studies, and quotidian interactions to shed light on the legal system's ability to shape evangelical subjectivities even when appeals to law are denied or avoided. In so doing, I hope to show that the rejection of legalistic, rights-based language is intimately linked not only to long-standing theological concerns over the relationship between the individual and the community, but to recent shifts in English law's management of religion. Thus, just as Talal Asad has encouraged us to approach the secular through its 'shadows',[9] I join with Weiner and others in seeking to explore the ways in which litigation can affect religious lifeways even in the absence of a personal experience with the pageantry of the court.[10]

Beginning with an account of relational evangelism,[11] I develop arguments introduced in chapter 2 to show how claims to rights are evaluated on the basis of their impact on one's relationships with others. These consequentialist evaluations foster an understanding of the 'true Christian' as someone who, following the example of Jesus on the cross, seeks to forgo his or her rights in the hope of bringing others to salvation. Such an ethic of sacrificial love is seen to be countercultural in a world which is imagined as increasingly individualistic, self-centred, and litigious. Yet this relational focus does not negate the fact that evangelical Christianity remains, in terms of salvation, highly individualistic. I suggest that this tension explains, in part, the ambivalent response that my Christ Church interlocutors have to the Christian discrimination cases pursued by the CLC. While the claimants were sometimes the recipients of both sympathy and admiration, with Christ Church members praising their courage in standing up for individual conscience, they were sometimes the subjects of disapproval, criticised for being seen to value their rights above the needs of others. I conclude that these responses reflect the somewhat paradoxical result of the English legal system's move towards protecting religious freedom as a positive right (as opposed to a negative liberty), a shift that seems to be experienced as a *lessening* of 'free religion' for English evangelicals.

Relational Evangelism

In evangelical theology, the unit of salvation is not the family or the church, but the individual Christian (a term which, for the members of Christ Church, is limited to those who are 'trusting in Christ for salvation'). Salvation, as Robbins puts it, 'cannot be shared'.[12] The gospel message, on the other hand, both can and should be, and many evangelicals see it as their Christian duty to engage with non-believers in the hope of welcoming them into the Kingdom.

As was suggested in chapter 2, one way that the members of Christ Church hope to achieve this is through the visible work of the Holy Spirit in them, which ought to encourage their non-Christian friends, family members, and colleagues to ask what enables their distinctive, grace-fuelled demeanour. However, for such an approach to bear fruit, it is not enough for a Christian to demonstrate God's grace to their fellow believers (although this, of course, is always expected). Nor is it enough to live a gracious life in the hope that non-Christian strangers will find it appealing (although this would be very much welcomed). Rather, the congregation was encouraged to develop trusting, meaningful friendships with non-Christians in the hope that these relationships would lead to 'gospel opportunities', that is, naturally arising opportunities to share Jesus' message of forgiveness and eternal life. An understanding of this evangelistic strategy is necessary before we can understand the church's approach to rights-based litigation.

One of the settings where I heard frequent reference to the importance (and the difficulty) of developing meaningful friendships with non-Christians was during meetings with my women's Bible study group, which I began attending in the autumn of 2013. By this point in my fieldwork, I had already been studying the Bible 'one on one' with Carol, a nurse in her fifties, and Leah, a solicitor in her twenties. However, given that it is almost impossible to overstate the importance of the Bible for my interlocutors, who view it as the foundation of their faith, I was always eager to increase my exposure to Scripture. Further, Bible study groups are the backbone of evangelical life. In addition to offering opportunities for in-depth, close text analysis of biblical passages, they allow for the building of strong, supportive friendships, the development of accountability networks, and the sharing of prayer requests. As the anthropologist James Bielo puts it, 'what happens in Bible study' ought not 'stay in Bible study', but should '[inform] the logic and decision making of participants as they leave the group setting to be mothers, fathers, spouses, bosses, workers, and citizens'.[13]

One of several study groups that met in the church building on Monday mornings, my group of eight was made up of women in their thirties, forties, and fifties. Our meetings began in the church lounge, where the thirty or so women who were part of a Monday group would collect cups of tea or coffee from volunteers in the church kitchen before spending a few minutes chatting about the previous and coming weeks. We were then read the church notices—'Please keep praying for those coming to Christianity Explored; we need more volunteers for mums and tots; does anyone have a spare buggy they could lend to x and y, our mission partners in Cambodia, who will be visiting London in July?'—before breaking up into our study groups. Mine met in a small room at the back of the church, where we would sit around a collapsible table on orange plastic chairs with a plug-in blow heater directed at our feet (the room's location was such that it rarely got much sunlight, and could therefore be quite chilly; as the autumn progressed, we found that many of the layers of clothing that one might normally remove upon entering a building—scarves and coats, for example—were re-appropriated as blankets draped over our laps). Despite the majority of Christ Church members being English, my group was surprisingly international, with members from South Africa, Australia, and the United States (although all, barring Kristen, the American, had lived in England for many years). Most members had children, who ranged in age from Kristen's three under-fives to Catherine's two grown sons. While some had chosen (and had the resources) to stay at home with their children,[14] others were in paid part-time employment in fields including finance, special needs teaching, and university lecturing.

Although they always began with a chance to socialise over a cup of tea, our Monday morning Bible studies were not entirely informal affairs. They required—in theory at least, if not always in practice—advance preparation, and as one might expect from a church where services seemed to have more in common with academic lectures than effervescent assemblies, this preparation was text-based. We spent autumn 2013 working our way through 1 Timothy, a letter written by the Apostle Paul to the leader of the church at Ephesus. At the beginning of term, each of us had been given a soft-backed A5 booklet, the rosebud yellow cover of which read 'Studies in 1 Timothy'. Inside the booklet were questions based on the Bible passages we would be studying. The first question for our study on 1 Timothy 1:1–7, for example, was 'By what authority does Paul write this letter? Why is this important?' These questions were designed to encourage us to think through and engage with the text, and under each of the questions (of which there were seven to nine per study) was a space to write down our answers. In addition to these booklets, our group leader, Georgina, would sometimes quote to us from *Teaching 1 Timothy*, a paperback Bible commentary by Angus MacLeay, a Church of England minister.

We were not the only group using these resources. In fact, for the first time at Christ Church, all of the small groups—men's groups, women's groups, mixed-gender home groups, and student groups—were studying the same book of the Bible. Written to encourage Timothy in his leadership, it contains a number of verses that are controversial within the Church of England, including the requirement that women 'learn quietly with all submissiveness' and do not 'teach or . . . exercise authority over' men (1 Timothy 2:11–12), as well as condemning 'men who practice homosexuality' (1 Timothy 1:10). Given the debates over gender and sexuality then consuming the Church, 1 Timothy proved both timely and challenging. But although these particular verses were, of course, the subject of much discussion, the theme we returned to week by week was neither gender nor sexuality, but the importance of living grace-fuelled Christian lives as a means of attracting others to the church, and the development of the kind of relationships with non-Christians that would allow one to explain why Christians could live in such a distinctive, attractive way. After all, it was one thing for outsiders to be impressed by a Christian's loving relationships, forgiving attitude, or hardworking lifestyle, but quite another for them to understand that this was the result not of their own effort but of the presence of the Holy Spirit in them.

The connection between these two elements—living a gracious life in the hope of piquing a non-Christian's interest in the gospel, and cultivating the kind of relationships with non-Christians that would allow you to explain it— was brought out during a study we undertook one morning in November. We were looking at 1 Timothy 6:1–2, in which Paul asks those 'who are under a yoke as bondservants' to honour their masters, as this will bring glory to God. Question six of our study guide read 'What is at stake in the way we behave at work?' Catherine, a tall blond woman with a slight South African accent, answered: 'It's obviously God's good name.' Non-Christians will look at the lives of those professing to be Christian, and if they don't see any evidence of the work of God, they'll judge the gospel accordingly. Christians, she continued, must both 'behave well and be observed to behave well'. Linda, who worked part-time in London's financial district, agreed: 'I've always been told to remember that my boss is God.' Not only was she representing God, and therefore under an obligation to demonstrate His grace to those around her, but she was also accountable to Him, and ought to keep her words and actions consistent with her Christian faith. Everyone agreed that this was important to remember, because it focused on the need to work well even when one's colleagues weren't looking. Catherine laughed and suggested that we were to be as consistent as the gentleman who used a butter knife even when dining alone.

The group then moved on to a discussion of explicit evangelism. Kristen, who had recently moved to London with her husband and children from the American Midwest, suggested that Christians should be willing to 'incorporate' their faith into their work lives. This included being able to talk about the role it played outside of work: 'Talk about your weekend; say you went to church on Sunday.' Catherine agreed that one shouldn't 'hide' one's Christianity. After a short pause, she asked the group: 'Do you think people should try to evangelise at work in more overt ways?' Kristen was the first to respond. After acknowledging that her nationality meant her evangelising sensibilities might be slightly different to those of her English sisters, she explained that yes, she did think Christians should evangelise in the office. However, she stressed, this had to be 'friendship evangelism'. She differentiated friendship evangelism from the kind of evangelism where there was no pre-existing relationship between speaker and listener. 'Handing out pamphlets outside your work' was not 'honouring God', but developing real relationships of trust and friendship—the kind that would allow your non-Christian friends to notice your distinctiveness, and then allow you to explain its cause—was.

This conversation suggests a similar approach to evangelism as the one advocated by Carol in chapter 2, in which the Christian's loving, hardworking, gracious approach to life ought to point to their beliefs, thereby allowing evangelistic conversations to arise 'quite naturally, because of your good lives'. But as Kristen pointed out in our Bible study, these conversations were unlikely to occur without a pre-existing relational base. After all, a stranger with whom one had little meaningful contact was unlikely to notice one's grace-fuelled demeanour. Even if they did, they might mistakenly attribute it not to the grace of God but to the kind of legalistic, rule-keeping religion from which evangelicals try to distance themselves. It was for this reason that Kristen connected the grace-fuelled living spoken of by Catherine and Linda—the kind of consistent, using-a-butter-knife-even-when-dining-alone behaviour that could only be achieved by the grace of God—to relational evangelism.

Although a relative newcomer to Christ Church, Kristen was not its only proponent of friendship evangelism, or what sociologists have referred to as evangelicalism's 'personal influence strategy'.[15] As has been noted of Christian groups in the United States, an emphasis on relational witness has taken root alongside the growth of the 'seeker-friendly' church model, with diverse evangelical communities keen to spark interest in Christianity through displays of friendship and kindness.[16] Christ Churchites, on the whole, are not what Omri Elisha terms 'socially engaged' evangelicals, those who feel compelled to engage in charitable outreach as a result of their faith. Yet they would agree with Paul, one of Elisha's Tennessee-based activist interlocutors, when he declared: '"[Evangelicals] have always been good at proclamation evangelism—preaching sermons and handing out pamphlets and such—but we're terrible at loving people."'[17] Successful evangelism, in this understanding, requires acts of relational love. It was for this reason that Kay, a geography teacher from Hong Kong who was then studying Japanese in the hope of becoming a missionary, doubted that street preaching was an effective way of growing the Kingdom: 'I don't think it's very relational.' Her own approach, by contrast, was to build up friendships, first with Japanese people living in London and then with the locals in Sapporo, Hokkaido, 'the most unreached part of Japan'.

James, the curate, expounded a similar strategy during a sermon on Matthew 18:1–6. In these verses, Jesus tells His disciples that they must humble themselves like little children before they can enter the Kingdom of Heaven. James' message for the church was that because the Kingdom was for 'nobodies', Christians were not to set up artificial barriers that might prevent others from joining the church family.[18] Rather, they were to be welcoming, and one way to gauge how welcoming they were was to ask: 'How much time do we regularly give to those currently outside the Kingdom of God?' Christ Church was then gearing up for a nation-wide mission drive that was scheduled to take place in the week before Easter. Although this mission week was still six months away, James told the congregation that they ought to be 'investing' in their relationships with non-Christians now:

> We need to know people if we're to have any chance of welcoming them into God's Kingdom. . . . We have to be investing in friendships now in order to have any chance of being able to share the gospel with people in the future. How much time do we *really* give to those who are currently outside the Kingdom of God?

James stressed that Christians ought to have a 'genuine' (as opposed to 'superficial') interest in their non-Christian friends. It was this kind of relationship—the kind where you knew about a friend's financial troubles, ill health, messy love life, or recent bereavement—that would allow you not only to demonstrate God's love in practical ways, but to share the gospel with them.

James' question was no mere rhetorical device. Indeed, it was the kind of question with which many of his listeners were already struggling. As Anna Strhan has argued of wealthy evangelicals in London's financial district, this is partly to do with their tacit acceptance of secular norms of privacy, as well as class-based assessments of what constitutes polite conversation.[19] It was for this reason that Georgina, who led our Bible study, found it easier to witness to relative strangers than she did to those in her immediate social circle. After all, the social cost involved in offending a stranger or social other by explaining that he or she was, by nature, deserving of hell was easier to deal with than alienating a cherished friend—or even a socially significant acquaintance—with the same message.

But it was also understood in terms of their own sinfulness. The conflict between wanting to see outsiders saved and not wanting to offend them with the message that 'all have sinned and fall short of the glory of God' (Romans 3:23) was internalised as a source of shame for many of my evangelical interlocutors. Diana expressed a common concern when she said: 'I don't know any Christian that would say that they evangelise as much as they could do. I definitely don't think I do.' Many church members could recount moments when they knew they ought to have shared the gospel but had failed to do so. Even Kristen, the American who had advocated 'friendship evangelism' in the workplace, once told us of an old school friend with whom she had been reluctant to speak about Jesus. Although they had known each other throughout school and university, it took her ten years to broach the subject of the gospel. Afterwards, he had asked her why, if her faith was so important to her, she'd waited so long to share it with him. Years later, his question still weighed heavy on her heart: 'I was ashamed when he me asked that, because I didn't have an answer.'

Further, as the church well knew, the desire to cultivate friendships in the hope of creating gospel opportunities could be interpreted as tokenistic or insincere by outsiders. Church members were aware, as James pointed out, that no one wanted to be thought of as a project: 'Biblical evangelism, friends, is sharing the gospel with *people*, not seeing people in our office as projects.' Relational evangelism, then, is lauded in theory but difficult in practice. The desire to see one's friends coming to Christ, but the worry that one might alienate them in the process, meant that getting one's relationships 'right' was a priority. Did spending time with a non-Christian friend in the hope of later inviting them to church mean you saw that person as a 'project'? If someone turned down one evangelistic advance, how long did you have to wait before making another? And—most guilt-inducing of all—at what point did your concern not to alienate non-Christians become an excuse not to boldly proclaim the gospel? In the following section, I argue that Christ Church's emphasis on developing good relationships with others as a means of both demonstrating God's grace and creating opportunities for the exposition of that grace plays a key role in their evaluation of the concept of rights, as reliance on these rights may have an impact, whether positive or negative, on the relationships that ought to be giving rise to gospel opportunities.

Rights Forgone

Although evangelical Protestantism posits salvation as an individual matter, even bounded individuals exist in webs of relationship to one another. This can create a tension between Christian individualism, on the one hand, and one's obligation to kith and kin on the other. Such a tension is masterfully explored by Joel Robbins in his study of Christian conversion among the Urapmin of Papua New Guinea. Drawing on Dumont's terminology of 'paramount values', the values that structure how the various elements of a society relate to one another, Robbins argues that Melanesian people are neither individualist nor holist (the two values analysed by Dumont) but 'relationalist'. By this he means that Urapmin society is structured neither in terms of individuals nor around social wholes, but in terms of relationships between people. The clash between the Urapmin's newly adopted Christian individualism, which condemns the expression of individual will as a failure to subjugate the self to God, and their traditional morality, which evaluates wilful acts on the basis of their effect on existing relationships, is a cause of great discontent among Urapmin converts.[20]

Robbins' emphasis on the individualism of Christianity is not without its critics.[21] Mark Mosko, for example, uses New Melanesian Ethnography to explore the dividuality of Christian personhood, arguing that 'Christianity . . . involves elicitive detachments and attachments among dividual persons (converts, God, Jesus, Holy Spirit, the Devil, etc).'[22] Outside of the Melanesian context, Girish Daswani has approached Ghanaian Pentecostal conversion in terms of ongoing partibility,[23] while Liana Chua's fieldwork in Malaysian Borneo shows that Christian individualism does not necessarily displace more relational forms of morality.[24] Even ethnographers working in regions known for their cultural individualism, such as the Protestant United States, have challenged our understanding of the indivisibility of Christian salvation, as Fenella Cannell's account of collective notions of 'religious work' among Latter-day Saints shows.[25]

Robbins' Dumontian terminology, however, remains relevant for my interlocutors, who strongly identify with what Mosko terms 'the bounded, possessive individual of Western ideology' (even as they seek, on occasion, to suppress it).[26] As with the Urapmin, they experience a conflict between the values of individualism and relationalism. However, whereas Urapmin relational sociality is challenged by Christian individualism, my informants see the individualism of rights discourse as a potential threat to Christian relationalism. Further, while the Urapmin learned to interpret all wilful actions as sinful regardless of their outcomes, the Christ Church ministry team encourage an explicitly consequentialist approach to standing on one's rights. This consequentialist approach, which evaluates the desirability of insisting on one's rights on the basis of their relational impact (as opposed to one's inherent entitlement to so insist) suggests that although they refer to themselves as having the 'right' to undertake certain actions, the idea of a 'human right' to freedom of religion—that is, a pre-existing, inviolable privilege guaranteed by the state—has little purchase for church members.

This was most evident in a number of sermons preached throughout summer 2013, during which Luke, the minister, asked the question with which this chapter began: 'Do Christians have rights?' Christ Church sermons, which are expository in style and typically last twenty-five to thirty minutes, are usually delivered as part of a 'series' devoted to a certain biblical book. This approach had the benefit, I was often told, of making sure that the whole Bible was 'faithfully preached': if ministers went through the Bible book by book, chapter by chapter, verse by verse, they were unable to skip or gloss over its more uncomfortable, challenging, or confusing portions. Christ Church sermons usually feature a detailed, close-text analysis of the verses in question, a call to repentance for listeners who are 'not yet' Christian, and practical advice on how to apply the passage for those who are. This preaching style has been popular in conservative evangelical churches since the 1930s.[27]

The sermons discussed in the following section were part of a series preached by Luke on the book of 1 Corinthians. It was aimed at helping the congregation develop a framework for biblically-based decision making. On many matters, of course, the Bible is seen to give direct and easily applicable guidance about one's life choices. As regards sexual morality, for example, there is thought to be little room for interpretation: passages from Genesis, the Gospels, and the Epistles were all taken to confirm that the only legitimate place for sexual expression was within a lifelong, heterosexual marriage.[28] Yet there are some areas of life where the Bible is less specific. How should a Christian decide, for example, whether or not it was acceptable for them to attend a particular party? How could they determine whether or not it was all right for them to see a particular film? 'There's no chapter or verse in the Bible that I can take you to help you make those decisions, and yet our lives are full of decisions like that, aren't they?' Luke hoped to use 1 Corinthians to give the congregation a set of principles that they might apply in order to determine the acceptability of the choices they made on a daily basis.

Luke is an animated, enthusiastic preacher. He has little time for props or pictures; all he needs are his sermon notes, his pulpit, and his open Bible. As such, it was a mark of the importance of the issues we were dealing with that the sermon series on 1 Corinthians involved Luke projecting an image onto the screen that hung at the back of the church, which was usually reserved for song lyrics, church notices, and the occasional Bible verse. The image in question was a flow chart, which laid out a number of questions Christians ought to ask themselves before making a decision. The first thing a Christian ought to do, he told us, was to establish whether the Bible allowed them to make the choice in question. This was, unsurprisingly, the most important question to ask. If the Bible marked something out as a sin—theft, fornication, drunkenness—then the Christian could not, in good conscience, engage in that behaviour. If, on the other hand, the Bible did allow it, the Christian could move on to the second question, which was whether or not their conscience allowed it. Too often, Luke said, this is where we stop: if the Bible allows it and our conscience allows it, we go ahead and do it. But 1 Corinthians teaches us to ask three more questions. (Of the three questions Luke listed on his flow chart, this section examines the first two. We will return to the third in this chapter's conclusion.)

The first of the three additional questions, which we looked at during a sermon on 1 Corinthians 8, was: 'What is the effect of this decision on other Christians?' In the text in question, the Apostle Paul is writing to the Corinthian church about the acceptability of eating food offered to idols. The letter explains that, as monotheists, Christians know that the idols to which meat is sacrificed are not real. Therefore, Christians are free to eat this meat: 'We are no worse off if we do not eat, and no better off if we do' (1 Corinthians 8:8). Yet the fact that they are free to do so does not mean that they *ought* to. Weaker Christians—perhaps those who had only recently converted, or who had been deeply involved in the worship of idols before their conversion—might see stronger Christians eating meat offered to idols and become confused, compromised, or led back into idol worship as a result. 'Therefore', Paul writes, 'if food makes my brother stumble, I will never eat meat, lest I make my brother stumble' (1 Corinthians 8:13). Luke illustrated this principle with an example he thought more applicable to middle-class Londoners:

Take Josephine. Josephine's been an alcoholic for many years, and she's been wonderfully liberated from her alcoholism by the gospel of Jesus

Christ. And she comes to church and she comes to take communion, but the only wine that's being distributed at the Lord's Supper is alcoholic, and she can't go near alcohol without causing her to stumble. And every communion service is a struggle for her inwardly. . . . Are Christians free to drink wine? Absolutely. In our Lord's Supper, yes, at home, yes. But what would be the loving thing of that church leadership to do? Surely it would be to find some way of serving non-alcoholic wine, so that Josephine, and possibly others, would not be caused to stumble.[29]

Unlike actions which would be met with a 'no' when subjected to Luke's first question, 'Does the Bible allow it?', which were deemed unacceptable by virtue of their inherently sinful nature, the validity of a Christian's actions in a situation like the one imagined above were approached from a gospel-shaped, consequentialist perspective. It's tempting, Luke noted, to ask, 'Am I allowed to do this as a Christian?', but a better question, he thought, was 'is this a loving thing to do as a Christian?' Christian freedom, in other words, ought to be understood *relationally*.

A similar approach was evident in the next of the questions on Luke's flow chart: 'How does this further the gospel?' This was the subject of a sermon on 1 Corinthians 9, in which Paul tells the Corinthians that as a full-time Christian worker, he has the right to receive a salary from those he preaches to: 'those who proclaim the gospel should get their living by the gospel' (1 Corinthians 9:14). And yet, so concerned was he that people heard the Good News that he was willing to forgo this right to payment. With this in mind, Luke argued, Christians should be 'regularly forgoing' their rights in the hope of welcoming others into Christ's Kingdom. Luke asked us to think about the 'rights' we held so dear— 'the right to a Sunday evening, the right to watch cricket on Sunday morning, the right to time with friends, the right to a holiday, the right to respectability and everyone thinking well of us'[30]—and to compare them with what Paul had given up. He concluded with a prayer asking for forgiveness for those times 'when we have stood on our rights when we should have forgone them, and when we have not shared Christ's concern and love for lost men and women'.

In the above sermon, Luke explicitly linked the denial of oneself for the sake of others with the spread of the gospel. When faced with a decision, Christians should always 'think gospel', prioritising the salvation of others over their own rights. Indeed, standing on one's rights when they should have been waived was seen as a failure to share 'Christ's concern and love for lost men and women', as such an approach revealed the Christian in question to be more concerned with themselves than with the eternal fate of others. This was, Luke reminded us, not the behaviour of a true Christian:

You see, as long as defending our rights is the lodestar that orders our priorities, I'm not sure we're really Christians. Because of all people, we

Christians know the ultimate example of someone abandoning their rights. And it's not supremely Paul. It's the Lord Jesus Christ.

He hoped the congregation would have 'that same willingness to let go of our rights, that same desire to do whatever we can to win whoever we can, that same preparedness to inconvenience ourselves' so as to bring others to God.

Although framed by Luke in terms of rights, the above examples are not, of course, the same kinds of rights as those handled by the Christian Legal Centre. Luke's focus was less on legally codified rights than on actions to which a Christian might feel entitled to take by virtue of their apparent acceptability within a biblical framework (and, of course, the law of the land). They were not so much positive rights as negative liberties, in that they are freedoms not curtailed by the Bible or the state. Yet a similar logic was applied to some of the cases argued by the Christian Legal Centre under rights-based law. For example, a few months after Luke's series on 1 Corinthians, James (the curate) gave a sermon on Matthew 17:24–27. In these verses, Jesus is asked if He will pay the temple tax, a tax required of all Jewish men for the upkeep of the temple. Jesus explains that although He is exempt from this tax, just as a prince is exempt from the taxes of the king, He will pay it so as 'not to give offence' (Matthew 17:27). James preached that Jesus was giving a pattern for Christians to follow in their own lives. In his words, 'Jesus limits His freedom to serve a larger purpose. . . . He limits His freedom for the sake of the lost':

> Christian people, we are free people. Free from sin, free from the bur-den of the law, free from guilt, free from what people think of us. It's liberating. Yet the challenge, to each and every one of us here this eve-ning, is how we exercise that freedom for the greater good of the gospel.

James continued: 'You see, I'm free to wear a cross at work, but I might choose not to for the offence that it causes. That could be an example of [forgoing our] gospel freedom for the sake of the gospel.'

As we have already seen, the members of Christ Church are wary of Chris-tians who seek to enforce their right to wear religious symbols at work. James' choice of example, then, was hardly surprising. For our purposes, however, what is interesting about this application was its explicitly relational bent. Sit-ting in a café together a few months after he had given this sermon, I asked James if he could explain the sort of situation he had in mind when he sug-gested that wearing a cross might limit the spread of the gospel. Taking out his Bible (as my interlocutors often did), he reread Matthew 17 before offering me a hypothetical. Imagine you're trying to win your Muslim colleague for the Kingdom, but 'a big sticking point' for them is the crucifixion. Your colleague thinks that if Jesus were the Son of God, it would be absurd for Him to have been crucified. In that instance, James explained, wearing a cross around your neck might actually act as a 'barrier' between you and your colleague. You would still be free to wear it, but really, why would you? 'I've got the right for many things, but I want to deny that right, the rights that I have, for the sake of other people.'

Another example of this principle related to those seeking to enforce a right not to work on Sundays. This had been the subject of a recent CLC case, *Mba v London Borough of Merton*. Celestina Mba, a children's care home worker, argued that she had been discriminated against by her employer, Merton Council, when it sought to enforce her contractual obligation to work Sunday shifts (an obligation she thought had been overridden by an informal agreement with the Council).[31] She lost her case at first instance, appealed, and lost again. The Court of Appeal's ruling had been released to widespread press coverage just weeks before James and I sat down for our interview,[32] and it was perhaps for this reason that the following hypothetical came so easily to his mind:

> If you're working for a firm that says you need to work shift work on a Sunday, to [then] assert your right to not work on a Sunday, well, you knew that when you signed up for that company. Is it possible to find another place of work? Because that's going to be an offence. That's going to really hack off your manager and maybe your other colleagues, as they're having to work the roster so that you have Sunday off. That's not going to do the gospel any favours. It's just going to make you look like a really difficult person.

He went on to argue that those who insisted on their rights in a belligerent way—to be 'provocative' or 'cause a stink'—were not promoting the gospel, but damaging its reputation. Unlike the ideal Christian employee discussed by my Bible study group, who knew that her ultimate boss was God and that she ought to represent Him well, Christians who sought to 'cause a stink' were neither living gracious lives nor building up solid relationships with their non-Christian colleagues. Instead, they were placing their individual desires ahead of the salvation of others, mirroring the selfishness of the unconverted.

Recall from chapter 1 that James believes Christians throughout the UK are coming under increasing pressure at work, and that they ought not be surprised by state-backed persecution in the future. He even wondered whether evangelical preachers like him might soon end up in prison for proclaiming the gospel. Yet he did not feel that rights-based claims were an appropriate way to counter this trend. Instead, he worried that standing on one's rights meant one was buying into the individualistic logic of what Luke had labelled an 'ever more litigious society' in which 'everyone is insisting on their rights' to the detriment of others. James' and Luke's aversion to this sort of litigation stems from the tension between the values of individualism, here imagined as a selfish, stubborn attempt to enforce one's rights at the expense of one's colleagues, and Christian relationalism, portrayed in terms of building meaningful friendships with non-Christians and denying one's rights for their sake.

Rights-denying relationalism was to be preferred to rights-insisting individualism. Their advice to the congregation was to look to Jesus as the perfect model of this rights-denying attitude: 'Jesus loved you enough to put aside His rights in order to die for you, and trusting in Him you and I are called to be like Him, putting aside our rights.'

Now, in light of the emphasis on grace that we saw in chapter 2, Luke's flow chart approach to Christian living might seem somewhat surprising. Following a checklist seems to advocate exactly the kind of legalistic morality that an evangelical ought to reject. Further, evaluating the acceptability of one's actions on the basis of their potential consequences seems to grate against my interlocutors' understanding of moral absolutes. It is for this reason that we must remember that these relational, consequentialist questions—what is the effect of this on other Christians, and what is the effect of this on the spread of the gospel—were ultimately secondary; they were the questions one was to ask once one had already determined that an action was not discouraged or forbidden by the Bible. Indeed, Luke himself recognised the risk of legalism inherent in this approach when he acknowledged that 'the Pharisee in us' always seeks out rules and regulations to follow. He tried to guard against this by stressing that the flow chart ought to be approached lovingly, not legalistically. He was offering principles, not mandates.

Yet the sheer flexibility of a religion that rejects rules and regulations can sometimes leave the faithful crying out for guidance, for conventions to be given or virtuous models to aspire to. Robbins writes that the Urapmin, by abandoning the complex regime of taboo observance they had practiced before their conversion to Christianity, now inhabit a world of moral discontent. Although they are pleased to live in 'free time', in which they are no longer bound by ritual law, the loss of the ritual system means they are now unable to understand themselves as moral subjects. Unlike the taboo system, which provided 'a very workable framework for regulating the will', Christian sin is so all-encompassing that any expression of wilful behaviour is seen to threaten their salvation. Ironically, this led one pastor, a Bible college graduate named Kiki, to encourage his congregation to be as self-controlled as someone living under the strictest of the Urapmin taboo regimes: 'the image of someone following a stringent version of its taboos [was] the most compelling model he [could] find for a life of moral rectitude.'[33] Luke's flow chart, I suggest, indexes a similar tension between freedom and its use. By laying out a step-by-step approach to the decision-making process and encouraging a relationalist, consequentialist ethic, it functioned to curb the excessive freedom associated with free time, reminding the Christian that although he or she had been liberated from the power of sin, this liberation entailed relational responsibilities.

In addition to elaborating the somewhat paradoxical relationship between Christian freedom and the strict moral code adhered to by my informants, in which grace both liberates one from the law and gives one a deep desire to keep it, the ministry team's tips for ethical decision making also tell us something about the Christ Church congregation's approach to rights per se. As regards the Christian discrimination cases, it was in relation to those situations where one would have to answer 'no' to the first or second of Luke's questions—does the Bible allow it, does my conscience allow it—that support for Christian claimants was most strongly expressed. This was most evident in cases involving service provision to LGBTQ+ persons. In particular, great sympathy was expressed for 'conscientious objectors' such as Peter and Hazelmary Bull,[34] B&B owners who would not let double bedrooms out to couples who were not in heterosexual marriages.[35] Yet even where my interlocutors felt a great deal of compassion for the people involved, they were not spoken of as the victims of human rights violations. Rather, they were seen as the early casualties of the dismantling of Britain's 'Christian heritage', from which its traditional civil liberties were thought to flow.

This was brought out during a conversation with Leah and Lucy, both solicitors, with whom I met one summer's morning to discuss a number of real and hypothetical legal cases over iced coffee. Both women came armed with their Bibles (Lucy's, which was hot pink and decorated with Christian fish stickers, was particularly memorable) and made frequent reference to them throughout the morning. The first case we discussed was that of Lillian Ladele, a registrar who had resigned when her employer, Islington Borough Council, refused to accommodate her objection to registering same-sex civil partnerships.[36] Ladele had been a registrar well before civil partnerships were introduced. When she took the job, she could not have known that she would be expected to perform them. As such, both Lucy and Leah were extremely sympathetic to her case. As far as they were concerned, she had been right to politely refuse to facilitate the formation of civil partnerships; as Bible-believing Christians, they would have done the same.

But although they expressed disappointment at the fact that Islington Council would not accommodate Ladele's religious beliefs, the very fact of the court's decision meant that they no longer expected to be able to rely on conscientious objection as a 'right'. Her case had clarified the law, and although they disagreed with it, they accepted that the judgment represented the 'conventional wisdom' of an 'increasingly secular' Britain. As with professions that would require the Christian to go against his or her conscience in any other way, for example, through exaggeration or lying (Lucy gave the example of being an estate agent, which she thought would require dishonesty), being a registrar had simply been added to the growing list of jobs which Bible-believing Christians, in good conscience, would no longer choose to apply for. Although 'a lot of these cases focus on issues that are very controversial, like homosexuality', Lucy argued that there were any number of issues that might prevent her taking any particular job: 'These things make the headlines, but I couldn't take a job even as an estate agent.' She explained this inability to take a job as an estate agent or a registrar not as an infringement of an inviolable 'right' to work in these professions, but as a choice she simply would not make. In the terminology of Luke's flow chart, this was because it was forbidden by both the Bible and her conscience. Leah agreed, stating that not applying for a job 'because of your faith or your conscience' was not a form of discrimination, but an active choice.

To repeat, this is not to say that Leah or Lucy agreed with the Employment Tribunals that found against Christians seeking exemptions from workplace duties on the grounds of conscience. On the contrary, they thought it both unfair and disproportionate that Christian registrars could not be accommodated, and that Christian B&B owners were no longer able to set their own guest policies. In an ideal world, they would prefer Christians to be able to work in all legal professions (all the better for relational evangelism). What is important for my argument, however, is that the language used was that of resignation, sadness, and disappointment at the way things were going, not outrage or indignation at an inviolable right denied. While the CLC publicises their cases in an effort to cultivate what Ronald Niezen refers to as the 'indignation' associated with rights-based activism, particularly among conservative Christians, those at Christ Church—who form, we can safely assume, a part of this target audience—have accepted them as the inevitable result of secularisation.[37] If indignation suggests the possibility of real reform, *resignation* suggests an acceptance of the inevitability of the status quo.[38]

Given that those at Christ Church tend to understand the nation's tradition of civil liberties, such as freedom of speech, assembly, and religion, to be at least partly rooted in its 'Christian heritage', it was of little surprise to them that, as the state moved away from its ostensibly Christian foundations, these liberties would increasingly come under threat. The idea of an enforceable right to freedom of religion had not filled this vacuum. This suggests that the move towards codifying freedom of religion as a 'positive legal right', as opposed to the traditional common law approach of respecting religious freedom as a 'negative accommodation',[39] has come to be understood by conservative evangelicals as a weakening of their religious liberty. Indeed, one could argue that it is due to their *lack of faith* in the human rights project that the members of Christ Church take the consequentialist approach to rights outlined above, in which—so long as it did not violate what was taken to be biblical law—the rightness or wrongness of a Christian's decision to rely on their rights was evaluated not according to their inherent entitlement to do so, but according to its impact on gospel-spreading relationships.

Conclusion: Individuals in Relationship

In a world in which 'everyone is insisting on their rights'—not least in the self-interested city of London[40]—the members of Christ Church are encouraged to go against the grain, prioritising their gospel-spreading relationships over and above their own desires and freedoms. This is understood to be as countercultural as giving up one's time to teach Sunday School, arguing for the exclusivity of Christ, or saving one's first kiss for one's wedding day. By deflecting attention from one's own needs on to the needs of others, both grace-fuelled living and relational evangelism encourage the Christian to, as Luke would say, 'think gospel'. Yet the relational element of 'thinking gospel' was not always easy, particularly as Christianity itself views the person as an individual-in-relation-to-God.[41] The emphasis on relationships was never an attempt to deny or challenge the individual nature of salvation.

That the individual-in-relation-to-God remained in tension with the individual-in-relation-to-others was most clearly articulated by Naomi. An optician in her twenties, Naomi is both naturally friendly and exceptionally eager to evangelise. She would often approach me if she noticed me sitting alone at church, and seemed particularly keen to help me find God during my research. However, it was not just me that Naomi hoped to help on the journey to faith. She was deeply conscious of her duty to share the gospel with every- one she met, and experienced real frustration when she felt that this was not possible or appropriate.

Naomi and I were sitting together on the Sunday evening when James gave the sermon summarised above, in which he challenged his listeners to re-evaluate how much time they '*really*' gave to those 'outside the Kingdom of God'. We continued sitting in the pew long after the service had finished, chat- ting and drinking the cups of tea that had been brought to us by volunteers on the coffee rota. Naomi explained that she was already following James' advice about investing in relationships. She had built up strong friendships with her non-Christian colleagues and had had many gospel conversations as a result. But she only worked closely with three people, she told me, and that just didn't seem like very many. 'If this is true'—and she was convinced that it was—then telling three people just wasn't enough. She ought to be telling everybody. She sighed in frustration as she repeated the core point of James' sermon: that she should spend more time serving those who weren't yet Chris- tians. But how, she asked, was she supposed to do that? She volunteered with the church youth group on Fridays, attended church twice on Sundays, went to a Bible study group on Wednesdays, and worked full time, often on Saturdays. Although she tried to see her non-Christian friends during the week, some- thing had to give. 'Should I leave my Bible study group?' she wondered aloud. But if she were to do that, what about her own spiritual growth? Wouldn't her relationship with God suffer as a result?

Naomi was not the only Christian who worried about striking a balance between, as Girish Daswani puts it of Ghanaian Pentecostals, her 'individual aims' and her 'moral obligations to others',[42] and the sort of bind she felt her- self to be in was not unknown to the Christ Church leadership team. It is in this context that we return to the final question on Luke's flow chart. As noted above, after determining that an action is neither forbidden by the Bible nor the individual's conscience, the Christian was encouraged to ask three more questions. 'Chapter 8 made us ask: what is the effect of this decision on other Christians? Chapter 9 made us ask: how does this further the gospel?' The third question, which Luke examined in relation to 1 Corinthians 10, was 'how will this decision affect my spiritual life? In the Christian race, will this decision slow me down or speed me up?' Luke reminded the congregation that it was important they safeguard their own relationship with God. Winning someone for the Kingdom at the expense of one's own holiness was to be avoided. In the words of Will, a Bible college student and church apprentice: 'being a Christian is fundamentally something for an individual. . . . It is something that's done in community, but it is an individual thing.' For Naomi at least, the tension between individualism and relationalism was never fully resolved. She felt herself to be at a crossroads and continued to debate the relative merits of leaving her Bible study group, cutting down on her church service, or even quitting her job, so that she could more fully devote herself to evangelism without compromising her own spiritual growth.

Nor was the tension between individualism and relationalism fully resolved at the level of the Christian-interest cases. Robbins writes that paramount values not only structure the relations between different elements of a society, but 'determine what cultural form something has to take in order even to be eligible to be reckoned as good'.[43] For many members of Christ Church, the claimants in the legal cases appeared to be the subjects of ambivalence precisely because they created a conflict between two paramount values, making it difficult for them to be 'reckoned as good'. They were simultaneously admired for standing up for their biblical values and chastised for failing to do so in a relational way. Kate, for example, whose complicated evaluation of her own role in a CLC case we will examine in the next chapter, found that she sometimes thought the clients were 'brilliant' for 'standing up' for Christianity—a positive evaluation rooted in individualism—but sometimes thought the cases went 'too far' and were ultimately 'detrimental' to Christian witness—a negative evaluation rooted in relationalism. Even James, who gave such short shrift to those he thought were putting their needs before the gospel by insisting on the right to wear a cross or have Sundays off, was much more sympathetic to claimants who were asked to act against their individual consciences. And as we saw with Shirley Chaplin in chapter 2, many of those involved in Christian-interest litigation frame their cases in relational terms, as efforts to protect the rights of *all* believers—now and in the future—rather than theirs alone. But in a context in which 'God's agenda' was increasingly seen to come into conflict with that of the government, deciding whether the gospel was better served by forgoing one's rights and resigning quietly or insisting on them through a highly publicised court case was becoming increasingly difficult to determine.

These micro-level community reflections cannot be understood in abstraction from the macro-level legal context in which they occur. Rather, they show how local theological categories and nation-wide legislative shifts can bleed into one another, thereby impacting religious subjectivity at the level of the individual. I suggest that the ambivalence noted above points to a lack of confidence in 'rights' per se, a lack that is linked to recent changes in the law's regulation of religion. Since the coming into force of the Human Rights Act 1998, Article 9 of which enshrines a positive right to religious freedom, the kind of Christianity practiced at Christ Church—conservative evangelical Anglicanism—has come to occupy two slightly contradictory positions in public life. It cleaves with Crown power as the nation's established faith, yet it is also governed by rights-based law (just like any other 'religious' position). Under this regime, it is made relative twice over: first, in relation to other religions; but second, in relation to the other 'protected characteristics' recognised in antidiscrimination law, including gender, race, and sexual orientation. Its cultural heft, of course, remains substantial, but it has also been substantially diminished. Religion—even *established* religion—no longer takes priority. Indeed, with Article 9 claims as likely to *remove* Christian practices from the realm of the culturally defensible as they are to ensure their protection, it made sense for Luke to argue that 'the gospel is more important than rights'.

CHAPTER FIVE

Communicative Doubt

Set a guard, O Lord, over my mouth;
keep watch over the door of my lips!

—PSALM 141:3

Weddings and Third Wheels

Throughout my time at Christ Church, I was often asked what I found most 'surprising' or 'different' about the lives of my Christian interlocutors. It was a question I found difficult to answer; although it was asked partly out of cross-cultural curiosity, an anthropological yearning to have the familiar rendered strange by an outsider, I also knew that my new acquaintances were looking for confirmation that they were living the kind of distinctive lives in which the work of the Holy Spirit was both visible and attractive to non-Christians (see chapter 2). It was with some trepidation, then, that I sought to answer Isabel, a bubbly maths graduate in her early twenties, when she asked me what I found most 'unusual' about evangelicals. It was a Tuesday evening in November, and Isabel and I were sitting around my small kitchen table with Stephen, her husband, and Will, both of whom were Bible college students and church apprentices. We had just finished dinner, and although their commitment to moderation meant my guests would not let me top up their wine glasses, we had settled into an amicable postprandial discussion about church life.

Deciding to focus on the particular rather than the general, I told my guests that I had recently attended the wedding of a Christian friend named Carrie, whom I'd met through Christian Concern. It had been a large wedding—never one to cut corners, Carrie had had ten bridesmaids, two flower girls, and approaching three hundred guests—and had been seen as an explicit 'gospel opportunity' by the bride and groom. After the ceremony, the couple's friends and family had crowded into the church's adjacent lounge for a celebratory afternoon tea. We happily indulged in the homemade spread (many of the guests had contributed cakes, biscuits, and other sweet treats to the celebration) while the groom, Rob, stood to make a speech. As with most wedding toasts, it was an ode to his new bride. Unlike any toast I'd ever heard, however, it was also an ode to Jesus Christ. Rob explained that his love for his new wife was grounded in the fact that 'she loves Jesus'. Carrie, for her part, echoed this in her own toast, telling the assembled crowd that the only thing better than having married Rob was having a relationship with her Saviour. Even the best man's speech—typically a vehicle for crude jokes and embarrassing anecdotes—had focused on Rob's growth as a Christian. It was the first 'Christian' (in my interlocutors' sense of the term) wedding I had ever attended, and as I explained to Isabel, Stephen, and Will, I had been surprised that the toasts focused so much on God and so little on the couple themselves.

Isabel nodded; she knew exactly what I meant. Like Carrie and Rob, she and Stephen had also seen their wedding as an evangelistic opportunity. Unlike Carrie and Rob, however, they had worried that too heavy an emphasis on Jesus might be confusing or off-putting for their non-Christian friends. For this reason, they had sought to make their references to God as 'accessible' as possible to the unchurched. Perhaps inevitably, some things still seemed to have been lost in translation. One non-Christian uncle, for example, did not understand why they had vowed to love one another 'until death do us part or Christ returns'. Isabel laughed heartily as she recounted a friend's reaction to Stephen's speech, in which he had explained that he knew Isabel loved Jesus more than she loved him. This friend, apparently unfamiliar with 'Christian things', had spent the rest of the evening in a state of utter confusion; *if Stephen knew Isabel loved someone else, why on earth was he marrying her?*[1]

Isabel's efforts to render her wedding ceremony 'accessible' to non-Christians while keeping Jesus at its core is but one example of the difficulties evangelicals face as they seek to introduce others to their faith without evoking incomprehension, apathy, or even hostility. Having explored the value placed on relational evangelism in the previous chapter, I now turn to the aesthetics of evangelical speech in what my interlocutors imagine to be a rapidly de-Christianising country. As studies of global Christianities have shown, speech—words spoken, written, sung, and even left unsaid—is central to Christian practice.[2] For conservative evangelicals, the primacy of words is shaped through their understanding of the Bible as being both an historical document, one whose cultural context must be understood so as to appreciate the import of a particular passage, and a body of divine revelation that is inspired by God, perfect in its totality, and coherent in its message. It is through the words of the Bible that these Christians meet with the Word made flesh, and it is incumbent on them to speak these words to non-believers in the hope that they too will be granted eternal life. But if speech has potentially eternal consequences, how does one gauge the success of communication with those who do not (yet) have access to the evangelical tongue?

This chapter explores this question through the frames of doubt and ambiguity. In so doing, I hope not only to highlight the 'contingencies, ambivalences and variations in people's engagements with truth claims' that are, according to the anthropologist Mathijs Pelkmans,[3] all too often edited out of the ethnographic record, but to suggest that lived ambiguity might play a productive role in my interlocutors' grace-based theology. It presents two case studies which foreground the experience of what I call 'communicative doubt'. In the first section, I discuss the language used in relation to (then) proposed changes in marriage law as an example of the difficulties faced by religiously-motivated social reformers as they seek to enter the public sphere. These difficulties are not, of course, limited to conservative Christians.[4] But in a context in which the use of theological justifications for political positions has been rendered 'inconceivable',[5] I suggest that the doubt, hesitation, and ambivalence my informants express in relation to the use of both religious and secular speech is indicative of a central tension at the heart of evangelical activism.[6] The staff of Christian Concern agitate for (their understanding of) a biblical approach to gender, sexuality, and family life on the basis that following God's 'blueprint' will benefit all people, Christian and non-Christian alike. Yet they also believe that meaningful socio-political change cannot be wrought without Christian conversion. This results in a Catch-22 situation, wherein religious language is deemed inappropriate, yet secular language lacks the transcendental force necessary for spiritual transformation. As such, efforts to convince the nation of the universality of God's 'blueprint' seemed to function, paradoxically, to reaffirm its Christian particularity.

In the second section, I focus on one Christ Church couple, Kate and Jim, and their experience of Christian speech in a setting some conservative evangelicals identify as hostile to their faith: the secular university.[7] Kate and Jim provide a useful intersection between my two field sites, as they are both Christ Church members and former clients of the Christian Legal Centre. They had found themselves involved with the CLC as a result of their membership of the University of Exeter's Christian Union, which was accused of discriminating against Christians of non-evangelical persuasion by the university's Students' Guild. The couple were marked by a profound ambivalence towards their experience in the public eye. I conclude by asking whether or not it is possible to speak of such experiences in terms of meaning, and suggest that this communicative doubt can be approached in terms of evangelicalism's theological rejection of religious legalism.

Words and the Word

Written, spoken, and sung words are central to Christian practice. This is, perhaps, particularly so among conservative evangelicals, who view the sixty-six books of the Protestant Bible as containing the inerrant Word of God. Although the members of Christ Church understand the Bible to have been penned by human authors, they also view it as 'God breathed', the inspired result of divine intervention. It is regarded as the ultimate authority in all matters, both spiritual and mundane. This means that, as Luke put it during a sermon on the book of Leviticus (part of the Old Testament Holiness Code, which enjoyed a surprisingly high media profile during my fieldwork on account of its condemnation of same-sex sexual relationships), the fact that something is written in the Bible ought to be 'a good enough reason' for the Christian to accept it as true: 'If God says something, it's true. We don't have to question Him.' Reading the Bible is equated to spending time with God Himself. Christian friends spoke of 'meeting with Jesus' in the pages of what were often well-thumbed, highlighted, annotated, and dog-eared Bibles. (If not dog bitten. Anne, who often drove me home from church, once recounted in fits of laughter how her new puppy had recently torn one of her Bibles to pieces. Still, what mattered was not the physical object, but the message it contained.) It was patiently explained to me that my 'red letter' Bible, in which the words of Jesus are printed in a contrasting colour to the rest of the text, was theologically suspect; the *entire* Bible was the Word of God, and although some passages might be weightier than others, all might as well be red (and, more importantly, *read*).

To say that the members of Christ Church view the Bible as their ultimate authority is not, of course, to say that they are unthinking in their approach to Scripture. Many church members devote a great deal of time and energy to determining the meaning and application of Bible verses, both through individual and group study and through the use of Bible companions ('Explore' Bible notes were particularly popular), prayer diaries, and theological commentaries. The church encourages the academic study of biblical hermeneutics and is affiliated with a local Bible college, from which it hosts church apprentices—including Will and Stephen, the dinner guests introduced at the beginning of this chapter—during the course of their study. Sunday sermons typically involve a detailed deconstruction of the passage under discussion, complete with biblical cross-references, historical overviews, and occasional forays into the etymology of ancient Greek words. The many Bible studies I undertook, both as part of my women's Bible study group and 'one-on-one' with individual Christians, always began with a prayer that we would *really* hear, understand, and take on board the Truths that God wanted to communicate to us through His Word. These prayers are necessary not only because an uninspired student risks misinterpretation—or, rather, as Carol J. Greenhouse found among her Baptist interlocutors, *misunderstanding*[8]—but because Bible passages resonate differently depending on the circumstances of the reader, which might refer to one's 'age and stage' (for example, one's employment or marital status), one's maturity as a Christian, or one's ongoing battle with a particular sin.

Understanding the Bible, then, is thought to require training, discipline, and effort. The point I would like to make here, however, is that the evangelical tendency to locate the Truth of the Bible in the divine inspiration of its human authors sits uneasily with an ideology of public debate that purports to evaluate claims according to their merits, not their makers. As Matthew Engelke notes, the English chattering classes have retained a 'lasting commitment' to the idea that 'public things' ought to be free of '"personal agendas"', including religious conviction.[9] The evangelical emphasis on divine personality—the fact that, as Luke put it, an idea's presence in the Bible ought to be 'a good enough reason' to accept it as true—troubles the bourgeois ideal of the public sphere, in which private people make 'public use of their reason' without reference to the received wisdom of traditional authorities.[10] Nor can it be easily accommodated by what Jürgen Habermas posits as the public sphere's degenerate contemporary form, in which public debate is reduced to the negotiation of special interest groups, bureaucracies, and political parties (and their subsequent manipulation of public opinion).[11] If anything, my interlocutors' emphasis on absolute Truth suggests a desire to return to Habermas' idealised—and much critiqued—bourgeois archetype, in which public debate is deployed not to seek concessions but 'to discover laws immanent to . . . society'.[12] But while eighteenth-century public intellectuals might have preferred to uncover these laws through rational-critical debate, my Christian interlocutors believe them to be readily accessible in the divinely inspired text of the Bible.[13]

The belief that the Bible contains laws for human behaviour, combined with the conservative evangelical assertion that it is both possible and desirable to interpret these laws according to the will of God, has led to a profusion of temporal vocabulary relating to what my interlocutors call 'biblical clarity'. Church members speak of the Bible as containing 'timeless Truths' for all of humanity, Truths that are 'eternally' relevant to the lives of both Christians and non-Christians. They are also aware, however, that their insistence on the infinite applicability of the Bible marks them out as *behind the times, stuck in the past*, or simply *old fashioned*. For some commentators, this temporal disjunction is not only historic, but personal, with Christians understood to be perpetually immature; childishly unable, in Charles Taylor's words, to 'face the void'.[14] As Fenella Cannell, drawing on Taylor, has observed, this Nietzschean intellectual inheritance is evident in the pronouncements of prominent atheist spokespeople, such as Richard Dawkins, who view religious belief as 'evidence of ignorance, credulousness, [and/or] emotional weakness'.[15] Perhaps as a result of the popularisation of this view through such anti-theistic bestsellers as *The God Delusion*, many church members had come across non-Christians who viewed their Christianity as a sort of 'crutch' or safety blanket, something 'needed' by the Christian but not—heaven forbid!—by their mature, secular counterparts.

Indeed, throughout the course of my fieldwork, accusations of temporal inertia were levelled at conservative Christians not only by atheists and sceptics, but by those who might otherwise be thought to endorse my friends' 'traditional' or 'old-fashioned' values. Over a post-school-run coffee one week-day morning, Bethany, the minister's wife, and I discussed comments made by the Conservative Prime Minister, David Cameron, in relation to the Church of England's (then ongoing) debate over the appointment of women bishops. Although both liberal and conservative wings of the Church agreed that women would, eventually, join the episcopate, legislating for this eventuality had proved a complicated process for both pragmatic and theological reasons.[16] Conservative evangelicals and Anglo-Catholics sought guarantees that they could remain within the Anglican Communion without being subject to the authority of a woman bishop, while liberal Anglicans had begun to reject legislation accommodating these concerns on the grounds that it was unworkable in practice (and unpalatable in theory). In the autumn of 2012, following another round of failed discussions, Cameron waded into the fray, directing the Church to 'get with the programme' on gender equality.[17] Bethany had been deeply disappointed by these remarks. Conservative evangelicals, she explained, were not natural contrarians, holding to what others saw as outdated views with the intention of dividing the Church. They were simply seeking to submit to Scripture. Cameron's invitation to 'get with the programme' amounted to an invitation to ignore the unchanging Word of God. To Bethany, it was the height of hubris.

Nor was this the only area where such hubris was on display. During my fieldwork, one particularly prominent dispute centred on the nature of marriage. For many conservative Christians, heterosexual marriage is a sacred covenant with theological implications, an institution stretching back to Creation and pointing forward to the union of Christ and the Church. Some view marriage between partners of the same sex as a contradiction in terms. (Once, while filing literature related to equal marriage at the Christian Concern offices, I made a number of labels that said 'SSM'—same-sex marriage—and attached them to the outside of the plastic boxes I had just filled. A few days later, I noticed that someone had altered the labels so that they now read 'SS"M".') It was unsurprising, then, that when the Conservative-Liberal Democrat coalition government launched a consultation on the extension of marriage rights to gay and lesbian couples, it was conservative Christians who spearheaded the opposition.

Members of both my field sites were involved in this campaign. Christian Concern was a founding member of the Coalition for Marriage (C4M), a not-for-profit company established to campaign against the Marriage (Same-Sex Couples) Bill. At the church level, members of Christ Church were among the almost 670,000 people who signed a C4M petition protesting marriage's 'redefinition',[18] and the congregation were encouraged to write to their Members of Parliament to register their opposition to the change. Political scientist Andrea Hatcher has recently argued that a 'stark difference' between UK and US evangelicalism is that 'there [is] no politics' in British congregations.[19]

However, this was simply not the case when it came to the marriage bill (at least with conservative congregations). Not only was the issue repeatedly raised from the pulpit, but the Christ Church website provided a template letter for congregants to print, sign and send to their MPs.

Given the overwhelmingly evangelical make-up of the C4M's governing board,[20] it is fair to extrapolate that its founding members' opposition to same-sex marriage was grounded in the biblical belief that 'a man shall leave his father and his mother and hold fast to his wife, and they shall become one flesh' (Genesis 2:24). In an effort to make the campaign more accessible to non-Christians, however, C4M used non-biblical language to argue that same-sex marriage would be detrimental for British society as a whole. Although the campaign appealed to an essentialised understanding of marriage— 'Throughout history and in virtually all human societies marriage has always been the union of a man and a woman'—this essentialism was not rooted in the words of Genesis. Rather, C4M used the language of civil rights ('Civil partnerships already provide all the legal benefits of marriage so there's no need to redefine marriage'), free speech ('People should not feel pressurised to go along with same-sex marriage just because of political correctness. They should be free to express their views'), and the slippery slope of unforeseen consequences ('If marriage is redefined once, what is to stop it being redefined to allow polygamy?') to argue against extending marriage rights to gay and lesbian couples.

The Coalition for Marriage was not the only 'religious' organisation to downplay its theological concerns. As Steven Kettell has shown, although the most consistent opposition to proposals to legalise same-sex marriage came from religious organisations, their use of theological arguments in public debate was 'comparatively rare' (though many groups, including Christian Concern, adopted a 'public/private distinction', with materials addressed to their supporters more likely to feature biblical language).[21] As such, it is likely that Britons of 'all faiths and none', as the Coalition put it, were among the hundreds of thousands who voiced their opposition to the bill by signing C4M's petition. But what did this 'strategic secularism'[22] mean for those signatories who held the relationship between husband and wife to be not only society's building block, not only a guarantee of freedom of conscience, and not only a bulwark against polygamy, but *also* a reflection of the union of Christ and His bride? While Kettell analyses the mobilisation of non-biblical arguments in terms of macro-level shifts in secularisation, in what follows I offer a micro-level account of this phenomenon that emphasises the double-bind faced by evangelicals as they confront the public sphere.

The tension between secular accessibility and biblical clarity was brought out during my first week of fieldwork, when I joined Andrea and two CLC clients at the Church of England's General Synod (see Introduction). Also in our party was Adam, an American law student completing a Blackstone Legal

Fellowship summer internship, who was spending his six-week placement period at the CLC.[23] An Arizona native, Adam is tall, slim, and impeccably turned out; during his six weeks in London, he was never without a sharp suit and crisp shirt. Although he identified as an evangelical Protestant, Adam had chosen to study law at the University of Notre Dame—a Catholic university—because he wanted to be able to talk about the biblical roots of American law 'without people thinking I'm crazy, and I thought they'd be more open to that'.

Adam and I had come to York primarily to see a debate on the place of Christianity in public life. However, Andrea invited us to extend our stay so as to attend an event organised by Anglican Mainstream, a conservative organisation which exists 'to re-state and support traditional understandings of marriage, the family and human sexuality in the face of erosion of these values in church and society',[24] at which a life peer (Member of the House of Lords) I will call Lord Jameson was due to give a short speech. The Anglican Mainstream meeting came after what had been a disappointing morning for Synod's conservative contingent. While the previous evening's debate on Christianity in public life had been a success, the morning session on women bishops—in which an amendment to give greater protection to parishes opposed to women in church leadership had failed—had been deeply frustrating for 'complementarians'.[25] The mood lightened considerably, however, when Lord Jameson joked that it was a pleasure to be associated with 'the fringes' of Synod. His presentation defined marriage as an institution that centred on the production and welfare of children. Taking his cue from Prime Minister Cameron's assertion that extending marriage rights to gay and lesbian couples ought to be celebrated as an expression of 'commitment', he argued that commitment was not the only necessary ingredient of a marriage. There already existed various classes of people in loving, committed relationships who were unable to marry. For example, although Mr Cameron was, no doubt, committed to his children, he could not marry them. In Lord Jameson's understanding, same-sex couples fell into a similar legal category.

Following the speech, there was a short question and answer session. The first question came from a man who said that, as a Christian with a 'biblical worldview', he agreed that same-sex couples were ineligible for marriage. However, how could he convince those *without* this biblical worldview? Lord Jameson answered that this had been the point of his talk, which had explained that there already existed certain categories of people who were prohibited from marrying. A C4M activist then spoke. She announced that she had just received a letter from the Home Secretary in response to the first 500,000 signatures on the Coalition for Marriage petition. The letter said that the government would not prevent people getting married unless there were very strong reasons to do so, and being gay, lesbian, or bisexual did not constitute such a reason. Building on the previous question, she asked how Christians should respond to this logic. Another audience member asked a similar question, phrased in terms of convincing those who lacked a 'Judeo-Christian worldview' of the folly of same-sex marriage. In response to each of these questions, Lord Jameson repeated the core of his argument: marriage is about the production and welfare of children, and there will always be categories of people, including those in loving, committed relationships, who are ineligible to enter into it. But it seemed that, even to an audience who already held this view, his argument was found somewhat lacking.

On the afternoon train back to London, I asked Adam what he had thought of the meeting. He told me that he had been disappointed by the question and answer session, in which Lord Jameson had seemed to 'deflect' the legitimate questions he'd been asked. Adam suggested that, by removing any reference to the Bible, Jameson was trying to be inoffensive, 'trying not to step on anyone's toes'. I found this a surprising point to make, and told Adam that many people would find a comparison between same-sex relationships and incest—both of which fell into his categories of ineligibility—to be very offensive indeed. Adam clarified that, by focusing on the legal system, Lord Jameson had avoided talking about 'moral absolutes'. Christians, he continued, believe in absolutes, and these absolutes are found in the Bible. A Christian's beliefs about marriage, the family, and sexuality should flow directly from these Biblical Truths. However, if you *don't* believe in moral absolutes, then it's difficult to explain the heterosexual exclusivity of marriage. To Adam's mind, to discuss same-sex marriage without reference to the Bible's stance on sexual morality was to hollow out the argument. To secularise it—to make it about legal categories, to 'deflect' references to moral absolutes, to try 'not to step on anyone's toes'—was to miss the point.

I initially took Adam's disappointment with Lord Jameson's deflections to be indicative of what Keane posits as an archetypically Protestant concern with 'sincerity as a moral norm', in which the Christian's thoughts, words, and deeds ought to be a true reflection of her subjectivity.[26] Adam, I supposed, was uncomfortable with what he saw as a disingenuous disjuncture between reasons given and thoughts 'really' held. Writing of the controversy surrounding the decision of Danish newspaper *Jyllands-Posten* to publish cartoons depicting the Prophet Muhammad, Asad posits that European commentators had difficulty grasping the Islamic understanding of blasphemy—which punishes not the fact of disbelief, but the risk that one will '[seduce]' others into this 'false commitment' through its public promulgation—on account of their biblically-inflected understanding of truth and interiority.[27] Contra Christianity, which requires the disciplining of sinful thoughts through, for example, the act of confession, Islamic jurisprudence considers (dis)belief itself to be inscrutable. Asad suggests that Islam's emphasis on the social consequences of the blasphemer's *words*, as opposed to the blasphemer's incorrect *belief*, troubles the secularised Christian assumption that because coerced belief is 'insincere', its public pronouncement must be 'irrational'.[28] Perhaps, I thought,

Adam associated the secularisation required by Lord Jameson's desire 'not to step on anyone's toes' with the irrationality of articulating a belief not held.

Yet Adam's critique seemed to extend beyond the risk of insincerity. While Asad's Islamic jurists fear the pernicious social effects of seduction into false-hood, Adam seemed to worry that the use of secular logic might deprive non-Christians of the opportunity to submit to ultimate Truth. If anything, Lord Jameson's words appeared to be *insufficiently* seductive. After all, Adam held that non-biblical arguments against same-sex marriage reflected valid con-cerns. These arguments—that it would turn a child-centred institution into an adult-centred one; that it might be used to limit freedom of speech; that if gender was declared irrelevant to marriage, so too might age, number of par-ticipants, or the fact of consanguinity between them—made intuitive sense to him. Yet he also thought they were unlikely to win over those who had not yet accepted the Bible's moral absolutes.

Adam's disappointment in Lord Jameson's ability to answer the questions asked of him suggests that Christian campaigners operate within a Catch-22 situation, one in which religious language is thought inadequate to convince outsiders, but in which secular arguments, by failing to reference biblical absolutes, are deemed equally insufficient. His firm belief in the rightness of a particular moral proposition, even one rooted in a holy text, did not negate the experience of uncertainty as he sought to communicate that position to others. Indeed, the argument's ultimate rooting in the Truth of the Bible seemed to have rendered it particularly ambiguous: did mentioning the Bible risk putting off non-Christians, who might consider it *outdated* prejudice? Or did failing to mention it mean those same non-Christians would be denied its *timeless* Truth?

Writing of registrars with a 'conscientious objection' to marrying same-sex couples in the Netherlands, scholar of religion Marco Derks argues that such persons were repeatedly constructed in public debate as motivated solely by 'religious' concerns. Indeed, it seemed that 'the only reason many opponents of [these registrars] could *imagine* for . . . such conscientious objections' was their presumed religiosity.[29] In the UK context, this lack of imagination seemed to be shared by both supporters and opponents of the bill. Despite the C4M's use of non-theological language, and despite these campaigners' acceptance of the validity of non-'religious' arguments against gay marriage, opposition to the bill continued to be associated with a religious rationale—including by the Christian activists unsure of how to convince those lacking their 'biblical worldview'. Somewhat paradoxically, the use of non-biblical arguments in public debate seemed to confirm the very *Christianness* of the C4M's position. In seeking to assert the heterosexual exclusivity of marriage as a general principle, Christian activists had confirmed the religious specificity of this particular moral stance.

In this context, Engelke's reminder that public speech 'creates awkward conditions for the presence of God' bears repeating.[30] My interlocutors are aware that, regardless of whether one imagines the public sphere as a site for reasoned debate or negotiated settlements, their inability to yield on matters of biblical clarity risks leaving them unintelligible to those lacking a conservative evangelical theology. This, I suggest, is part of the challenge of inhabiting what Tanya Luhrmann calls a 'double register' of certainty and scepticism.[31] Conservative evangelicalism suggests a 'closed' system of Truth, one in which revelation is final and unassailable. In the words of theologian J. I. Packer, such a system takes as its starting point 'the Bible's account of itself'.[32] Yet these Christians are also members of an 'open' society, one in which everything is vulnerable to revision. As Keane suggests, religious logic might 'reinforce authority by offering it an apparently transcendental position from which to speak', but Christians are equally likely to find that decontextualised Bible verses cast doubt on the legitimacy of their arguments, rendering them 'problematic, even morally troubling'.[33]

The three questions asked of Lord Jameson highlighted this difficulty by seeming to challenge and accept the norms of secular public speech in equal measure. By rooting the reason for their opposition to same-sex marriage in the divine authorship of the Bible, the audience had implied that Lord Jameson's secularised account had somehow missed the point. And yet, by recognising that alternative arguments might be required for those whose worldview did *not* spring from the Bible, they also suggested that their religious language was, to some extent, unconvincing. Taylor suggests that efforts to remove religious speech from public life are often premised upon a perceived 'epistemic distinction' between 'secular reason' and the 'special languages' of faith. In this ideology, religious logic is seen to suffer from epistemic fragility, rendering it unlikely to convince those who do not already subscribe to it.[34] For Lord Jameson's audience, however, the epistemic distinction between the claims of the secular and the divine was less to do with the inclusivity (or otherwise) of religious or secular speech, and more to do with the ontological transformation that allows fallen hearts and minds to understand the obvious Truth of a religious position. In this understanding, the truly universal is not the 'common language' of the secular. Rather, it is the biblical law written on the hearts of all men and women, including those who currently deny it.

Indeed, according to many Christian campaigners, real social change may well be impossible without mass conversion. This understanding of the relationship between conversion and social change was expressed most clearly by Maria, a CLC solicitor, in the quote below. A slight brunette with fashionable blue-framed glasses, Maria had come to the CLC via the Lawyers' Christian Fellowship, the organisation from which the CLC had emerged. This made her, along with Andrea, their longest-serving member of staff. One Sunday afternoon, as we sat drinking herbal tea together in a south London teashop, Maria outlined Christian Concern's raison d'être:

> The real reason why we do this work, as much as we want the nation to be changed, we know that ultimately the only way people and this nation will be changed is by the gospel saving them. For example, changing the law on abortion. Someone is not going to wake up one day and say, 'Oh, I see the light, abortion is actually murdering a child' unless they're saved and they understand that God creates life and God takes life away.
>
> Of all the things that we do, what we want most of all is that people would see that the only way that people can have a happy and fulfilling life is by knowing their Creator God, by being saved and building the right relationship with Him. And everything flows from that. But while we're in a nation where not many people are good Christians, I think the next best thing we can do is to preserve the freedoms which give people the opportunity to speak about the gospel and to fight those cases where Christians have been maligned and discriminated against because they stood up for their faith.

Maria's comments reflect longstanding concerns among Christian reformers. Indeed, her words echo those of the eighteenth-century evangelical campaigners who made up William Wilberforce's influential Clapham Sect: '"Christ the lawgiver," declares [Clapham Sect member Henry] Venn, "will always speak in vain, without Christ the saviour is first known."'[35] Of course, as noted in chapter 1, God can always intervene in human affairs, regardless of whether Bible-believing Christians make up a nation's majority.[36] Yet this virtuous circle suggests a tension at the heart of Christian campaigning. If conversion is essential but the use of 'religious' language in public debate is, in Asad's terms, 'inconceivable', then neither 'religious' nor 'secular' logic (if this distinction can be maintained) will be enough to convince non-Christians to support biblically-motivated socio-political positions. It was for this reason that Adam, although he found non-biblical arguments against same-sex marriage to be valid, sensible, and accurate, *still* thought they were unlikely to convince non-believers.

For evangelical observers, then, the kind of doubt that takes prominence in public policy debates is communicative, highlighting the conflict between accessibility and doctrinal purity.[37] It reflects an anxiety about the point at which one draws the line between, on the one hand, using secular arguments to promote God's 'blueprint' for living and, on the other, unashamedly proclaiming the gospel, even if doing so risks undermining one's credibility in the public sphere. In such instances, the Bible seems to function as an index of both moral certitude and relational ambiguity, as Christians find themselves struggling to explain the transcendent to those who, with disappointing frequency, seem to lack 'ears to hear' (Matthew 11:15). The remainder of this chapter discusses this issue from a different angle, one which moves from the micro-level of the individual Christian's duty to graciously evangelise their friends, colleagues, and neighbours to the macro-level at which Christians seek to ensure their continued freedom to spread the faith outside of these intimate, relational spheres.

An 'Absurd Case'

Sunday evening services at Christ Church are relaxed affairs. Or, more accurately, they are as relaxed as a Christ Church service gets; although the minister will have removed his tie, an evening service's prayers are equally heartfelt, its sermon equally academic, and its call to repentance equally urgent. It was to such a service that I headed one evening in November 2013, to hear Greg, a tall, floppy-haired curate, speaking on the tricky subject of church discipline. Greg began his sermon with a story of two sisters, Charity and Clarity. Charity and Clarity divided public opinion. Many people preferred Charity. Charity was 'accepting', whereas Clarity was 'discriminating'; Charity was 'warm', whereas Clarity was 'cold'; 'Charity said, "Come in!", whilst Clarity said, "Technically, you shouldn't be here."' Others, however, preferred Clarity. Clarity was 'effective', while Charity got nothing done; Clarity was a 'realist', while Charity was an 'idealist'; Charity *meant* well, but Clarity *did* well.

The apparent incompatibility of these two virtues, Greg continued, was often implied in discussions of Christianity:

> These days, few would question the legitimacy of religious charity, but religious clarity? Well, many say that's impossible. In fact, that's evil. Those who draw clear lines between right and wrong, in and out, saved and lost, they're narrow-minded bigots, blatant transgressors of their supposed Lord's command to love. Perhaps you remember that absurd case of the Exeter and Birmingham Christian Unions a couple of years back. They got kicked out of their Student Unions because these CUs were requiring people to sign a declaration of faith, thereby excluding membership from those who were of other faiths. And it seems obvious [that members of a Christian Union would sign a declaration of faith], doesn't it, but that, apparently, was appalling.

Greg was referring to a number of disputes between local chapters of the University and Colleges Christian Fellowship (UCCF) and their university Guilds or Student Unions, disputes which had made headlines between 2006 and 2008.[38] UCCF is 'the most influential and most popular umbrella organisation' for Christians at British universities.[39] It is unashamedly evangelistic, teaching its members to view the university campus as a potential mission field.[40] Conservative in its theology, it is known among my informants as a biblically sound organisation, one whose Doctrinal Basis—which affirms that the Bible 'is the inspired and infallible Word of God' and 'the supreme authority in all matters of belief and behaviour'—was one they would readily sign up to. Which was, as it happened, just as well: many university CUs required their members to do just that.

Unfortunately for UCCF, not all self-identified Christians proved willing to do so. In 2006, an Orthodox Christian student at the University of Exeter complained that his Orthodox theology rendered him unable to sign the declaration and, therefore, ineligible for membership. As a result of his complaint, the Students' Guild temporarily disaffiliated the Christian Union, claiming that its Doctrinal Basis discriminated against Christians of non-evangelical persuasion. The situation quickly escalated. The CU's bank account was frozen. It was no longer allowed to host events on University property. Lawyers were instructed, public debates were held, and mediation attempts failed. The CU protested that their right to freedom of religion was being curtailed; the Guild countered that student organisations must be open to all. Following a University-wide vote, the CU was required, against its wishes, to rebrand itself as the *Evangelical* Christian Union (ECU). It was the sort of story that caused the 'small c' conservatives at Christ Church to sadly shake their heads; *what was the world coming to when an 'equal opportunities' policy mandated that a non-Christian could apply to lead the Christian Union?*[41]

As always, my ears pricked up at Greg's mention of what I knew to be a CLC case.[42] Generally speaking, though, the spate of cases involving university Christian Unions were not ones I often heard about. They rarely came up in conversation with church members, and although this particular controversy had garnered a significant amount of media attention at the time, the Exeter dispute had never actually reached a courtroom. Less than a week later, however, I was to find myself puzzling over the strange case of the Exeter Evangelical Christian Union. The Friday after Greg's sermon, I was part of a group of volunteers who had offered to help out at the youth group's annual Guy Fawkes' Night fireworks display. The event was hosted by a couple who had volunteered their large (and, due to the inclement November weather, waterlogged) garden for the occasion. The gathering was, of course, evangelistic in nature. Regular members of the 11–14 youth group had been encouraged to invite non-Christian friends along for an evening of fun, fireworks, finger food—and a short talk on John 3:16. While the men among us busied themselves outside, hauling garden furniture into a makeshift barrier between the sodden grass and the patio, the women, myself included, retreated to the kitchen to cook hotdogs and hamburgers for the teenagers.

As I applied myself to the task of frying onions with which to garnish the food, I chatted with Kate, a fellow kitchen volunteer. Kate's good humour and 'servant-heartedness' were immediately obvious. Not only was she wearing the sort of jumper by which it was impossible to remain uncheered on a wet November evening (a red knitted number replete with smiling penguins), she was slicing hotdog and hamburger buns with an enthusiasm I had never before seen applied to a bag of bread rolls. Our conversation followed the pattern that such conversations usually took. I learned that she was in her midtwenties; that she worked for the National Trust; and that she attended church with her husband, Jim, who was out in the swampy garden trying to spark the fireworks. She learned that I was an anthropologist; that I lived within walking distance of the church; and that I was interested in evangelical legal activism. Having given a broad outline of my research, I asked if she had any interest in the Christian discrimination cases. 'Actually', she replied, 'yes. My husband and I were involved in one.' As it turned out, Jim and Kate had been President and Vice-President, respectively, of the Exeter ECU during their final year of university. Yet the case was not something they often discussed with their church friends. It was for this reason that, despite voicing my interest in Christian legal activism to every church member I met, no one had ever directed them to me.

Why was this the case? Of the ten CLC claimants I met through Christian Concern, almost all viewed their CLC experience as an important part of their Christian journey. Even more so than testimonies (the spiritual life stories that play such a key role in evangelical culture), their accounts often read like narratives of vocation to the religious life, reflecting a sense of having been chosen for a particular task or mission. Like the young Catholic nuns studied by Rebecca Lester, these clients had '[reordered and restructured] their understandings of their own personal histories' to showcase the centrality of this mission to their lives.[43] Lesley Pilkington, for example, who had come to the CLC after providing ex-gay therapy to an undercover journalist,[44] told me that God had used her life experience prior to the case as a time of preparation, 'strengthening me for that time of trial': 'I felt at the time, it just wasn't random, it just wasn't . . . From the beginning, I felt that it had been planned by God.' Others went further still. Gary McFarlane, who had lost his job as a relationships counsellor after expressing a possible conscientious objection to offering psychosexual therapy to same-sex couples, saw his case as the result of a prayer he had once prayed: 'Lord, I want my life to count. I want to make a significant impact upon this earth before I die. Amen.' Nor was Gary the only CLC client who viewed his legal difficulties as an answered prayer. Dr Richard Scott, who had been disciplined by the General Medical Council for encouraging a depressed patient to turn to Jesus, explained his case as the result of what he jokingly called 'a dangerous prayer', one in which he had asked to be 'significant'.

Kate and Jim offered a different perspective. A number of months after our first meeting, they invited me to their home to discuss the case over tea and chocolate biscuits. (The biscuits, I was told, were a late addition to our spread, an uncharacteristically empty kitchen cupboard having necessitated an early morning run to the shop.) Sitting in their bright front room, the spring sunshine pouring in through the large windows, Kate explained that she and Jim had 'inherited' the controversy from their predecessors. It was in their first year at university that a discrimination complaint had been made, and it was in response to their disciplining by the Guild that the Christian Union's Executive Committee had sought legal advice from the Lawyers' Christian Fellowship (the body out of which Andrea was then running the Christian-interest cases). The advice they received was that, in the context of a belief-based organisation, their disaffiliation from the Guild violated their human rights. As Jim explained, the Committee had a certain amount of time to decide whether to file legal papers or let the issue lie. They decided to file the papers, 'which sort of kicked off a massive storm, as you can imagine'. The Guild allowed them back, but grudgingly, making it clear that they were contravening Guild law and could be removed at any time. 'From then on', Jim continued, 'it would sort of simmer along, and every year there would be a spike where it was brought up and it reared its ugly head, and then it would go back down.'

The issue reached breaking point in their final year at Exeter, when Jim was President and Kate was Vice-President of what was then the Evangelical Christian Union. The Guild issued an ultimatum. The ECU, in consultation with their lawyers, responded by presenting the Guild with 'a paper which kind of backed up, legally, where we thought we stood'. This plan, unfortunately, backfired: 'They really didn't like the fact that we had this legal element to it.' The Guild stopped communicating. Jim, who 'just wanted the issue to be gone', agreed to a University-wide debate on whether faith-based organisations ought to be allowed to require their members to sign a statement of belief. Then began what the couple described as a 'hate campaign' against the ECU.

Although they received support from churches around the country, Kate and Jim remembered this as a distressing time. The Guild's attacks felt personal. Jim, who had initially seen the debate as a chance to have a productive discussion, quickly realised that 'we wouldn't be going to win, we'd be going to explain ourselves'. As expected, his motion to allow faith-based societies to restrict membership on the basis of belief failed to pass. Still, he received surprisingly positive feedback from non-Christians on his performance; given that 'people were sort of expecting me to be like a far-right Nazi', he was pleased to hear that 'it was the clearest way the problem had been communicated'. After the debate, the ECU had little appetite to keep fighting. They dropped the campaign to reinstate their belief-based membership policy, and the issue faded from campus prominence. As Kate explained, 'I think it was time. It had been three years.'

Coming under public attack is not unusual for those involved in Christian-interest cases. Lesley Pilkington, for example, had been humiliated and embarrassed by the newspaper articles written about her (and the ex-gay movement more broadly), which she felt had mocked, misrepresented, and distorted her position. But while Lesley viewed her case as having been 'orchestrated' by God, with even her abuse understood as a lesson about the spiritual state of the nation, Jim and Kate expressed a profound ambivalence about their roles in the ECU controversy. With the benefit of hindsight, Jim said:

> Looking back at it, it was actually a really difficult time, wasn't it, in terms of working out what was the right thing to do. . . . Like, our mission here, or the idea of the Christian Union, is to help people to communicate the gospel, and is this in the background going to help? But then you're also in a position where you're thinking, well, if you just sort of whimper out and just leave the Guild, then that is kind of conceding, you know, it's basically saying Christians don't have a place in any sphere of life, for whatever reason, and it's accepting that maybe you should be marginalised or that that's okay, you know?

Jim's comments suggest the difficulty of straddling the divide between principles and particulars. He had identified a conflict between his principled commitment to ensuring the continued spread of the gospel through the maintenance of laws and institutions friendly towards it, and his personal duty to witness to those in his sphere of influence. On the one hand, he was unwilling to forfeit the biblical clarity that required Christians to acknowledge the difference between, as Greg's sermon had it, 'right and wrong, in and out, saved and lost', particularly if making such a concession now would result in the increasing marginalisation of Christians in the future. He knew that he was called to work towards a world in which Christians could lead 'peaceful and quiet [lives], godly and dignified in every way' (1 Timothy 2:2). On the other hand, he worried that, in this *particular* instance, framing the dispute as an insurmountable divide between the Guild and the ECU might just do more harm than good.

The university setting seemed an ideal context for this ratcheting up of rhetoric, with religious freedom repeatedly framed as a threat to equality. Students were encouraged to align themselves with one or other of these apparently incompatible values. This polarisation led to the juxtaposition between 'religion' and 'equality' being extended far beyond the UCCF's Doctrinal Basis. Despite their having nothing to do with the initial dispute (which was, at heart, an intra-religious debate focused on the ostensibly exclusionary nature of the evangelical-inflected Doctrinal Basis, which proved a theological bar to Christians from other denominations), the ECU was also accused of sexism, homophobia, and racism. They were portrayed as being, in Jim's words, 'against equal opportunities of *any* type'. Such a reputation was, they knew, unlikely to win converts for Christ.

Speaking of his meetings and phone calls with Andrea and barrister Paul Diamond, who were then advising the ECU, Jim said:

> [Andrea] was kind of 'bigger picture' in terms of Christian rights in the UK, and . . . my impression is that she would fight any battle, you know, in terms of that, because she didn't want to lose ground, as it were. That was my impression, that she'd fight tooth and nail and that she'd go for it in a legal way. Whereas I think our ideal would have been to be able to sit down and talk with the Guild and come up with some sort of solution. But equally, how realistic would that have been? I don't know.

Jim felt that the legalisation of the ECU's language had diminished the possibility of a mediated solution. (The anthropological evidence bears this out: studies of dispute resolution suggest a positive association between the parties' desire to maintain their relationships and efforts to deescalate confrontation.[45]) He spoke of the submission of legal papers as '[kicking] off a massive storm', and pointed out that the Guild 'really didn't like' the legal element. The divergence of Andrea and Jim's preferred modes of speech—the formal, adversarial language of the court versus the informal, conciliatory language of mediation—highlights the ambiguous relationship between what Veena Das, in her account of quotidian ethics, calls the 'actual everyday' and one's ability, through ethical conduct, to influence the 'eventual everyday'.[46] Andrea's legal language reflected her fear that the 'eventual everyday' would be one in which Christian freedoms had been diminished beyond the point of no return. Jim, on the other hand, wondered whether a conciliatory ethic in the 'actual everyday' might bear a more fruitful eventuality.

For her part, Kate was able to point to one positive offshoot of what had otherwise been an 'almost traumatic' experience. The publicity surrounding the debate meant that the ECU's annual mission week—seven days of student-friendly evangelistic outreach—was extremely well attended. From this perspective, the ultimate success or failure of the case might be realised years hence, when a former student who had attended their mission week understood what it *really* meant to claim the exclusivity of Christ. Conversion, after all, can be a slow process. Yet even on this level, Jim remained doubtful. To be sure, the dispute had given him many chances to speak about the ECU. But given that he saw the ECU's role as one of introducing students to Jesus, discussions about membership policies and Guild politics were ultimately conversations about which he 'couldn't give a toss'.

But if the couple's reflections on their experience do not lend themselves particularly well to notions of success, nor can they be dismissed as failure. Although neither Jim nor Kate could be sure that 'legalising' the dispute had been the correct path to take, *nor could they be sure it hadn't*. Jim was unwilling to come down on either side: 'I'd go through it again if it was the right thing, but it's very fifty-fifty, for me, whether that was the right thing to do or not. I have no idea.' Five years later, what remained was ambivalence. Had they been right to assert, on principle, that the ECU ought to be able to determine its own membership policy? Had they been wrong, in terms of their own personal witness, to distract from the gospel? They simply couldn't say. Their struggle to resolve principles and particulars was a poignant reminder of the conflict Greg, the curate, had highlighted just days before I met Kate: they were torn between Clarity and Charity, and couldn't be sure which sister's lead ought to have been followed.

That Kate and Jim expressed doubt, hesitation, and ambivalence in relation to the case, however, does not negate their having a meaningful orientation towards it. Rather, their experience draws attention to the fact that, for conservative evangelicals, there are many situations in which there simply isn't a 'Christian' or 'unchristian' way of doing things. Indeed, their unwillingness to resolve the case as a success or failure can be approached in terms of their theology. As we have already seen, emic evangelical theology rejects rule following, box ticking, and religious legalism (traits which they associate with highly caricatured readings of non-Protestant traditions, particularly Judaism and Catholicism). From this perspective, experiencing occasional doubts as to the rightness or wrongness of one's actions suggests a spiritually sensitive disciple, one who is seeking to make godly decisions on the basis of grace rather than law. As such, the lack of resolution experienced by Kate and Jim can be said to have a meaningful quality, as it reorients its participants to divine grace. In a context in which Christians understand themselves to be morally fragmented beings, the ever-imperfect foil of their coherent, integrated, and ever-perfect God,[47] the ambiguity experienced by Jim and Kate might be made meaningful by the recognition that although they cannot know whether their choices in this instance were correct, nor do they necessarily need to; *they can't, but God can.*

And what of the difference between Kate and Jim's experience and those of Lesley Pilkington, Gary McFarlane, and Dr Richard Scott, all of whom deemed their CLC cases to have been ordained by God? Part of the explanation must lie in the circumstances in which the case arose. Although they were deeply involved in the dispute's final escalation, Kate and Jim saw themselves as the 'inheritors' of the case, not its instigators. The fact that the participants in the ECU/Guild dispute had become associated with larger values—religious freedom versus equality—meant that, at the time, they 'had this feeling that being part of the Guild was absolutely everything'. But it also meant that, when they left the fishbowl of what they called 'studentville', Kate and Jim achieved the sort of distance that other clients, perhaps, have been unable to attain. Although they certainly suffered during the lead-up to the debate, they did not take this harm with them when they left university. Unlike those

clients whose unwillingness to concede a principle had cost them their liveli-
hoods (or resulted in their names being dragged through the national press),
perhaps Kate and Jim can afford the ambivalence they continue to experience.

This somewhat reductive approach to certainty, however, is not the only
possible explanation. That Kate and Jim were unable to reconcile principle
and practice in this instance does not mean that others in their situation would
be rendered equally ambivalent, particularly if those others have a different
understanding of the actual everyday's relationship to the eventual. Writing
of a very different socio-political context, Elizabeth Povinelli has encouraged
anthropologists to attend to the differences in personality, experience, and
sheer will that allow some members of disenfranchised groups to 'endure'
while others, tragically, are ground down by the realities of late liberalism.[48]
While the circumstances of my interlocutors are, of course, radically different
from those of Povinelli's Australian Aboriginal friends, the commitment that
both groups show to living in a way that could be categorised as 'otherwise'
suggests that the concepts of will and endurance may have some purchase for
clients like Lesley, Gary, and Richard. Indeed, if they did experience doubt
about their cases, perhaps it supplied what Pelkmans terms 'the energy needed
to produce conviction'.[49] Given the comparatively brief time I spent with the
clients I met through the CLC (and due to my desire to avoid uninformed psy-
chologising), I can only hint at this possibility here; but I would suggest that,
in a theological context in which the Christian's choice to take legal action
is neither inherently wrong nor inherently right, a client's 'will to be otherwise' may indeed play a role in managing, if not quashing, ambivalence, doubt,
and uncertainty. The same, of course, could be said of the Christian activists
we have met throughout this book: people like Andrea, Andrew, Carrie, Jake,
Louise and Maria.

Conclusion: Doubt and the Divine

This chapter has explored the ways in which conservative Christians express
doubt and ambivalence in speaking 'Christianly' in public life. In recounting the communicative doubt expressed by Adam, the American law student, I have sought to explain the difficulty my interlocutors associate with
efforts to convince non-Christians of the truth of policy positions that are
experienced as being both common sense—*marriage, as an institution ori-
ented towards the production and welfare of children, can only be contracted
between men and women*—and divinely ordained—*which is why God made it
so*. Within this framework, Christian representations of the family are seen
to exist 'beyond ideology' or cultural context.[50] But as the inhabitants of a
double register of scepticism and certainty, my interlocutors are aware that
what is common sense to one person is contestable to another. Thus, evangelicals mobilise non-religious arguments to convince their opponents of the

correctness of biblically-informed opinions, even as these efforts function to confirm their hearers' suspicion that only conservative Christians could hold such views. From within this feedback loop (in which only conversion enables true comprehension of the Bible's moral positions), neither overtly 'religious' nor ostensibly 'secular' language is thought entirely convincing. Christians are still called to speak, as Bethany once put it, 'graciously and wisely' on matters of public interest, but what is really required is divine intervention from a speaking God.

As it happened, many of my Christian friends had experienced just this sort of dramatic intervention.[51] These experiences ranged from the jarring words that prompted Lucy, a solicitor, to begin her search for Truth—'the words were, "something is *deeply* wrong with your life, something is missing from your life"'—to Dominic, a church apprentice, opening the Bible to Romans 5:8—'and the verse says, "God showed His love for you in this, that while you were still sinners Christ died for you"'—on the day of his conversion. Sitting on the platform at York Railway Station, waiting for our train to London, Adam told me that he too had been addressed by the divine. We had been discussing my own religious history, and Adam, seeking, perhaps, to encourage me, explained why he had never doubted his faith. A childhood experience in which God had spoken directly to him meant he could never doubt His existence. Yet the fact that God had spoken to him was, Adam knew, a bit like conservative biblical exegesis: it required an inductive interpretation to be properly understood. After all, although he described both hearing and feeling God's voice, 'It's not like anyone else in the room would have heard Him.'

By addressing Adam personally, God had become both more real and more *private*. The temporality Adam longed for me to inhabit as I approached the words of the Bible, then, was neither one of timeless Truth nor outdated prejudice. Rather, it was a radical rupture in space and time, the same sort of 'discontinuity', in Robbins' terms,[52] that he had experienced when God Himself had broken into the everyday and Adam had heard His voice. While awaiting this possibility for his non-Christian friends, perhaps all he could really do was seek to maintain the channels that allowed Christians to evangelise, so that, if God did choose to speak, the hearer would know by Whom they were being addressed.

But as Kate and Jim's reflections on the contrast between principle and practice suggest, tensions sometimes emerged between the actions taken to protect the freedom to evangelise in the future and the actual impact these actions might have on a Christian's gospel witness in the here and now. This contrast suggests that, in addition to inhabiting Luhrmann's double epistemic register of faith and doubt, conservative evangelicals also navigate a temporal divide, one in which the language an individual Christian uses in the 'actual everyday' might have an impact, either positive or negative, on the 'eventual everyday' faced by Christians throughout the nation.

Pelkmans writes that it is difficult to imagine people 'resting in doubt', which he describes as being 'always on the move'.[53] Unresolved doubt, he suggests, can only be tolerated under certain circumstances, in which it ceases to be the focus of attention, is reinterpreted, or is denied.[54] I have argued that what makes Kate and Jim's ongoing ambivalence bearable is that they rest not in doubt, but in God. Their doubts as to the case were neither denied nor resolved—indeed, Jim implied that resolution was impossible—but reflected the theological truism that while God is coherent, complete, and omniscient, humans are incoherent, hesitant, and fallible. In what Pelkmans might class as a 'reinterpretation' of doubt, the distance between their human ambivalence and the complete coherence of God means Kate and Jim can live with the fact that the 'meaningful attitude' provided by a religious experience—whether that experience involves a ritual, a prophet, or even a legal case—can never provide all the answers. Nor is it necessarily supposed to.[55]

Ambiguity, then, has its pros. Writing of early twentieth-century Catholic Spain, historian William Christian argues that the Church's unwillingness to categorise dead parishioners as definitively saved or damned served a social purpose, '[directing] behaviour by establishing rewards and disincentives with indulgences and jubilees in much the way modern states use tax codes'.[56] The threat of damnation maintained the ethical order even as its uncertainty left hope for the grieving relatives of known sinners. Flexibility, then—ambiguity by another name—can be productive. And what is true of the Church may also be true of the law. Although courts are typically associated with the desire to move beyond reasonable doubt, there is a certain benefit to keeping legal controversies murky. Many lawyers, and certainly those at the CLC, believe that the rule of law cannot deliver justice unless it is clarified, that is, unless a judgment has been made on an otherwise ambiguous situation. One staff member thought that 'clarity tends to help confidence', as legal clarity would allow Christians to know where they stood. But by demanding a resolution and setting a precedent, test cases also have the potential to reify the issues under consideration, fuelling the construction of what Tamir Moustafa has recently termed a 'rights-vs-rites' binary.[57] In the move from general ethos to prescriptive rules, the space for compromise in untested areas of law becomes ever smaller.[58]

Lest the above be read as resolving ambiguity, however, this chapter must end by recognising the continuing discomfort that doubt causes for those for whom salvation requires firm belief. While much of this book has discussed the difficulties faced by evangelicals seeking to render their faith *legible* to law and politics, it is important to remember that they are primarily concerned with rendering it *convincing* to the individual men and women who are subject to these worldly institutions. In the end, it is the question of individual salvation that matters most; and it is the (un)saved state of their friends, family, colleagues, and neighbours that evangelicals find most difficult to deal with.

This brings us back to Isabel, Stephen, and Will, the dinner guests who asked what I found most 'unusual' about the members of Christ Church. As noted above, I was often uncomfortably aware that questions focused on Christian distinctiveness required me to evaluate my interlocutors' ability to live in such a way that the indwelt presence of the Holy Spirit was visible and attractive to non-Christians. Questions about what was most 'unusual' or 'different' about Christians functioned as subtle references to my own status as someone who was, in the words of the church, 'not *yet*' Christian, an outsider looking in. As was explained in chapter 2, Christ Churchites' distinctiveness ought to have sparked in me an openness to the gospel, a desire to understand the cause of their attractive, grace-fuelled lives. From within this framing, my continuing membership among 'the lost' challenged them to ever greater efforts to reflect the grace of God to me before it was too late; forcing me, as Carol once put it, with a heartbreakingly pained expression on her face and the beginnings of tears in her eyes, to grapple with the fact that *as things currently stood, she would not be seeing me in heaven.*

To offer Isabel a fuller and, perhaps, more honest answer to the question she asked that Tuesday evening, what really struck me as surprising—and, indeed, touching—about the Christians I came to know was the way in which I, and my own ongoing *doubt*, seemed to function as a measure of their (in)ability to meet the standards they set themselves; standards which, as I hope to have shown, were nothing short of divine.

Good Things Worth Sharing?

ON CHRISTMAS DAY 2012, Lucy found herself in tears.

Lucy, the charity lawyer who had first introduced me to Christ Church, was spending the holiday with her parents and sisters. They had just finished their Christmas lunch and were sitting down together in front of the television to watch Queen Elizabeth II deliver the Royal Christmas Message. A tradition dating back to 1932, the monarch's festive speech is something of an institution; Lucy called it the 'hallmark' of Christmas in Britain. Still, it wasn't something they always managed to watch together as a family. It was for this reason that Lucy, when she heard the content of the speech, was especially pleased that they had done so this year:

> This is the time of year when we remember that God sent His only Son 'to serve, not to be served'. He restored love and service to the centre of our lives in the person of Jesus Christ. It is my prayer this Christmas Day that His example and teaching will continue to bring people together, to give the best of themselves in the service of others.
>
> The carol, 'In the Bleak Midwinter', ends by asking a question of all of us who know the Christmas story, of how God gave Himself to us in humble service: 'What can I give Him, poor as I am? If I were a shepherd, I would bring a lamb. If I were a wise man, I would do my part.' The carol gives the answer: 'Yet what I can, I give Him—give my heart.'
>
> I wish you all a very happy Christmas.

So unused was she to hearing the name of her Saviour on television in an evangelistic context—popular programming, in her experience, tended to feature the words 'Jesus Christ' only in their capacity as profanity—that Lucy, an evangelical sitting among the non-Christian relatives with whom she longed to share the gospel, was moved to tears.[1]

This book opened with a debate held at the Church of England's General Synod, in which a member of the House of Laity asked his fellow Anglicans:

'If I can manifest my faith publicly with a *donkey*, seriously, what do the rest of you want to do?' The absurdity of the speaker's illustration—the Palm Sunday procession of a donkey around Trafalgar Square's Nelson's Column, that most literal and iconic example of the public square—and the exasperation, albeit good-humoured, with which he expressed it, suggested that anyone who felt unable to 'manifest' their faith in public must be unreasonable, unhinged, or otherwise beyond the pale.

For conservative evangelicals like Lucy, however, the question he raised was no mere rhetorical device. Her tears, recounted to me the following January, were an expression of the almost paradoxical situation in which English evangelical Protestants feel themselves to live. Protestant Christianity, after all, is—or *remains*—at the heart of national life. Queen Elizabeth II, whose Coronation Oath requires her to 'maintain the Laws of God and the true profession of the gospel', is a potent symbol of the interlinking of church and state. But the nation's sympathy for Christian symbolism is no substitute for salvation, and the trappings of Christendom are meaningless without acknowledgement of the Kingdom. If Protestantism remains an element of national identity, it seems to do so *as* remains: a shell or husk; a body from which the animating force has largely departed.

For people like Lucy, Christianity seems increasingly, but perplexingly, spatialised. As an aspect of selfhood, it is defined as (and protectable so long as it continues to be) private, internal, and depoliticised. Yet its language and imagery seemed acceptable, even desirable, when deployed in public rituals of nation-building or the affirmation of tradition. Perhaps public 'manifestations' were only tolerable when they were assumed to *diverge* from private convictions, when references to Christianity indexed cultural heritage rather than converted hearts? Perhaps Lucy's conservative religiosity, unlike that of the St Martin's donkey, did not fit the domesticated space allocated it by the liberal state? In this context, the strange blend of publicity and privacy represented by the Queen's Christmas Message—in which a national figurehead broadcasted public religion into her family home—was particularly meaningful for Lucy, whose efforts at witnessing within this quintessentially private space had met with little success. (Indeed, her non-Christian sister had once threatened to pull out of a family holiday unless Lucy agreed not to mention Jesus for its duration.) With evangelism in the private sphere having proved so relationally unsettling that she was now reliant on public figures to share the Good News with those closest to her, Lucy's Christmas story belies the incredulity of the Synod speaker, highlighting the complexity of expressing an evangelical identity in a nation that is variously portrayed as Christian, de-Christianising, and anti-Christian all at once.

This book has explored the ways in which conservative Christian activism is both a response to and constitutive of the ever-shifting relationship between Christianity and the state. By focusing on a group of conservative Protestant campaigners and a conservative evangelical church community, I have suggested that Christian-interest litigation and lobbying work to reframe beliefs and practices that were once commonplace as manifestations of 'religion'. So construed, this activism might well contribute to the secularisation it seeks to challenge, for 'religion', as Richard Amesbury has recently argued, is a fundamentally *secular* category.[2] Cases and campaigns emphasising the 'religious' nature of certain beliefs and practices risk constructing these phenomena as the niche interests of a legally-defined minority group; and the interests of a minority are, by definition, set apart from the concerns of most Britons. As such, efforts to promote Christianity's place in national life might well reduce its reach, as the general public increasingly associate it with a narrow range of duties, desires, and dogmas (not least, as Linda Woodhead and Andrew Brown have argued, a particular understanding of sexual ethics).[3]

In this conclusion, I hope to draw together the threads of this argument by focusing on the following themes: evangelism in the public sphere, emergent trends in Christian activism, and the changing place of Christianity in English law.

Legal Theology and the Evangelistic Impulse

In recounting my interlocutors' reflections on the nature, content, and desirability of public witness, I have tried to shed light on both the routes through which this publicity is pursued and the ways in which it is challenged, countered, and otherwise complicated by those in whose name it is being sought. Despite their conservative theology and shared set of socio-political concerns, including a self-described 'countercultural' approach to sexuality and gender, the staff of Christian Concern / Christian Legal Centre and the congregation of Christ Church sometimes come to different conclusions—or inconclusions—as to how best to express these convictions in public life. These are questions, as Engelke puts it, of the 'legitimate and legitimating forms of proclamation' through which religion goes public in the contemporary world.[4] In my interlocutors' reflections on these ambivalent spaces, where different forms of legalised proclamation can appear legitimate and illegitimate at once, what comes to the fore is rarely either the straightforward embrace or the outright rejection of muscular evangelism. Rather, what emerges is a searching consideration of their gospel-spreading obligations as responsible Christian subjects.

In principle, the members of both Christ Church and Christian Concern agree that they are called upon to publicly disavow sin, whether individual, corporate, or national. In practice, though, the desire to both *live out* and *live up to* God's Word results in the emergence of tensions between, for example, one's duty to publicly proclaim the gospel and one's class-based internalisation of what constitutes appropriately reserved behaviour; between the explication of grace and the maintenance of God's law; between individual salvation and one's relational obligations to others; between the desire to use Christian language in the hope of 'convicting' one's listeners and the worry that this language will be incomprehensible to unsaved ears. The ethnographic record suggests that efforts to adhere to absolute truths are inevitably qualified through 'lived practice'.[5] But when, my interlocutors might ask, does pragmatic qualification become problematic compromise? With the Christian's every action bearing a potential soteriological weight, the division between the two may have eternal significance, rendering clear lines exceptionally difficult to draw.

It is on account of this soteriological weight that the members of Christ Church feel a special burden in their interactions with others. This relational burden is evident in the efforts they go to in order to render theological Truths accessible to non-Christians. These efforts can be both great, such as the temporal and financial expense involved in cooking dinner for those who attend their evangelistic courses, and small, such as the minister announcing, during services attended by non-Christians, the pages on which the verses he will be preaching from can be found in the pew Bibles. (Page numbers are not announced at the monthly prayer meeting, when it is assumed that those present will know their Obadiah from their Hosea.) This burden can also be seen in their oft-voiced fears that non-Christians, inured to the specificity of conservative evangelical theology through the promulgation of a religious pluralism in which all 'faiths' are essentially one, misunderstand the nature of salvation. Indeed, the fear that their theology is distorted by efforts to render it intelligible to the court underlies my Christ Church informants' critique of those cases that are seen to blur the distinction between (salvation by) grace and law, such as those focusing on a legalistic adherence to the Sabbath or the visible display of religious symbols.

These concerns amount to a form of shared anxiety on the part of my Christ Church interlocutors. In positive terms, as a church apprentice once told me, the desire to introduce others to Jesus was simply a much more intense experience of the desire he felt to tell people about a great pub he'd just discovered. *Good things*, he explained, *are worth sharing*. But the issue was more often expressed negatively. With heaven and hell hanging in the balance, failing to tell someone about Jesus was like letting them stumble into a crisis that you not only foresaw, but had a means of preventing; that a Christian who didn't evangelise was like someone who had found the cure for cancer, only to keep it to themselves.

In this context, high-profile legal cases and political campaigns have come to occupy an awkward conceptual space for conservative evangelicals: were they *too* high-profile to be effective? Was it better to be a bull in a china shop or a chameleon who blended in? Did one catch more flies with honey than vinegar, or was this simply an excuse not to proclaim the gospel? With overly enthusiastic proselytism sometimes thought to be self-defeating, getting the balance right was no easy task. Of course, from a theological perspective, it is God who saves. The failure of His people to evangelise does not limit His ability to do so. Still, the impossibility of ever fully meeting their gospel duties whilst maintaining their own spiritual growth could lead to the sort of guilt stirred up in Naomi, the young optician, when she pictured non-Christians being led to hell on Judgment Day: *Why didn't you tell us, Naomi? Why didn't you tell us?*

The Anthropology of Christian Activism

In addition to providing an account of the relational anxieties faced by contemporary English evangelicals in their efforts to spread the gospel to a nation deemed antagonistic to it, I have sought to elucidate the relationship between conservative Christian campaign groups, on the one hand, and the conservative church communities to which they appeal for spiritual and financial support on the other.

Anthropologists have provided incisive analyses of Christian campaign groups, businesses, and charities, ranging from Jerry Falwell's use of prophetic speech as leader of the Moral Majority, to the generation of 'biblical publicity' by the British and Foreign Bible Society, to American evangelicals' involvement with anti-LGBTQ+ campaigns around the world, to the divergent worldviews of US-headquartered officials and local staff in a Christian aid organisation in Zimbabwe.[6] Further, the burgeoning anthropology of Christianity has provided a wealth of ethnographically rich and geographically diverse accounts of Christian communities worldwide, many seeking to answer Cannell's oft-quoted question: 'What difference does Christianity make?'[7] This body of literature includes ethnographies focused on churches in countries noted for their apparent secularity, such as Sweden, the Netherlands, and the United Kingdom.[8] While the existence of contentious Christian activism is often referenced as part of the background noise against which these communities construct themselves—Strhan, for example, argues that conservative Anglicans can be critical of activists who hold non-Christians to Christian standards,[9] while Harding has explored conservative 'transevangelicals' who reject the 'bipolar, us/them, culture war' rhetoric of the US Religious Right[10]—rarely are the two analysed coterminously. This book has brought these two strands together, putting the experience of Christian activists into direct conversation with those of one conservative church community.

As was stressed in the Introduction, there are many informal links, both personal and theological, between Christian Concern / Christian Legal Centre and Christ Church. With its conservative doctrine and full church coffers, Christ Church represents an ideal source of both spiritual and financial support for an organisation like Christian Concern, which must, after all, devote a considerable amount of energy to the solicitation of donations from like-minded supporters to continue operating. Yet the relationship between conservative evangelicals 'on the ground' and campaigners at the legal coal-face is one of complexity. Many church members support evangelical-fronted political campaign groups, such as the Coalition for Marriage, of which Christian Concern was a founding member. They often critique the 'absurd' behaviour of those represented as secular authorities. They have great sympathy for many CLC clients. Yet they also express doubts as to the efficacy of Christian-interest case law. While some cases are critiqued according to the specifics of evangelical doctrine—such as the Protestant iconoclasm suggested by the statement that 'wearing a cross doesn't make you a Christian'—others, and particularly those relating to issues framed in terms of conscience, are less clear-cut.

In an essay titled 'Cool Passion: the Political Theology of Conviction', the anthropologist Thomas Blom Hansen argues that despite anthropological critiques of disembodied notions of belief, the idea of 'conviction'—that is, the 'dramatic interior life' articulated by political and religious activists—has become a universalised understanding of interiority, a means by which activists the world over frame their identity in terms of deep-seated beliefs and the moment they came to 'embrace' them.[11] Such conviction, he argues, is genealogically rooted in two ethical models. He posits the 'ethics of sincerity' as beginning to emerge in Europe from the sixteenth-century onwards, a time when the proliferation of Protestant sects, increasing geographic mobility, and changing social hierarchies led to a concern with authenticity and credibility. By contrast, an 'ethics of consequence' emerged from the late eighteenth century onwards as revolutionary groups, such as the Jacobins, sought 'the coming utopia'. From within a revolutionary ethics of consequence, the important factor is not merely an individual's sincerity, but their commitment to the 'larger vision of transformation' of society.[12]

Without wanting to stretch the analogy, perhaps this distinction illuminates the differences of approach evident in my two field sites. Although the members of both Christian Concern and Christ Church are people of conviction, their conviction is demonstrated in different ways. At Christian Concern, where an ethics of consequence is emphasised, the 'test of conviction' is 'the ability to break norms' and run strategic risks, to support one's cause over and above one's family, friends, or reputation.[13] For these campaigners, 'permissive' legislation is challenged on what are understood to be socially motivated, compassionate grounds. After all, the rejection of God's Word is thought to have negative consequences both at a micro level—for example, in the heartache and relational dysfunction caused to individual men and women by abortion or 'homosexual practice'—and at a macro level, with society's moral foundations increasingly eroded by the law's encouragement of such sins as infanticide and sexual licence. Faced with the propinquity of permissive legislation and sinful acts, Christian activists are motivated by what I have referred to as an urgent theology, one in which engagement is prioritised over reflection.

Regardless of whether they are rejected as unwelcome prophets or vindicated as moral reformers, they are compelled to take a stand for Christ and His Word.

As conservative evangelicals living in a world deemed hostile to the gospel, the members of Christ Church share these worries. They are wary of the relativist approach to life's 'big questions' so prevalent among their non-Christian colleagues, friends, and neighbourhood anthropologists. (I was often taken to task for expressing this relativism, with my methodological agnosticism a particular point of contention.) But they are also influenced by an individualising mindset that questions the believer's right to impose God's standards on a disbelieving world. As Strhan has convincingly shown, middle-class evangelical Londoners' desire to combat sin in all its forms is tempered by socially-mandated responses to pluralism that stress inclusivity, respect for personal autonomy, and the tolerance of different lifeways. Like those at Christian Concern, Christ Churchites long to see God's Word upheld in the nation, and they desire—or desire *to* desire—to speak this Word to the non-Christians in their lives. Yet they find themselves hampered by the risk of relational discomfort inherent in submitting non-Christians to ideas that outsiders often dismiss as anachronistic, unpleasant, or both. At Christ Church, then, where the ethics of sincerity reigns, the test of conviction is one of remaining true to one's beliefs, even when publicly challenged or shamed.

It is important to stress the specificity of my account. While Strhan's work with wealthy evangelicals in London's financial district suggests that these ambivalent responses may be common to London's primarily white, middle-class conservative evangelical community, it is by no means clear that they would be held by the members of, for example, churches with greater ethnic or racial diversity; immigrant-majority churches; churches whose members are primarily low-paid; or churches with an alternative theology, such as an explicitly Dominionist approach to political engagement. Given the theological and social spread of Christian Concern's support base, this diversity may prove a fruitful direction for further research. Ethnographic investigation of different churches' responses to such movements would greatly enhance our understanding of both conservative Christianity and Christian activism in contemporary England, shedding light, for example, on the possible relationship between economic and racial exclusion and the appeal of the rhetoric of marginalisation, or possible variances between members of non-established congregations and their Church of England counterparts.

While recognising the class- and race-based privileges and particularities of Christ Church, however, the reflections of both staff and clients of the Christian Legal Centre suggest that ambivalence towards legal theology spans England's denominational spectrum. Staff members who worshipped at Anglican, Baptist, and low evangelical churches all knew of fellow church members—and, in at least two cases, family members—who questioned the confrontational strategy of organisations like Christian Concern and the CLC (even as they might strongly sympathise with their aims), while some clients found the greatest challenge in coping with their cases to be the mixed responses they received from fellow believers. Recognising this diversity of opinion provides a useful corrective to sociological accounts of conservative Christianity that view it as a reactionary response to changing values, in which the march of secularisation is seen to result in what the historian Callum Brown calls 'increasing commitment from decreasing numbers'.[14] As the ethnographic literature shows, a firm commitment to conservative values does not negate complex individual evaluations of public Christianity, nor varying degrees of agreement with or acquiescence to the secular norms of public discourse often presented as hostile to their faith.

Along with stressing the heterogeneity of a group often spoken of in terms of a presumed shared zealotry, I have also sought to complicate the idea that conservative Christian activism should be understood as a 'backlash'—again, to use Brown's terms—against its own 'irrelevance'.[15] This paradigm presents the rise of conservative Christianity as proof of (one understanding of) the secularisation thesis, in which religion has become extraneous to the life of the nation and conservative Christians, having lost their previous social clout, are mobilising against this change.[16] In addition to its popularity among secularisation theorists, a version of this position is sometimes expressed by other Christians, particularly those who identify as theologically liberal, who worry that conservative activists have confused the dismantling of historic privilege with the beginnings of persecution.

It is certainly true that Christian Concern staff members decry the passing of what is referred to as Britain's Christian heritage. They fear, in Durkheimian fashion, that the loss of a shared Christian metanarrative will result in the fragmenting of society; or, worse still, in its usurpation by a competing, and less desirable, 'worldview' (typical examples being secularism or Islam). In this sense, their goals *are* defensive. They view themselves as mobilising to 'protect' this heritage. Yet it would be a mistake to reduce their activism to a purely reactionary desire to return to an idealised Christian past. That nineteenth-century law used to reflect Christian Concern's preferred understanding of marriage, for example, does not mean that all nineteenth-century Britons had a saving faith in Jesus. Thus, although references to an ahistoric Christian Britain are a key part of the lexicon of Christian activism, their campaigns and cases are also strongly future-oriented. As I have argued in relation to their critique of rights-based language, these initiatives reveal a desire for what Griffith, writing of the United States, describes as a 'once and future' Christian nation in which individual recognition of the Truth of the Bible leads to corporate human flourishing.[17] Rather than a knee-jerk reaction to Christianity's decreasing cultural privilege, this alternative vision of human flourishing is, at least from an emic perspective, equal parts restitutionary and revolutionary. In relying on secular legal tools that work to separate out Christianity from the everyday, however, efforts to ensure this revolution may well be its undoing.

Liberty in History

An implicit aim of this book has been to give an account of English law's transition from framing religious freedom as a negative liberty—that is, the law's 'protection' of religion from state encroachment—to one in which it is seen as a positive right requiring state enforcement. As scholars from a range of disciplinary backgrounds have shown, contemporary ideas of religious freedom—despite frequently being presented as the primordial foundation of the liberal state—are often the result of fairly recent political developments. Ethnographic data highlight the ways in which 'religious liberty' is produced in everyday life, such that religiously motivated 'conscientious objections' may be brought into being by the law's efforts to protect them.[18] Recognising that this liberty is always socially constructed, this book has sought to stress the particularities of a transitional moment in which the law's preference for establishment Anglicanism gives way to a universal 'right' to religious freedom.

As we have seen, opponents of Christian Concern and the Christian Legal Centre sometimes describe them as having an 'American' approach to religious liberty, even as being at the forefront of a British 'Religious Right'.[19] For those who make these comparisons, 'American' has negative connotations: zealous, aggressive, and generally unsuited to a nation defined by its stiff upper lip. This comparison, of course, should not be overstated. English evangelicals have long agitated for socio-political reform. Many have used Parliament and the courts to do so. Further, it is hardly unusual for opponents of a social movement to claim that it is a foreign imposition incompatible with national values. Yet there is an element of truth to narratives that paint these organisations as American-inspired. This is so not only in relation to Andrea's personal testimony and the groups' professional links with US-based organisations, but in terms of their willingness to argue (and publicise) controversial religious liberty test cases. Indeed, one of their lawyers' personal websites describes a CLC case in which he was involved as being interesting from a 'First Amendment perspective'; an odd claim to make, perhaps, for a dispute settled under UK equality law.

Given structural differences in the regulation of religion in the United States and the UK, Christian Concern's approach raises questions of both legal and cultural fit. The First Amendment, which aims to protect religious freedom, in part, by *separating* church and state so as to prevent one religious community being favoured above others, makes quite different assumptions from Article 9 of the UK's Human Rights Act (which does not view church establishment as an a priori violation of such freedom). Freedom of religion cases in the United States tend to confirm that Protestant Christianity 'counts' as religion when it comes to the second of the First Amendment's religion clauses—that is, free exercise—but not its first, non-establishment.[20] So conceived, these cases carve out protections for Christianity when its norms diverge from those of the ostensibly secular state, even as the quotidian over-lap of these norms facilitates the occlusion of Protestantism as a form of unof-ficial establishment.

Of course, framing Christianity as 'culture' rather than 'religion' also hap-pens in Europe, occasionally in high-profile legal cases—of which the *Lautsi* case is the most (in)famous—but more often in claims that, say, Christian places of worship represent 'heritage' rather than religion.[21] This move is, per-haps, particularly significant in countries that valorise *laïcité* (recent discus-sions over the rebuilding of Notre-Dame de Paris are a case in point).[22] In the UK, however, Christian establishment is a fact. As such, cases rarely arise in which an act is found troubling because it is 'religious' in and of itself; rather, these acts are deemed problematic because of their coming into conflict with aspects of personhood—primarily gender or sexual identity—that have recently been designated 'protected characteristics' under human rights and equality law. In such circumstances, Christians are required to frame them-selves as embodying *another* 'characteristic' protected by this rights-based regime: that of religion. This is a designation they share with the various other 'faith communities' who must buy into the state's definition of religiosity to protect their distinctive lifeways. Indeed, it is a challenge faced by everyone who chooses—or feels compelled—to engage in legal theology.

In a 1993 lecture, Sir Thomas Bingham (later Lord Chief Justice and Senior Law Lord) suggested that the incorporation of the European Conven-tion on Human Rights into domestic law would 'help reinvigorate the faith, which our eighteenth and nineteenth century forebears would not for one instant have doubted, that [liberty and justice] were fields in which Britain was the world's teacher, not its pupil'.[23] Not long after he gave this speech, Lord Bingham had his wish: the European Convention was incorporated into UK law as the Human Rights Act 1998. UK residents no longer had to appeal to Europe to argue rights-based claims. For my activist interlocutors, how-ever, there is no necessary connection between nineteenth-century notions of justice and the 'equality and diversity' agenda that they believe has 'hijacked' the human rights project. As was suggested in chapter 4, it is perhaps for this reason that conservative evangelicals seem to be experiencing the legal sys-tem's move towards a more robust, positive understanding of human rights as a *weakening* of their ability to freely express their religion. Contra the hopes of Lord Bingham, then, the law's new emphasis on rights has done little to 'reinvigorate' their 'faith' in its ability to dispense justice.

Yet conservative Christian activists continue to put forward rights-based claims. I have presented this strategy as both pragmatic—one must work within the law as it stands—and prophetic—an attempt to reveal the under-lying incoherence of a system that seeks to protect competing rights without a comprehensive vision of the good. In this way, my activist interlocutors use the weight of the law against itself, highlighting its inconsistency to spark calls for reform. The range of theologies represented by Christian Concern's support base means that the organisation does not take an official position on what will be the ultimate outcome of their work, that is, whether the nation will (re)turn to God. As noted in chapter 1, they feel compelled to act regardless of worldly success or failure, often reminding themselves and their supporters of the fact that 'God's economy' is not the world's. The immediacy of this urgent theology, in which the actual ends of activism are held in temporal abeyance, can account for both success and defeat in the courts. On the one hand, God is known to favour the blameless, granting victory to those who uphold His laws. On the other, as Candida Moss puts it of ancient Christian martyrdom, 'martyrdom authenticates mission'.[24] A client's willing sacrifice of reputation, relationships, and financial remuneration can prove the righteousness of their endeavour.

As we have seen, these activists face an uphill battle. Those looking to protect England's Christian heritage are, in part, responding to social and demographic changes beyond their control: increasing ethnic, cultural, and religious diversity; decreasing adherence to traditional forms of authority, whether religious, political, social, or generational; value pluralism; and other challenges to Protestant hegemony. These shifts all impact the place of majority religion in contemporary England. Yet, by stressing the particularly *religious* nature of the words, beliefs, and actions for which they seek protection, Christian activists also contribute to these changes. Pursuing their claims under religious freedom legislation works to confirm that these are niche interests set apart from the everyday, thus invoking a secular distinction between the 'religious' and other spheres of life. In this context, some of their fellow believers have come to conclude that the Kingdom is best served not by theo-legal activism, but by personal holiness.

As I conclude, however, it is important to stress the subtlety of this position. That God's people are obliged to provide a positive Christian witness even in a hostile world, and that they ought to rejoice in doing so, does not negate the sadness with which they may respond to this perceived hostility. While finishing the doctoral thesis on which this book is based, I told Lucy that I intended to conclude by quoting the Queen's speech that had moved her so greatly. I mentioned that I would be framing her experience in terms of what I saw as a conceptual paradox: that Christianity could be 'at the heart of national life' even as its public proclamation was unusual enough to bring her to tears. Gently correcting my interpretation, Lucy clarified:

> I wouldn't say that Christianity is at the heart of national life. I fear it is anything but. It is at the heart of everything we've historically built our national life upon, but the nation seems to be turning away from that—morally in any event—at every opportunity and at an astonishing rate.

'That', she explained, 'also brings a tear to my eye.'

Introduction. Palm Fronds in the Public Square

1. The Church of England (Anglican Church) can broadly be divided into three theological strands: 'liberal' Anglicans ('mainline Protestants', in the American terminology); evangelicals, the most significant subgroup of whom are conservative evangelicals; and Anglo-Catholics, who traditionally favour a 'High Church' approach to ritual. Conservative evangelicals and Anglo-Catholics tend towards the conservative end of the social and theological spectrum, rejecting, *inter alia*, the ministry of women and LGBTQ+ priests. These terms are, of course, somewhat porous; there are also liberal Anglo-Catholic and evangelical Anglican congregations. Readers looking for an introduction to these divisions may find Andrew Brown and Linda Woodhead's *That Was the Church That Was* a useful, albeit polemical, primer.

2. Most Church of England funding comes from its parishes, but it also receives government funding for the upkeep of historic church buildings.

3. Neither Caroline Petrie nor Olive Jones are Anglican. Both attend Baptist churches.

4. This book focuses on England, one of the four countries or regions that makes up the United Kingdom of Great Britain and Northern Ireland. While some Acts of Parliament apply equally to England, Northern Ireland, Scotland, and Wales, some legislation is geographically specific, and England, unlike Northern Ireland, Scotland, or Wales, has an established church. Many people who live in England prefer to call themselves 'British' rather than 'English', and they sometimes refer to 'Britain' or 'the UK' when they are speaking, primarily, about England. As such, the book variously references the United Kingdom, Britain (which comprises England, Scotland, and Wales), and England as relevant, with apologies for the inevitable slippage between terms that this involves.

5. This shift is usefully charted in Russell Sandberg's *Law and Religion*.

6. I have taken this term from Helge Årsheim and Pamela Slotte's *The Juridification of Religion?*

7. Christian Concern, 'About Us'. In mid-2019, Christian Concern updated their website. As such, there are some differences in phrasing between quotes taken from the website before this redesign (some of which I collected during my doctoral studies) and the wording on the website now. The ideas, however, remain the same.

8. See statistics compiled by Faith Survey, 'Christianity in the UK'.

9. Christians in Parliament, *Clearing the Ground Inquiry*, 44. It is worth pointing out that, as with all polls, these data should be treated with some caution; respondents are likely to be self-selecting. However, this possible selection bias does not negate the fact that some (although certainly not all) British Christians feel themselves to be under attack in public life.

10. Donald, Bennett, and Leach, *Equality and Human Rights Commission Research Report 84*, 111–112.

11. Christians in Parliament, *Clearing the Ground Inquiry*, 9–23.

12. Former prime minister Tony Blair's 'spin doctor', Alastair Campbell, caused a media stir when he announced to a journalist that 'we don't do God'. See Engelke, *God's Agents*, xvii–xix, for an exploration of the cultural significance of this phrase.

13. This theological dabbling is not limited to cases involving Christianity. In the Jews' Free School case, for example, the UK Supreme Court ruled that the School's admission policy was discriminatory. See Rubens, '"Something Has Gone Wrong": The *JFS* Case and Defining Jewish Identity in the Courtroom'.

14. Lord Justice Laws in *McFarlane v Relate* at [23]. It is worth noting that Laws LJ identifies as a Christian. His reflection on the subjective nature of religious belief does not preclude that belief being true.

15. The term '"legal" religion' comes from Sullivan's seminal *The Impossibility of Religious Freedom*, which engages these questions from a First Amendment perspective.

16. Sullivan, Yelle, and Taussig-Rubbo, *After Secular Law*, 16.

17. See Mahmood, *Religious Difference in a Secular Age*; Asad, *Formations of the Secular*; and contributions to Sullivan, Yelle, and Taussig-Rubbo, *Politics of Religious Freedom*.

18. Given the lack of comparable organisations in the UK, Christian Concern and the Christian Legal Centre would be easily identifiable on the basis of their campaigns and legal cases. For this reason, I have not anonymised these organisations. Nor have I anonymised those staff members who are public figures, such as co-founders Andrea Minichiello Williams and Ade Omooba. I have, however, anonymised staff members who are not in the public eye.

19. Hatcher, *Religious and Political Identities of British Evangelicals*, 12.

20. Sandberg, *Law and Religion*, 192.

21. Rivers, *The Law of Organized Religions*, ix. See also Sullivan, 'Comparing Religions, Legally', on English law's pre-HRA approach to religion as a category.

22. Christian Concern, 'About Us'.

23. Amesbury, 'Is the Body Secular? Circumcision, Religious Freedom and Bodily Integrity', 5.

24. Sullivan, *Impossibility*; Hurd, *Beyond Religious Freedom*; McIvor, 'Carnal Exhibitions'.

25. Sullivan, *Impossibility*, 7.

26. Fernando, 'Intimacy Surveilled: Religion, Sex and Secular Cunning'.

27. Walton, Hatcher, and Spencer, *Is There a 'Religious Right' Emerging in Britain?*, 57; see also Jamie Doward and Seb Wheeler, 'Christian Legal Centre Fights More than 50 Religious Discrimination Cases'. The association of 'American' with unwelcome forms of Christianity is not limited to the UK. The Swedish press, for example, has been highly critical of 'the political conservatism, unabashed prosperity theology and outright Americanism' of Swedish branches of the charismatic Word of Life church. See Coleman, '"Right Now!"', 438.

28. Theologian John Warwick Montgomery, for example, has suggested that Christian Concern is heavily influenced by 'American fundamentalism' and the 'Puritan-Calvinist' values of the Moral Majority. *Defending the Gospel in Legal Style*, 277.

29. Bebbington, *Evangelicalism in Modern Britain*, 3.

30. Turnbull, *Shaftesbury: The Great Reformer*.

31. Morrison, 'Cultural and Moral Authority: The Presumption of Television', 120.

32. Morrison and Tracey, 'American Theory and British Practice: The Case of Mrs Mary Whitehouse and the National Viewers and Listeners Association', 38.

33. Bebbington, *Evangelicalism in Modern Britain*, 265.

34. Mary Whitehouse, for example, was instrumental in securing the 9pm 'watershed', which requires all programming before 9pm to be suitable for a general audience (including children).

35. Hatcher, *Religious and Political Identities*, 14.

36. Bebbington, *Evangelicalism*, 8.

37. Coffey, 'Evangelicals, Slavery and the Slave Trade: From Whitefield to Wilberforce'; Gerbner, *Christian Slavery: Conversion and Race in the Protestant Atlantic World*.

38. Hatcher, *Religious and Political Identities*, 14; Guest, 'The Emerging Church in Transatlantic Perspective', 43.

39. See Lewis, *The Rights Turn in Conservative Christian Politics;* Bennett, *Defending Faith*.

40. Sullivan, 'Comparing Religions'.

41. Sandberg, 'The Right to Discriminate', 157–158; Hill, Sandberg, and Doe, *Religion and Law*; Morris, 'Part One: Establishment in Great Britain Now', 17–22; Sandberg, *Law and Religion*, 17–29.

42. Sullivan, 'Comparing Religions', 916.

43. Isaiah Berlin, *Two Concepts of Liberty*.

44. Sullivan, 'We Are All Religious Now', 1185. As Sullivan's work shows, however, the expansive 'protections' offered religion in the United States are themselves of relatively recent origin.

45. Sullivan, *Impossibility*, 1.

46. Sullivan, 'Comparing Religions', 916.

47. Andrea's testimony, as recounted here, comes from a mix of sources, including a taped interview and numerous presentations.

48. Christian Concern posits the 1960s as the decade in which British Christianity was significantly undermined. Interestingly, this is also the position of historian Callum Brown's *The Death of Christian Britain*, which attributes this titular demise to the sexual revolution and the 'discursive death of pious femininity'.

49. Harding, *The Book of Jerry Falwell*, 190. This is a fairly recent association. By contrast to the preacher-led movements of the late twentieth century, mid-nineteenth-century campaigns to criminalise abortion were organised by the newly minted American Medical Association, which, by linking the availability of abortion to population decline and degeneracy, sought to reduce competition from midwives, local healers, and abortionists. See Ginsburg, *Contested Lives*, 24–27.

50. Cannell, 'Concepts of Parenthood', 681.

51. Sidewalk counselling is a form of non-violent activism in which volunteers attempt to persuade those entering abortion clinics to rethink their decision to terminate a pregnancy.

52. Strhan, *Aliens and Strangers?*; Engelke, *God's Agents*, 115.

53. Soper, *Evangelical Christianity in the United States and Great Britain*, p.1.

54. Sullivan's *Impossibility* remains the clearest articulation of the law's power to define certain actions as failing to meet its standards of religiosity.

55. Durkheim, *Elementary Forms of Religious Life*, 62.

56. Malinowski, *Crime and Custom in Savage Society*, 82–86.

57. Comaroff, 'Reflections on the Rise of Legal Theology', 195.

58. Sullivan, Yelle, and Taussig-Rubbo, *After Secular Law*, 3.

59. Comaroff, 'Reflections on the Rise of Legal Theology', 198.

60. Ibid., 202.

61. Casanova, *Public Religions in the Modern World*, 6.

62. The Lawyers' Christian Fellowship was founded in 1852 to support Christian lawyers in their efforts to live Christlike lives.

63. Christian Concern, 'About Us'.

64. Brown, 'Evangelicals Reverse the Ferret'.

65. It is possible that they hoped my research would offer a kind of 'proof' or affirmation of the validity of Christian Concern's position, a normative judgement that, as an anthropologist, I found myself unable to make (see the concluding section of this Introduction).

66. Walton, Hatcher, and Spencer, *Is There a 'Religious Right' Emerging in Britain?*; Kettell, 'The Collective Action Framing of Conservative Christian Groups in Britain'.

67. Although she is not currently a member of an Anglican church, Andrea was, at the time of my fieldwork, an elected member of the Church's House of Laity. She has previously worshipped at Anglican churches.

68. The Christian Institute, a campaign group with a similar set of concerns and lobbying interests, has also funded a number of high-profile cases. However, neither its caseload nor its ability to capture the media's attention can match that of the CLC.

69. See Kiska, 'The Unknown Client'.

70. Martin, *On Secularization*, 71.

71. A.M. Williams, 'Church Teaching Used as Evidence Against Christian in Court'.

72. For an example of a Christian-interest case featuring Catholic claimants, see the 'Scottish midwives' case, *Greater Glasgow Health Board v Doogan*.

73. See Bartley, *Faith and Politics After Christendom*.

74. Bychawski, 'UK Christian "Reactionaries" Mark 10 Years of Lobbying Against Women's and LGBT Rights'.

75. Walton, Hatcher, and Spencer, *Is There a Religious Right' Emerging in Britain?*, 56.

76. Alliance Defending Freedom, 'Our First Freedom'.

77. The Blackstone Legal Fellowship is a summer internship programme for aspiring Christian lawyers.

78. See Walton, Hatcher, and Spencer, *Is There a 'Religious Right' Emerging in Britain?*

79. For ethnographies of Christian communities in England, see Jenkins, *Religion in English Everyday Life*; Daswani, 'Transformation and Migration'; Coleman, 'Pilgrimage as Trope for an Anthropology of Christianity'; Strhan, *Aliens and Strangers*. On Christianity's interaction with politics and law in the UK and United States, see Engelke, *God's Agents*; Harding, *Book of Jerry Falwell*; Greenhouse, *Praying for Justice*; Crapanzano, *Serving the Word*.

80. That this unwillingness was ethnographically interesting in and of itself (proof of a slightly embattled feeling among certain sections of the conservative Christian community) was of little comfort.

81. Conley and O'Barr, 'Legal Anthropology Comes Home'.

82. Malinowski, *Crime and Custom in Savage Society*, 71.

83. I use the English Standard Version (ESV) of the Bible, which is Christ Church's preferred translation, for Bible citations.

84. GAFCON, 'About GAFCON'. Herriot, *Warfare and Waves* gives some detail about these organisations, albeit from a polemical, critical position.

85. See Taylor, *A Secular Age*, 589; Cannell, 'Imaginary Friends'.

86. Engelke, *God's Agents*, xix.

87. Braunstein, *Prophets and Patriots*, 11.

88. Sociological studies, such as Strhan, *Aliens and Strangers?* and Hatcher, *Religious and Political Identities of British Evangelicals* have highlighted the ambivalence English evangelicals feel about the politicisation of their faith. My account, however, combines church ethnography with research among legal activists.

89. The idea that Christians are 'under attack' is common to many contemporary evangelicalisms. See Smith, *American Evangelicalism*.

90. Sandberg, 'The Right to Discriminate', 181.

91. Harding, 'Representing Fundamentalism'.

92. This was especially so at Christ Church, where the congregation is largely homogeneous in terms of ethnic, social, and economic background. The staff and clients of Christian Concern, by contrast, represent a much more diverse constituency.

93. Robbins, 'What Is a Christian?', 192.

94. Engelke, 'The Problem of Belief'.

95. Lambek, 'Value and Virtue', 134.

96. Ibid.

97. Mahmood, *Politics of Piety*, 5.

98. Tarusarira writes primarily about forgiveness and peacebuilding in post-conflict contexts. See 'The Anatomy of Apology and Forgiveness'.

99. Sherwood, *Biblical Blaspheming*, 5.

Chapter 1. Confronting a Hostile World

1. In addition to conjuring images of both unfair dismissal and violent persecution, the phrase 'in the firing line' echoes the title of a Christian Concern publication. Written by former client Dr Richard Scott (who was disciplined for allegedly telling a depressed patient that 'the devil haunts people who do not turn to Jesus'), *Christians in the Firing Line* gives a summary of thirteen CLC cases.

2. In a 2011 speech, then prime minister David Cameron stated: 'Britain is a Christian country and we should not be afraid to say so.' See BBC, 'David Cameron Says the UK Is a Christian Country.'

3. Engelke, *God's Agents*, 103.

4. Mathewes and De Hart, *Sex, Gender and the Politics of ERA*, 243.

5. Christian Concern, 'About Us'.

6. 'Permissive legislation' is that which permits, rather than restricts, sinful behaviour.

7. The idea that Christianity might lead to the civilising of otherwise barbaric Others is, of course, an old one, but it gained a particular salience during the Age of Empire. An 1813 copy of the *Missionary Register*, for example, justifies colonialism by juxtaposing the formerly pagan state of Britain—'Your own ancestors, in this very Island, once worshipped dumb idols'—with its contemporary status as a Christian country, in which 'civil and religious liberty have grown up under the benign influence of the Gospel'. Two hundred years later, Andrea's comments seemed to echo this understanding of the relationship between Bible preaching, morality, and civil liberty. See Sugirtharajah, *The Bible and the Third World: Precolonial, Colonial and Postcolonial Encounters*, 62.

8. Omri Elisha, 'Moral Ambitions of Grace', 167–168.

9. Sherwood, *Biblical Blaspheming* 6.

10. Christian Concern/CLC does not promote a particular party, and its employees represent a range of political viewpoints. As a general rule, though, they are sceptical of the leading parties (the Conservatives, Labour, and the Liberal Democrats), none of which are thought to be interested in protecting the UK's Christian heritage. This can lead to either protest or pragmatic voting. In the 2015 general election, for example, one former staff member voted Conservative on the grounds that the Tory Party, with its emphasis on small government, was more likely to support local churches' voluntary work than the other parties. Others refused to vote Conservative in protest at the party's introduction of same-sex marriage. Christian Concern has not taken a stance on the UK's exiting the European Union (Brexit). However, it has been criticised for its links to the United Kingdom Independence Party (UKIP), one of the primary forces behind this move. See Symon Hill, 'UKIP's "Christian Manifesto" Will Be Repulsive to Many Christians'.

11. 'YouGov Survey Results', YouGov, http://cdn.yougov.com/cumulus_uploads /document/6quatmbimd/Internal_Results_140725_Commonwealth_Empire-W.pdf.

12. 'Cultural fundamentalism' is distinct from 'Christian fundamentalism'. The term 'fundamentalist' masks a complicated history of theological and denominational struggle in the context of early twentieth-century American Christianity. Because 'Christian fundamentalist' is often used in a pejorative sense, I do not use it here. That being said, members

of both field sites are broadly in agreement with the authors of 'The Fundamentals', the series of essays from which fundamentalism draws its name. See Packer, *'Fundamentalism' and the Word of God*.

13. Mathews and De Hart, 177.

14. Ibid., 177–9. See Harding, *Jerry Falwell*; and Griffith, *God's Daughters* for ethnographic accounts of American evangelical cultural fundamentalism, particularly as regards gender.

15. Robbins, *Becoming Sinners*, 164.

16. Harding, *Jerry Falwell*, 231.

17. Guyer, 'Prophecy and the Near Future', 414.

18. Thompson, *Waiting for Antichrist*; Webster, *The Anthropology of Protestantism*.

19. Strathern, 'Enabling Identity?', 39–41.

20. A.M. Williams, 'Modern Legal Thought Eliminates Christian Morality'.

21. Vallely, 'Christians: The World's Most Persecuted People'.

22. Census data suggest many Britons continue to identify with the label 'Christian'. Throughout this book, however, I adopt the understanding of my informants, for whom Christian means those 'trusting in Christ for salvation'.

23. Laidlaw, *The Subject of Virtue*, 150–155; cf. B. Williams, 'Moral Incapacity'.

24. See Sullivan, *Impossibility*, 7; Asad, *Genealogies*, 28.

25. Gordon, *The Mormon Question*, 135.

26. A.M. Williams, 'Is This Equality? As a Lawyer, I Never Thought I'd Have to Defend Christians in a Christian Nation'.

27. Smith, *American Evangelicalism*, 131.

28. Strhan, *Aliens and Strangers?*; cf. Brown and Woodhead, *That Was the Church That Was*; Herriot, *Warfare and Waves*.

29. This may be changing. At the time of writing, a number of CLC cases involving conflicts over alleged homophobic language are being appealed, and there is some evidence that the courts may be growing more sympathetic to these claims.

30. Herriot, *Warfare and Waves*, 9.

31. Brown, *The Death of Christian Britain*, 229.

32. See Riles, 'Anthropology, Human Rights, and Legal Knowledge: Culture in the Iron Cage', 59; Weber, 'Science as a Vocation', 144–145.

33. Harding, *Jerry Falwell*, 238.

34. Bebbington, *Evangelicalism*, 62.

35. Harding, *Jerry Falwell*, 240–245.

36. Ibid., 244.

37. This is not to say that everyone would be Christian—although John thinks that many more would be—but that national law would largely reflect Biblical morality.

38. Moss, *Ancient Christian Martyrdom*, 1.

39. Bartley, *Faith and Politics*.

40. B. Williams, 'Moral Incapacity'; Laidlaw, *The Subject of Virtue*; cf. Hansen, 'Cool Passion', 27.

41. One staff member's response was: 'An anthropologist? Surely not!'

Chapter 2. Grace and Law

1. Christianity Explored is a conservative evangelical version of the Alpha course, popularised by Anglican Nicky Gumbel in the 1990s. It differs from Alpha in giving greater prominence to sin and judgement in its teaching. See R. Warner, *Reinventing English Evangelicalism, 1966–2001: A Theological and Sociological Study*, 133.

2. Catholics, like liberal Anglicans, occupy a somewhat liminal space for conservative evangelicals. Although Catholic teaching is thought insufficient for salvation, the members of Christ Church agree with the Catholic Church's conservative stand on issues such as abortion, sexuality, and the role of women. While they accept that some Catholics are saved, they worry that the Church's emphasis on the sacraments means many Catholics are not true Christians.

3. Julian Pitt-Rivers, 'Postscript: The Place of Grace in Anthropology', 215. In the years since Pitt-Rivers raised this concern, increasing ethnographic interest in Christianity has somewhat filled this gap. Omri Elisha's essay on grace and accountability in American evangelicalism, 'Moral Ambitions', has been particularly influential in this regard. While the grace/law distinction is often relevant in contexts where Protestantism has been opposed to Catholicism and Judaism (and, increasingly, Islam), different ethnographic settings reveal different binaries. Michael Edwards and Neena Mahadev, for example, have focused on the opposition of grace to karma. See Edwards, *Real Change: Translating Salvation in Myanmar*; Mahadev, 'Economics of Conversion and Ontologies of Religious Difference'.

4. Cannell, 'The Christianity of Anthropology', 352.

5. There is some debate about evolution versus creationism at Christ Church. Luke, the minister, believes that the Bible speaks of a literal Adam and Eve.

6. Church Society, *An English Prayerbook*, 207.

7. Ibid.

8. Bebbington, *Evangelicalism*, 21–22.

9. Of the ten trainees, three were staff, four were former Wilberforce Academy delegates, one was a regular volunteer, one was a former CLC client, and one was an anthropologist.

10. The Trust disputed this.

11. This followed new guidelines released by the Department of Health.

12. Sikh staff members had been asked to remove *kara* bracelets, and although two Muslim doctors wore *hijab*, these were close-fitting sports *hijab* that did not require a brooch to pin them in place.

13. Much of the decision focused on how many individuals needed to be impacted by the policy before they constituted 'persons' for the purpose of indirect discrimination.

14. *Eweida v British Airways Plc* at [8].

15. *Chaplin* at [17].

16. As with many CLC cases, *Playfoot* was highly controversial. Her parents were both involved in the Silver Ring Thing movement. A school spokesperson suggested that the case was less about religious freedom than it was free publicity: 'I do wonder whether this action is brought more for the purpose of generating publicity for the Silver Ring Thing movement in the UK than for any practical outcome for Lydia, who leaves my school this month in any event.' See Alexandra Topping, 'Girl Takes School to Court Over Right to Wear "Purity" Ring'.

17. *Playfoot* at [23].

18. Sullivan, *Impossibility*, 6.

19. Sullivan, 'Comparing Religions', 923.

20. Sullivan, 'Religion, Law and the Construction of Identities: Introduction', 134.

21. Sullivan, 'We Are All Religious Now', 1185.

22. Sullivan, 'Competing Theories of Religion and Law in the Supreme Court of the United States', 207.

23. *R (Begum) v Denbigh High School*. See Tarlo, *Visibly Muslim*, 104–110, for an anthropological discussion of the *Begum* case.

24. During my fieldwork, one of the projects Christian Concern affiliates were involved in was opposition to the building of what they called a 'mega mosque' in east London. They justified this campaign by reference to the proposed mosque's connection to the Tablighi Jamaat movement.

25. *R (X) v Head Teacher of Y School*.

26. *R (Watkins Singh) v Governing Body of Aberdare Girls' High School*.

27. McIvor, 'Carnal Exhibitions'; Lourdes Peroni, 'Deconstructing "Legal" Religion in Strasbourg'.

28. BBC News, 'Cross Case Nurse Shirley Chaplin Plans to Appeal Ruling'.

29. The CLC maintains that Shirley would have accepted a compromise, but that no acceptable one was ever offered. Hannah, however, who knew one of the lawyers (a fellow evangelical) on the hospital's legal team, said that the general feeling from the hospital administration was that Shirley's representation had been 'quite unreasonable' in their demands.

30. Keane, *Christian Moderns*, 188.

31. Carol Greenhouse noted a similar approach among the confrontation-averse Baptists she worked with in Georgia.

32. See Donald, Bennett, and Leach, *Equality and Human Rights Commission*, 114, on 'the perils of quoting selectively from complex legal judgments'; also Nobles and Schiff, 'A Story of Miscarriage', on media reporting of miscarriages of justice.

33. Meyer, 'Aesthetics of Persuasion', 748; cf. Engelke, *A Problem of Presence*.

34. Keane, *Christian Moderns*, 77.

35. Ibid., 186.

36. Ibid., 7.

37. Duffy, *The Stripping of the Altars*, xiv.

38. See Mahmood, *Politics of Piety*; Hirschkind, *The Ethical Soundscape*; Janson, *Islam, Youth and Modernity*.

39. Keane, 'Sincerity, "Modernity" and the Protestants', 68.

40. Liberatore, *Somali, Muslim, British*, 205.

41. Ibid., 204.

42. Ibid., 207.

43. Keane, *Christian Moderns*, 211.

Chapter 3. Broken Cisterns

1. Sherwood, *Biblical Blaspheming*, 303.

2. Much of the material in this chapter was previously published in *Ethnos: Journal of Anthropology*. See McIvor, 'Human Rights and Broken Cisterns: Counterpublic Christianity and Rights-based Discourse in Contemporary England'. With thanks to *Ethnos* and the Taylor & Francis Group.

3. For an account of this phrase from the perspective of the British Humanist Association, see Engelke, 'Christianity and the Anthropology of Secular Humanism'.

4. Article 9's interiorised definition of religion, which guarantees freedom of belief but offers only qualified protection to its manifestation, makes proving a violation particularly difficult. In at least one case, an alternative legal strategy was actually pointed out by the presiding judge. See Justice Lang at paragraphs [67] and [80] of *Core Issues v Transport for London*.

5. Hauerwas, 'On the "Right" to Be Tribal', 238.

6. In discussing their claims to counterpublic status, it is worth remembering that my interlocutors distinguish themselves not only from non-Christians, but from liberal

Christians (many of whom they doubt are Christian at all). This is also true of those at Christ Church, who, despite identifying as members of the established Church of England, often feel marginalised within it.

7. David Little, *Essays on Religion and Human Rights*, 8.

8. Wolterstorff, 'Christianity and Social Justice', 221. See also Wolterstorff, *Justice: Rights and Wrongs*.

9. Asad, 'What Do Human Rights Do?'

10. By contrast to the foundation myth, the understanding of human dignity upon which these conservatives built was disturbingly compatible with ongoing anti-Semitism. See Moyn, *Christian Human Rights*, 77; Marco Duranti, 'The Holocaust, the Legacy of 1789 and the Birth of International Human Rights Law', 170.

11. Duranti, *The Conservative Human Rights Revolution*, 301.

12. Greenberg, 'Against Conservative Internationalism', 184.

13. See Ronan McCrea, *Religion and the Public Order of the European Union*, 53–56, for an overview of EU Treaty drafters' debates on whether or not to incorporate a reference to the Christian God into the Treaty; Johannes Morsink, *The Universal Declaration of Human Rights*, 81–90, for a similar account in relation to the UDHR.

14. The UK government has since solidified its opposition to the ex-gay movement, announcing in July 2018 that it would ban all forms of what it terms 'conversion therapy'.

15. This is neither typical nor atypical of a Christian Concern event. At this particular church, many attendees were older and white (although some younger Coptic Christians were also present). However, Christian Concern speakers are also invited to church youth groups, black-majority churches, Asian-majority churches, etc. In terms of its denominational, age, class, and ethnic make-up, their support base is extremely broad.

16. Asad, *Formations*, 158.

17. The coins suggested a link to the alleged profiteering of what Abort67 calls 'the abortion industry' (although BPAS is a not-for-profit registered charity).

18. Journalist Sarah Ditum, who spoke for the pro-choice side, wrote in a report for the *Guardian* that 'There was some regret from both sides that Minichiello Williams's opening remarks were largely a condemnation of abortion itself, as well as discomfort that she chose to show a film made by Abort 67, including explicit and gory images of terminations.' See Ditum, 'Can Anti-Abortion and Pro-Choice Campaigners Agree About Anything?'

19. Unfortunately, I was unable to meet Mr and Mrs Johns, who had returned to Jamaica by the time I began my fieldwork.

20. *Johns* at [6–7].

21. Ibid at [26–8].

22. Carl Stychin, 'Closet Cases', 34; Donald et al., *Equality and Human Rights Commission*, 82–83. For an account arguing that the current equality framework privileges religious rights over sexual orientation, see Rob Clucas, 'Religion, Sexual Orientation and the Equality Act 2010'.

23. Emphasis in original.

24. *Johns* at [32–106].

25. Rozenberg, 'Fostering Discrimination'.

26. Christians in Parliament, 44–45.

27. Wilson, 'Homosexuality, Christianity and Child Welfare'.

28. *Johns* at [93].

29. A.M. Williams, 'Permanent Exclusion and the Johns'.

30. Felski, *Beyond Feminist Aesthetics*, 167.

31. Warner, *Publics and Counterpublics*, 67. Emphasis in original.

32. Ibid., 115.

33. Hirschkind, *The Ethical Soundscape*.

34. *Johns* at [33].

35. Honneth, 'Integrity and Disrespect', 191.

36. Asad, *Formations*, 67.

37. Keane, 'The Evidence of the Senses', 116.

38. Although, as Julian Rivers reminds us, some Christians will reject a 'choice-model' understanding of their faith as much as they might reject 'an essentialising view of sexuality'. See Rivers, 'The Secularisation of the British Constitution', 390.

39. Warner, *Publics and Counterpublics*, 121.

40. Felski, *Beyond Feminist Aesthetics*, 168; Nancy Fraser, 'Politics, Culture, and the Public Sphere', 293.

41. Niezen, *Public Justice*, 47.

42. Andy had been arrested under s. 5 of the Public Order Act in June 2011 after refusing to remove a particularly graphic banner from an Abort67 demonstration. He was also charged, along with colleague Kathryn Sloane, with obstructing a police officer under s. 19 of the Police and Criminal Evidence Act 1984. A CBR newsletter later referred to Andy and Kathryn as having 'forced' the arrest in an effort 'to set up a test case in which to establish the right to expose the horror of abortion'. See Center for Bio-Ethical Reform, 'CBR-UK Court Victory in England!'

43. Abort67 is not affiliated to any church. Andy, however, is an evangelical Christian. Andy's church, Jubilee Community Church, Worthing, has been the target of counterprotests by an opposing group, Brighton Pro-Choice.

44. Sheldon, *Beyond Control*, 2.

45. See Rosie Kinchen, 'We Will Shock You'; Ben Quinn, 'Anti-abortion Groups Raise Stakes by Deploying US Tactics on UK Streets'.

46. A remark which the judgment records as being 'uncalled for'.

47. This is a status they also hold for American activists and politicians. See Tom Minnery, *Why You Can't Stay Silent*, 112–116; Charles Colson, *God and Government*, 106–121.

48. Kelly, 'The Cause of Human Rights', 728.

49. Riles, 'Anthropology, Human Rights and Legal Knowledge', 55.

50. Ibid., 55–61.

51. Fernando, 'Intimacy Surveilled'; cf. José Casanova, 'Secularisation Revisited', 27.

52. Asad, *Formations*, 138.

53. See Elizabeth Shakman Hurd's *Beyond Religious Freedom* for an account of this phenomenon in international relations.

54. Casanova, 'Secularisation Revisited', 28.

55. Wenger, *Religious Freedom*.

56. Ibid., 112.

57. Su, *Exporting Freedom*. I discuss both Su and Wenger's work in more detail in a review article, 'Religious Freedom and the Politics of Empire'.

58. Casanova, *Public Religions*, 234.

59. Wolterstorff, *Justice*, 388.

60. Louis Pojman, 'A Critique of Contemporary Egalitarianism', 496.

61. Christian Concern, 'Andrea Williams, CCFON, Giving her State of the Nation Address at St Aldate's Church'.

62. Stychin, 'Closet Cases', 34.

63. Warner, *Publics and Counterpublics*, 63.

64. Merry, 'Legal Transplants and Cultural Translation', 267.

65. Audre Lorde, *Sister Outsider*; Michael Warner, *The Trouble with Normal*.

Chapter 4. Getting Rights 'Right'

1. Much of the material in this chapter was previously published in the *Journal of the American Academy of Religion*. See McIvor, 'Rights and Relationships: Rhetorics of Religious Freedom among English Evangelicals'. With thanks to the JAAR and Oxford University Press.

2. As an anthropologist researching Christianity and human rights law, I was, no doubt, more likely than the average visitor to hear discussions of religious rights. I certainly initiated many conversations on the subject. However, the fact that a number of sermons dealt with these questions leads me to believe that the interest in getting rights 'right' was not imposed by me.

3. Wolterstorff, *Justice*, 3.

4. Troeltsch, *The Christian Faith*, 184.

5. Dumont, 'A Modified View of Our Origins', 94–95; cf. Mauss, 'A Category of the Human Mind'; Shanahan, *Towards a Genealogy of Individualism*.

6. Sharma, *Are Human Rights Western?*, 185; cf. Freeman, 'The Problem of Secularism'.

7. Webster, 'Praying for Salvation: A Map of Relatedness', 20.

8. Weiner, 'Corporately Produced Conscience', 35.

9. Asad, *Formations*, 16.

10. In addition to Weiner's article, see Engel, 'The Spirits Were Always Watching'; Nadia Fadil, 'not-/unveiling as an ethical practice'; Fernando, 'Intimacy Surveilled'; Anna Strhan, *Aliens and Strangers*?

11. Although my interlocutors usually referred to 'friendship evangelism' rather than 'relational evangelism', they often evaluated their actions in terms of whether or not they were 'relational'. This term is also used by Rob Warner in his study of post-1960s English evangelicalism to describe guest services, wedding preparation courses, and other forms of church outreach. See R. Warner, *Reinventing English Evangelicalism, 1966–2001*.

12. Ibid., 299.

13. Bielo, *Words upon the Word*, 8–11.

14. Groups that meet on Monday mornings are made up of mothers with young children, the retired, or those working part-time outside the home. As far as I am aware, I did not meet any stay-at-home fathers at Christ Church, but equivalent men's groups meet for Bible studies at 6.30 a.m. on weekday mornings. Women in full-time employment outside the home tend to meet in mixed-gender house groups on weekday evenings.

15. Smith, *American Evangelicalism*, 187.

16. Bielo, *Words upon the Word*, 116.

17. Elisha, *Moral Ambition*, 6.

18. Christ Church is a wealthy congregation. The association of conservative evangelicalism with the upper and middle classes is not a recent phenomenon; as early as the 1851 census, evangelical Christianity proved more popular among the wealthy than the working class (see Bebbington, *Evangelicalism*, 110). The staff team sometimes worried that a 'Christ Church type' had developed, and that the proliferation of this type—elite education, steady job—had led to a church culture that excluded those from less privileged backgrounds. This was something they hoped to change.

19. Strhan, *Aliens and Strangers?*, 54; 95–99.

20. Robbins, *Becoming Sinners*, 292–294.

21. For useful summaries of this debate, see Vilaça, 'Dividuality in Amazonia'; Bialecki and Daswani, 'What is an Individual?'

22. Mosko, 'Partible Penitents', 217; 'Unbecoming Individuals'.

23. Daswani, '(In-)Dividual Pentecostals in Ghana'.

24. Chua, 'Conversion, Continuity, and Moral Dilemmas'.

25. Cannell, '"Forever Families"'.

26. Mosko, 'Partible Penitents', 219.

27. Bebbington, *Evangelicalism in Modern Britain*, 261.

28. Although they took this to be self-evident, it should be noted that this interpretation is contested (including by many within the Church of England, of which Christ Church is a part).

29. By contrast to some branches of Anglicanism, Christ Churchites view 'the Lord's Supper' as purely symbolic.

30. It should be noted that these 'rights' reflect middle-class pastimes and leisure activities outside the reach of many Britons.

31. From the Council's perspective, this accommodation had been a temporary concession, not a binding agreement. The tribunal found for the Council.

32. See Legge and Withnall, 'Christian Woman Celestina Mba Loses Legal Challenge Over Right Not to Work on Sundays'; Owen Bowcott, 'Christian Care Worker Who Did Not Want to Work on Sundays Loses Legal Fight'.

33. Robbins, *Becoming Sinners*, 221.

34. See *Hall & Preddy v Bull & Bull*.

35. This case was handled by the Christian Institute, a similar organisation based in Newcastle.

36. See *Ladele v London Borough of Islington*.

37. Niezen, *Public Justice and the Anthropology of Law*.

38. Joseph Webster has also noted the use of the language of resignation among his Scottish interlocutors, who appear resigned to the 'national decline into godlessness'. See 'Praying for Salvation', 30.

39. Hill, Sandberg, and Doe, *Religion and Law*, 25.

40. Strhan's *Aliens and Strangers?* offers a detailed account of this trope, which is as prevalent at Christ Church as it was at Strhan's field site, St John's. The association of the non-Christian world with greed and selfishness is not limited to urban, English, or twenty-first-century Christians. Greenhouse's work among suburban Georgian Baptists also notes a presumed association between litigiousness, selfishness, and non-Christians. See Greenhouse, *Praying for Justice*. Nor is this association necessarily Christian. David Engel has noted a tendency among Thai Buddhists in Lanna for the customary law of injuries, which had previously been governed by reference to local spirits, to give way to a Buddhist conception of legal compensation as 'counterproductive, materialistic, and selfish'. See Engel, 'The Spirits Were Always Watching', 255.

41. Dumont on Troeltsch, 'A Modified View', 96.

42. Daswani, '(In-)Dividual Pentecostals', 275

43. Robbins, *Becoming Sinners*, 291.

Chapter 5. Communicative Doubt

1. Whether or not a guest at a UK wedding could really have been unaware of what was meant by Isabel's 'loving Jesus', that this story was recounted in this way indicates the depth of 'Biblical illiteracy' my interlocutors expect from non-Christians.

2. Tomlinson and Engelke, 'Meaning, Anthropology, Christianity', 6.

3. Pelkmans, 'Outline for an Ethnography of Doubt', 11.

4. Both the normative ideal of the public sphere as a site for reasoned discourse and its contemporary manifestations tend to be founded upon the exclusion of many voices, including women, the poor, and sexual, ethnic, racial, and religious minorities (see contributions to Calhoun, ed., *Habermas and the Public Sphere*).

5. Asad, 'Free Speech, Blasphemy and Secular Criticism', 57.

6. 'Secular' is, of course, a contested term. I use it here in an admittedly simplistic sense to indicate arguments that do not appeal to divine law.

7. Although it is primarily in relation to American Christians that one hears of conflicts between secular education and Christianity (a recent example is the 2014 evangelistic film *God's Not Dead*), this narrative is gaining traction among evangelicals in the UK. That being said, many of the university-educated Christians I met credited their student days with maturing a childhood faith.

8. Greenhouse, *Praying for Justice*, 81.

9. Engelke, *God's Agents*, xxii.

10. Habermas, *Structural Transformation of the Public Sphere*, 27–36.

11. Ibid., 179.

12. Calhoun, 'Introduction', 16.

13. This is not to say that these positions are necessarily incompatible. As Bebbington notes, Enlightenment-era English evangelicals associated Christianity with the rational and reasonable. Evangelical epistemology was 'permeated by Enlightenment influences', particularly in relation to the knowledge of God that could be gained through reason, logic, and the evidence of the senses. See *Evangelicalism in Modern Britain*, 57.

14. Taylor, *A Secular Age*, 589.

15. Cannell, 'Imaginary Friends'.

16. See Rees, 'Yes to Women Bishops—Yes to Women?'; Adam, 'Women Bishops and the Recognition of Others'.

17. Quoted in Wintour and Davies, 'David Cameron: Church of England Should "Get on with It" on Female Bishops'.

18. The petition read: 'I support the legal definition of marriage which is the voluntary union for life of one man and one woman to the exclusion of all others. I oppose any attempt to redefine it.'

19. Hatcher, *Religious and Political Identities*, 2.

20. Although the C4M marketed itself as 'an umbrella group of individuals and organisations in the UK . . . of all faiths and none', it was overwhelmingly evangelical in its leadership. Then Directors included Colin Hart of the Christian Institute, Don Horrocks of the Evangelical Alliance, Andrea Williams of Christian Concern, and Nola Leach of Christian Action Research & Education.

21. Kettell, 'I Do, Thou Shalt Not: Religious Opposition to Same-Sex Marriage in Britain', 248–251.

22. Engelke, 'Strategic Secularism'.

23. The Blackstone Legal Fellowship, on which Christian Concern's Wilberforce Academy is loosely based, is a nine-week training and internship programme for Christian law students. It is a ministry of the US-based Alliance Defending Freedom.

24. Anglican Mainstream, 'Who We Are'.

25. Complementarianism teaches that although men and women have equal value, they have different roles in church and family life.

26. Keane, *Christian Moderns*, 202.

27. Asad, 'Free Speech', 40.

28. Ibid., 45.

29. Derks, 'Conscientious Objection and the Marrying Kind', 216.

30. Engelke, *God's Agents*, xxii.

31. Luhrmann, 'A Hyperreal God'.

32. Packer, *'Fundamentalism' and the Word of God*, 130.

33. Keane, *Christian Moderns*, 15.

34. Taylor, 'Why We Need a Radical Redefinition of Secularism', 49.

35. Quoted in Bebbington, *Evangelicalism in Modern Britain*, 63.

36. A reviewer noted that the requirement for mass conversion sits uneasily with the place Wilberforce's anti-slavery campaign occupies for many Christian activists (in that the abolition of slavery was not preceded by national repentance). As noted in chapter 1, Christian Concern staff have differing views on the likely state of the world at the time of Christ's return (that is, whether things will have gotten 'better' or 'worse'), leading to an urgent theology in which activism is pursued regardless of outcome. It is in light of this theology that Maria's comments should be understood.

37. Steven Kettell's 'Collective Action Framing' argues that conservative Christians who use secular language to make religious points do not experience this as either inauthentic or paradoxical. However, as I hope to have shown in relation to Adam and Maria, the situation is not quite so clear-cut: an evangelical might hold that 'secular', scientific arguments validate their claims, but can also find these explanations less convincing than a transcendental narrative. They can also experience guilt at having failed to explain the issue from a biblical perspective.

38. In addition to disputes over CU membership at Exeter, Birmingham, and Heriot-Watt, the University of Edinburgh's CU was accused of discriminating against LGBTQ+ students when it sought to run 'Pure', a Christian course on sexuality.

39. Guest et al., 'Challenging "Belief" and the Evangelical Bias', 209.

40. Ibid., 218.

41. From the perspective of those who sought to convince the CU to change its membership policy, the issue was not one of discriminating against non-Christians but of discriminating against *non-evangelical* Christians, including Orthodox, Catholic, Mormon, and 'mainline' Protestant Christians.

42. The case was initially run from the Lawyers' Christian Fellowship (the body out of which the CLC eventually grew) but was managed by Andrea from the beginning.

43. Rebecca Lester, *Jesus in Our Wombs*, 227.

44. The journalist, Patrick Strudwick, had posed as a Christian seeking to move away from 'same-sex attraction'. See Strudwick, 'The Ex-Gay Files'.

45. Greenhouse, *Praying for Justice*, 116.

46. Ibid., 134.

47. Strhan's work provides an evocative account of the experience of incoherence among conservative evangelicals in London.

48. Povinelli, *Economics of Abandonment*; Povinelli, 'The Will to Be Otherwise'.

49. Pelkmans, 'Outline for an Ethnography of Doubt', 15.

50. Cannell, 'Concepts of Parenthood', 668.

51. Supernatural intervention often involves a touch of the dramatic, regardless of context. However, I would argue that this is especially so among middle-class Londoners, where public references to this sort of experience risk one being labelled, in Tony Blair's words, 'a nutter'. See BBC News, 'Blair Feared Faith "Nutter" Label'.

52. Robbins, 'Continuity Thinking'.

53. Pelkmans, 'Outline for an Ethnography of Doubt', 15.

54. Ibid., 20.

55. Engelke, 'Clarity and Charisma', 78. See also contributions to Engelke and Tomlinson, *The Limits of Meaning*.

56. Christian, *Visionaries*, 393.

57. Moustafa, *Constituting Religion*, 63.

58. Plant, 'Religion in a Liberal State', 11. See also Beaman, *Deep Equality in an Era of Religious Diversity*.

Conclusion. Good Things Worth Sharing

1. As head of the Church of England, it is not particularly surprising that the Queen would mention Jesus in her Christmas speech. However, many members of Christ Church feel that her Christmas messages have become increasingly evangelistic in recent years. This is a trend they strongly endorse.

2. Amesbury, 'Secularity, Religion, and the Spatialisation of Time', 592.

3. See Brown and Woodhead, *That Was the Church That Was*. While their analysis relates to the Church of England, I would argue that this association extends well beyond the established church.

4. Engelke, *God's Agents*, xix.

5. Lambek, 'Value and Virtue', 137.

6. Harding, *The Book of Jerry Falwell*; Engelke, *God's Agents*; McAlister, *The Kingdom of God Has No Borders*; Bornstein, *The Spirit of Development*.

7. Cannell, *The Anthropology of Christianity*, 1.

8. Coleman, *The Globalisation of Charismatic Christianity*; Knibbe, *Faith in the Familiar*; Strhan, *Aliens and Strangers?*

9. Strhan, *Aliens and Strangers?*, 164.

10. Harding, 'The Transevangelical Zone', 15.

11. Hansen, *Cool Passion*, 5.

12. Ibid., 14–16.

13. Ibid., 26.

14. Brown, *The Death of Christian Britain*, 198.

15. Ibid., 229.

16. Bruce, *Politics and Religion*, 138.

17. Griffith, *God's Daughters*, 31.

18. Weiner, 'Corporately Produced Conscience'; see also contributions to Sullivan, Hurd, Mahmood, and Danchin, *Politics of Religious Freedom*.

19. See Walton, Hatcher, and Spencer, *Is There a 'Religious Right'?*

20. Contributions to the Luce Foundation-funded project 'Politics of Religion at Home and Abroad', organised by Elizabeth Shakman Hurd and Winnifred Fallers Sullivan, argue this point in the context of American exceptionalism. See Sullivan and Hurd, 'Theologies of American Exceptionalism'.

21. Elayne Oliphant, 'The Crucifix as a Symbol of Secular Europe'. For an interesting Canadian example, see Mo, 'A Christmas Crisis'.

22. See Poirier, 'We Watched Notre Dame Burn'.

23. Thomas Bingham, 'The European Convention on Human Rights', 400.

24. Moss, *Ancient Christian Martyrdom*, 163.

Adam, W. 2014. 'Women Bishops and the Recognition of Orders'. *Ecclesiastical Law Journal* 16, no. 2: 187–204.

Alliance Defending Freedom. Not dated. 'Our First Freedom'. http://adflegal.org/issues /religious-freedom.

Amesbury, R. 2016. 'Is the Body Secular? Circumcision, Religious Freedom and Bodily Integrity'. *Journal of the British Association for the Study of Religion* 18: 1–10.

———. 2018. 'Secularity, Religion, and the Spatialisation of Time'. *Journal of the American Academy of Religion* 86, no. 3: 591–615.

Anglican Mainstream. Not dated. 'Anglican Mainstream: Who We Are'. http://anglicanmain stream.org/anglican-mainstream-who-we-are/.

Årsheim, H., and P. Slotte. 2017. *The Juridification of Religion?* Leiden: Brill.

Asad, T. 1993. *Genealogies of Religion: Discipline and Reasons of Power in Christianity and Islam.* Baltimore: The Johns Hopkins University Press.

———. 2000. 'What Do Human Rights Do? An Anthropological Enquiry'. *Theory and Event* 4, no. 4. https://muse.jhu.edu/journals/theory_and_event/v004/4.4asad.html.

———. 2003. *Formations of the Secular: Christianity, Islam, Modernity.* Stanford: University Press.

———. 2009. 'Free Speech, Blasphemy and Secular Criticism'. In *Is Critique Secular? Blasphemy, Injury and Free Speech.* Edited by T. Asad, W. Brown, J. Butler, and S. Mahmood, 20–64. Berkeley: University of California Press.

Bartley, J. 2006. *Faith and Politics After Christendom: The Church as a movement for Anarchy.* Milton Keynes: Paternoster Press.

BBC News. 2007. 'Blair Feared Faith "Nutter" Label'. *BBC News,* 25 November. http://news .bbc.co.uk/1/hi/uk_politics/7111620.stm.

BBC News. 2011. 'David Cameron Says the UK Is a Christian Country'. *BBC News,* 16 December. https://www.bbc.com/news/uk-politics-16224394.

BBC News. 2013. 'Cross Case Nurse Shirley Chaplin Plans to Appeal Ruling'. *BBC News,* 15 January. https://www.bbc.com/news/uk-england-devon-21028691.

Beaman, L. G. 2017. *Deep Equality in an Era of Religious Diversity.* Oxford: Oxford University Press.

Bebbington, D. 1989. *Evangelicalism in Modern Britain: A History from the 1730s to the 1980s.* London: Unwin Hyman Ltd.

Bennett, D. 2017. *Defending Faith: The Politics of the Christian Conservative Legal Movement.* Lawrence: University Press of Kansas.

Berlin, I. 1966. *Two Concepts of Liberty.* Oxford: Oxford University Press.

Bialecki, J., and G. Daswani. 2015. 'What Is an Individual? The View from Christianity'. *HAU: Journal of Ethnographic Theory* 5: 1, 271–294.

Bielo, J. S. 2009. *Words upon the Word: An Ethnography of Evangelical Group Bible Study.* New York: New York University Press.

Bingham, T. H. 1993. 'The European Convention on Human Rights: Time to Incorporate'. *Law Quarterly Review* 109, no. 3: 390–400.

Bornstein, E. 2006. 'Rituals without Final Acts: Prayer and Success in World Vision Zimbabwe's Humanitarian Work'. In *The Limits of Meaning: Case Studies in the Anthropology of Christianity.* Edited by M. Engelke and M. Tomlinson, 85–104. New York: Berghahn Books.

——. 2005. *The Spirit of Development: Protestant NGOs, Morality and Economics in Zimbabwe*. Stanford: Stanford University Press.

Bowcott, O. 2013. 'Christian Care Worker Who Did Not Want to Work on Sundays Loses Legal Fight'. *The Guardian*, 5 December. http://www.theguardian.com/law/2013/dec /05/christian-care-worker-sundays-legal-fight.

Braunstein, R. 2017. *Prophets and Patriots: Faith in Democracy Across the Political Divide*. Berkeley: University of California Press.

British Humanist Association. 2012. Andrew Copson as panellist on *Sunday Morning Live*. YouTube, 28 September. https://www.youtube.com/watch?v=FhGgGUG1AVk.

Brown, A. 2011. 'Evangelicals Reverse the Ferret'. *The Guardian*, 2 March. https://www .theguardian.com/commentisfree/andrewbrown/2011/mar/02/evangelical-alliance-gay -derby-adoption.

Brown, A., and L. Woodhead. 2016. *That Was the Church That Was: How the Church of England Lost the English People*. London: Bloomsbury.

Brown, C. 2009. *The Death of Christian Britain: Understanding Secularisation 1800–2000*. London: Routledge.

Bruce, S. 2012. *Politics and Religion in the United Kingdom*. London: Routledge.

Bychawski, A. 2018. 'UK Christian "Reactionaries" Mark 10 Years of Lobbying Against Women's and LGBT Rights'. *Open Democracy*, 25 October. https://www.opendemocracy .net/en/5050/christian-concern-reactionaries-10-years-lobbying-women-and-lgbt -rights/.

Calhoun, C. 1992. 'Introduction: Habermas and the Public Sphere'. In *Habermas and the Public Sphere*. Edited by C. Calhoun, 1–48. Cambridge: MIT Press.

Calvin, J. 1845 [1536]. *Institutes of the Christian Religion*. Vol. 1. Translated by H. Beveridge. Edinburgh: T&T Clark.

Cannell, F. 2006. *The Anthropology of Christianity*. Durham, NC: Duke University Press.

Cannell, F. 1990. 'Concepts of Parenthood: The Warnock Report, the Gillick Debate, and Modern Myths'. *American Ethnologist* 17, no. 4: 667–689.

——. 2005. 'The Christianity of Anthropology'. *Journal of the Royal Anthropological Institute* 11, no. 2: 335–356.

——. 2006. Introduction. In *The Anthropology of Christianity*. Edited by F. Cannell. Durham, NC: Duke University Press.

——. 2013. 'The Re-enchantment of Kinship'. In *Vital Relations: Modernity and Persistent Life of Kinship*. Edited by S. McKinnon and F. Cannell, 217–240. Santa Fe: School for Advanced Research Press.

——. 2014. 'Imaginary Friends'. *Anthropology of This Century*, no. 11. http://aotcpress.com /articles/imaginary-friends/.

——. 2017. '"Forever Families": Christian Individualism, Mormonism, and Collective Salvation'. In *New Directions in Spiritual Kinship: Sacred Ties Across the Abrahamic Religions*. Edited by T. Thomas, A. Malik, and R. Wellman, 151–170. Cham: Palgrave Macmillan.

Casanova, J. 1994. *Public Religions in the Modern World*. Chicago: University of Chicago Press.

——. 2006. 'Secularisation Revisited: A Reply to Talal Asad'. In *Powers of the Secular Modern: Talal Asad and His Interlocutors*. Edited by D. Scott and C. Hirschkind, 12–30. Stanford: Stanford University Press.

Center for Bio-Ethical Reform. 2012. 'CBR-UK Court Victory in England!' *CBR Communique*. http://www.abortionno.org/wp-content/uploads/2012/11/N1209Web.pdf.

Christian, W. 1996. *Visionaries: The Spanish Republic and the Reign of Christ*. Berkeley: University of California Press.

Christian Concern. 2009. 'Andrea Williams, CCFON, Giving Her State of the Nation Address at St Aldate's Church, Oxford'. Christian Concern Media, 20 February. http://www .christianconcern.com/media/andrea-williams-ccfon-giving-her-state-nation-address -st-aldates-church-oxford-starts-soundtra?page=98.

———. 2012. 'Andrea Williams at BPAS 2012 Debate'. YouTube, 14 September. https://www .youtube.com/watch?v=g1nmUoRg4N8&feature=youtu.be.

———. 2013. 'Andrea Williams' Christmas Message'. YouTube, 20 December. http://www .youtube.com/watch?v=COq3Qrv3UKM.

———. Not dated. 'About Us'. Christian Concern. http://www.christianconcern.com/about.

Christians in Parliament. 2012. 'Clearing the Ground Inquiry: Preliminary Report into the Freedom of Christians in the UK'. http://www.eauk.org/current-affairs/publications /upload/Clearing-the-ground.pdf.

Chua, L. 2012. 'Conversion, Continuity, and Moral Dilemmas among Christian Bidayuhs in Malaysian Borneo'. *American Ethnologist* 39, no. 3: 511–526.

Church of England. 2012. Reports of Proceedings: July 2012 Group of Sessions Audio Files. Church of England. https://www.churchofengland.org/media/1497781/jul1212.mp3.

Church Society. 1994. *An English Prayer Book*. Oxford: Oxford University Press.

Clements, B. 2015. *Religion and Public Opinion in Britain: Continuity and Change*. Basingstoke: Palgrave Macmillan.

Clucas, R. 2012. 'Religion, Sexual Orientation and the Equality Act 2010: Gay Bishops in the Church of England Negotiating Rights Against Discrimination'. *Sociology* 46, no. 5: 936–950.

Clucas, R., and K. Sharpe. 2013. 'Women Bishops: Equality, Rights and Disarray'. *Ecclesiastical Law Journal* 15, no. 2: 158–174.

Coffey, J. 2007. 'Evangelicals, Slavery and the Slave Trade: From Whitefield to Wilberforce'. *Anvil* 24, 97–119.

Coleman, S. 2000. *The Globalisation of Charismatic Christianity*. Cambridge: Cambridge University Press.

———. 2011. '"Right Now!": Historio-Praxy and the Embodiment of Charismatic Temporalities'. *Ethnos* 76, no. 4: 426–447.

———. 2014. 'Pilgrimage as a Trope for an Anthropology of Christianity'. *Current Anthropology* 55, supp. 10: S281–S291.

Colson, C. 2007. *God and Government: An Insider's View on the Boundaries between Faith and Politics*. Grand Rapids, MI: Zondervan.

Comaroff, J. L. 2009. 'Reflections on the Rise of Legal Theology: Law and Religion in the Twenty-First Century'. *Social Analysis* 53, no. 1: 193–216.

Conley, J. M., and W. M. O'Barr. 1993. 'Legal Anthropology Comes Home: A Brief History of the Ethnographic Study of Law'. *Loyola Law Review* 27, 41–64.

Crapanzano, V. 2000. *Serving the Word: Literalism in America from the Pulpit to the Bench*. New York: New Press.

Das, V. 2012. 'Ordinary Ethics'. In *A Companion to Moral Anthropology*. Edited by D. Fassin, 133–149. Malden, MA: John Wiley & Sons.

Daswani, G. 2010. 'Transformation and Migration Among Members of a Pentecostal Church in Ghana and London'. *Journal of Religion in Africa* 40, 442–474.

———. 2011. '(In-)dividual Pentecostals in Ghana'. *Journal of Religion in Africa* 41, no. 3: 256–279.

Dawkins, R. 2007. *The God Delusion*. London: Transworld Publishers.

Derks, M. 2017. 'Conscientious Objectors and the Marrying Kind: Rights and Rites in Dutch Public Discourse on Marriage Registrars with Conscientious Objections Against Conducting Same-Sex Weddings'. *Theology and Sexuality* 23, no. 3: 209–228.

Ditum, S. 2012. 'Can Anti-Abortion and Pro-Choice Campaigners Agree on Anything?' *The Guardian*, 14 September. http://www.theguardian.com/commentisfree/2012/sep/14/can-anti-abortion-pro-choice-campaigners-agree.

Doe, N. 1996. *The Legal Framework of the Church of England: A Critical Study in a Comparative Context*. Oxford: Clarendon Press.

Donald, A., K. Bennett, and P. Leach. 2012. 'Equality and Human Rights Commission Research Report 84: Religion or Belief, Equality and Human Rights in England and Wales'. Equality and Human Rights Commission Research Report Series. http://www.equalityhumanrights.com/sites/default/files/documents/research/rr84_final_opt.pdf.

Doward, J., and S. Wheeler. 2011. 'Christian Legal Centre Fights More than 50 Religious Discrimination Cases'. *The Guardian*, 1 May. http://www.theguardian.com/world/2011/may/01/christianity-rights-colin-atkinson.

Duffy, E. 2005. *The Stripping of the Altars: Traditional Religion in England 1400–1580*. New Haven: Yale University Press.

Dumont, L. 1980. *Homo Hierarchicus: The Caste System and Its Implications*. Translated by M. Sainsbury, L. Dumont, and B. Gulati. Chicago: University of Chicago Press.

———. 1996. 'A Modified View of Our Origins: The Christian Beginnings of Modern Individualism'. In *The Category of the Person: Anthropology, Philosophy, History*. Edited by M. Carrithers, S. Collins, and S. Lukes, 93–122. Cambridge: Cambridge University Press.

Duranti, M. 2012. 'The Holocaust, the Legacy of 1789 and the Birth of International Human Rights Law: Revisiting the Foundation Myth'. *Journal of Genocide Research* 14, no. 2: 159–186.

———. 2017. *The Conservative Human Rights Revolution: European Identity, Transnational Politics, and the Origins of the European Convention*. Oxford: Oxford University Press.

Durkheim, E. 2008 [1912]. *The Elementary Forms of Religious Life*. Translated by C. Cosman. Oxford: Oxford University Press.

Edwards, Michael. 2018. 'Real Change: Translating Salvation in Myanmar'. Ph.D. thesis, The London School of Economics and Political Science. London, UK.

Elisha, O. 2008. 'Moral Ambitions of Grace: The Paradox of Compassion and Accountability in Evangelical Faith-Based Activism'. *Cultural Anthropology* 23, no. 1: 154–189.

———. 2011. *Moral Ambition: Mobilisation and Social Outreach in Evangelical Megachurches*. Berkeley: University of California Press.

Engel, D. M. 2011. '"The Spirits Were Always Watching": Buddhism, Secular Law, and Social Change in Thailand'. In *After Secular Law*. Edited by W. F. Sullivan, R. A. Yelle, M. Taussig-Rubbo, 242–260. Stanford: Stanford University Press.

Engelke, M. 2002. 'The Problem of Belief: Evans-Pritchard and Victor Turner on "the Inner Life"'. *Anthropology Today* 18, no. 6: 3–8.

———. 2006. 'Clarity and Charisma: "On the Uses of Ambiguity in Ritual Life"'. In *The Limits of Meaning: Case Studies in the Anthropology of Christianity*. Edited by M. Engelke and M. Tomlinson, 63–84. New York: Berghahn Books.

———. 2007. *A Problem of Presence: Beyond Scripture in an African Church*. Berkeley: University of California Press.

———. 2009. 'Strategic Secularism: Bible Advocacy in England'. *Social Analysis* 53, no. 1: 39–54.

———. 2010. 'Number and the Imagination of Global Christianity; or, Mediation and Immediacy in the Work of Alain Badiou'. *South Atlantic Quarterly* 109, no. 4: 811–829.

———. 2013. *God's Agents: Biblical Publicity in Contemporary England*. Berkeley: University of California Press.

———. 2014. 'Christianity and the Anthropology of Secular Humanism'. *Current Anthropology* 55, no. 10: 292–301.

Engelke, M., and M. Tomlinson, eds. 2006. *The Limits of Meaning: Case Studies in the Anthropology of Christianity*. New York: Berghahn Books.

Erzen, T. 2006. *Straight to Jesus: Sexual and Christian Conversions in the Ex-Gay Movement*. Berkeley: University of California Press.

Fadil, N. 2011. 'not-/unveiling as an ethical practice'. *Feminist Review* 98: 83–109.

Faith Survey. Not Dated. 'Christianity in the UK'. https://faithsurvey.co.uk/uk-christianity.html.

Felski, R. 1989. *Beyond Feminist Aesthetics: Feminist Literature and Social Change*. Cambridge: Harvard University Press.

Fernando, M. 2014. 'Intimacy Surveilled: Religion, Sex, and Secular Cunning'. *Signs: Journal of Women in Culture and Society* 39, no. 3: 685–708.

Fraser, N. 1995. 'Politics, Culture, and the Public Sphere: Toward a Postmodern Conception'. In *Social Postmodernism: Beyond Identity Politics*. Edited by L. Nicholson and S. Seidman, 287–312. Cambridge: Cambridge University Press.

Freeman, M. 2004. 'The Problem of Secularism in Human Rights Theory'. *Human Rights Quarterly* 26, no. 2: 375–400.

GAFCON. Not dated. 'About GAFCON'. https://www.gafcon.org/about.

Gerbner, K. 2018. *Christian Slavery: Conversion and Race in the Protestant Atlantic World*. Philadelphia: University of Pennsylvania Press.

Ginsburg, F. 1989. *Contested Lives: The Abortion Debate in an American Community*. Berkeley: University of California Press.

Gordon, S. B. 2002. *The Mormon Question: Polygamy and Constitutional Conflict in Nineteenth Century America*. Chapel Hill: The University of North Carolina Press.

Greenberg, U. 2017. 'Against Conservative Internationalism'. *Dissent* 64:181–186.

Greenhouse, C. 1989. *Praying for Justice: Faith, Order and Community in an American Town*. Ithaca, NY: Cornell University Press.

Griffith, R. M. 2000. *God's Daughters: Evangelical Women and the Power of Submission*. Berkeley: University of California Press.

Guest, M. 2017. 'The Emerging Church in Transatlantic Perspective'. *Journal for the Scientific Study of Religion* 56, no. 1: 41–51.

Guest, M., S. Sharma, K. Aune, and R. Warner. 2013. 'Challenging "Belief" and the Evangelical Bias: Student Christianity in English Universities'. *Journal of Contemporary Religion* 28, no. 2: 207–223.

Guyer, J. 2007. 'Prophecy and the Near Future: Thoughts on Macroeconomic, Evangelical and Punctuated Time'. *American Ethnologist* 34, no. 3: 409–421.

Habermas, J. 2002 [1962]. *The Structural Transformation of the Public Sphere: An Inquiry into a Category of Bourgeois Society*. Oxford: Blackwell.

Hansen, T. B. 2009. *Cool Passion: The Political Theology of Conviction*. Amsterdam: University of Amsterdam Press.

Harding, S. F. 1991. 'Representing Fundamentalism: The Problem of the Repugnant Other'. *Social Research* 58, no. 2: 373–393.

———. 2001. *The Book of Jerry Falwell: Fundamentalist Language and Politics*. Princeton: Princeton University Press.

———. 2010. 'The Transevangelical Zone'. *Anthropology Now* 2, no. 3: 10–18.

Hatcher, A. C. 2017. *Religious and Political Identities of British Evangelicals*. Cham: Palgrave Macmillan.

Hauerwas, S. 1987. 'On the "Right" to Be Tribal'. *Christian Scholars Review* 16, no. 3: 238–241.

Herriot, P. 2016. *Warfare and Waves: Calvinists and Charismatics in the Church of England*. Eugene, OR: Pickwick Publications.

Hill, M., R. Sandberg, and N. Doe. 2011. *Religion and Law in the United Kingdom*. Alphen aan den Rijn: Kluwer Law International.

Hill, S. 2015. 'UKIP's "Christian Manifesto" Will Be Repulsive to Many Christian Voters'. *Ekklesia*. http://www.ekklesia.co.uk/node/21650.

Hirschkind, C. 2006. *The Ethical Soundscape: Cassette Sermons and Islamic Counterpublics*. New York: Columbia University Press.

Honneth, A. 1992. 'Integrity and Disrespect: Principles of a Conception of Morality Based on the Theory of Recognition'. *Political Theory* 20, no. 2: 187–201.

Hurd, E. S. 2015. *Beyond Religious Freedom*. Princeton: Princeton University Press.

Janson, M. 2013. *Islam, Youth and Modernity in the Gambia: the Tablighi Jama'at*. Cambridge: Cambridge University Press.

Jenkins, T. 1999. *Religion in English Everyday Life: An Ethnographic Approach*. Oxford: Berghahn Books.

Keane, W. 2002. 'Sincerity, "Modernity" and the Protestants'. *Cultural Anthropology* 17, no. 1: 65–92.

———. 2007. *Christian Moderns: Freedom and Fetish in the Mission Encounter*. Berkeley: University of California Press.

———. 2008. 'The Evidence of the Senses and the Materiality of Religion'. *Journal of the Royal Anthropological Institute* (N.S.) 14, no. 1: 110–127.

Kelly, T. 2011. 'The Cause of Human Rights: Doubts about Torture, Law and Ethics at the United Nations'. *Journal of the Royal Anthropological Institute* 17, no. 4: 728–744.

Kettell, S. 2013. 'I Do, Thou Shalt Not: Religious Opposition to Same-Sex Marriage in Britain'. *The Political Quarterly* 84, no. 2: 247–255.

———. 2017. 'The Collective Action Framing of Conservative Christian Groups in Britain'. *Politics and Religion* 10, 286–310.

Kinchen, R. 2012. 'We Will Shock You'. *The Sunday Times Magazine*, 4 November. http://www.thesundaytimes.co.uk/sto/Magazine/Features/article1155984.ece.

Kiska, R. 2019. 'The Unknown Client'. Christian Concern. 18 October. https://christianconcern.com/news/the-unknown-client-blessed-are-those-who-act-justly/.

Knibbe, K. 2013. *Faith in the Familiar: Religion, Spirituality and Place in the South of the Netherlands*. Leiden: Brill.

Laidlaw, J. 2014. *The Subject of Virtue: An Anthropology of Ethics and Freedom*. Cambridge: Cambridge University Press.

Lambek, M. 2008. 'Value and Virtue'. *Anthropological Theory* 8, no. 2: 133–157.

———. 2010. Introduction. In *Ordinary Ethics: Anthropology, Language, and Action*. Edited by M. Lambek, 1–36. New York: Fordham University Press.

Legge, J., and A. Withnall. 2013. 'Christian Woman Celestina Mba Loses Legal Challenge over Right Not to Work on Sundays'. *The Independent*, 5 December. http://www.independent.co.uk/news/uk/home-news/christian-woman-celestina-mba-loses-legal-challenge-over-right-not-to-work-on-sundays-8985681.html.

Lester, R. 2005. *Jesus in Our Wombs: Embodying Modernity in a Mexican Convent*. Berkeley: University of California Press.

Lewis, A. R. 2017. *The Rights Turn in Conservative Christian Politics: How Abortion Transformed the Culture Wars*. Cambridge: Cambridge University Press.

Liberatore, G. 2017. *Somali, Muslim, British: Striving in a Securitised Britain*. London: Bloomsbury.

Little, David. 2015. *Essays on Religion and Human Rights: Ground to Stand On*. Cambridge: Cambridge University Press.

Llewellyn, K. N., and E. Adamson Hoebel. 1978. *The Cheyenne Way: Conflict and Case Law in Primitive Jurisprudence*. Norman: University of Oklahoma Press.

Lorde, Audre. 1984. *Sister Outsider: Essays and Speeches*. Berkeley: Crossing Press.

Luhrmann, T. M. 2012a. 'A Hyperreal God and Modern Belief: Toward an Anthropological Theory of Mind'. *Current Anthropology* 53, no. 4: 371–395.

———. 2012b. *When God Talks Back: Understanding the American Evangelical Relationship with God*. New York: Vintage Books.

MacLeay, A. 2012. *Teaching 1 Timothy: from Text to Message*. Ross-shire: Christian Focus Publications Ltd.

Mahadev, N. 2018. 'Economics of Conversion and Ontologies of Religious Difference: Buddhism, Christianity, and Adversarial Political Perception in Sri Lanka'. *Current Anthropology* 59, no. 6: 665–690.

Mahmood, S. 2005. *Politics of Piety: The Islamic Revival and the Feminist Subject*. Princeton: Princeton University Press.

———. 2009. 'Religious Reason and Secular Affect: An Incommensurable Divide?' In *Is Critique Secular? Blasphemy, Injury and Free Speech*. Edited by T. Asad, W. Brown, J. Butler. and S. Mahmood, 64–100. Berkeley: University of California Press.

———. 2015. *Religious Difference in a Secular Age: A Minority Report*. Princeton: Princeton University Press.

Malinowski, B. 1970 [1926]. *Crime and Custom in Savage Society*. London: Routledge & Kegan Paul.

Martin, D. 2005. *On Secularization: Towards a Revised General Theory*. Aldershot: Ashgate.

Mathews, D., and J. S. De Hart. 1990. *Sex, Gender and the Politics of ERA: A State and the Nation*. Oxford: Oxford University Press.

Mauss, M. 1996 [1938]. 'A Category of the Human Mind: The Notion of Person; The Notion of Self'. Translated by D. W. Hall. In *The Category of the Person: Anthropology, Philosophy, History*. Edited by M. Carrithers, S. Collins, and S. Lukes, 1–25. Cambridge: Cambridge University Press.

McAlister, M. 2018. *The Kingdom of God Has No Borders: A Global History of American Evangelicals*. Oxford: Oxford University Press.

McCrea, R. 2010. *Religion and the Public Order of the European Union*. Oxford: Oxford University Press.

McDannell, C. 1995. *Material Christianity: religion and popular culture in America*. New Haven: Yale University Press.

McIvor, M. 2015. 'Carnal Exhibitions: Material Religion and the European Court of Human Rights'. *Ecclesiastical Law Journal* 17, no. 1: 3–14.

———. 2018. 'Religious Freedom and the Politics of Empire'. *Religious Studies Review* 44, no. 1: 57–63.

———. 2019. 'Human Rights and Broken Cisterns: Counterpublic Christianity and Rights-Based Discourse in Contemporary England'. *Ethnos: Journal of Anthropology* 84, no. 2: 323–343.

———. 2019. 'Rights and Relationships: Rhetorics of Religious Freedom among English Evangelicals'. *Journal of the American Academy of Religion* 87, no. 3: 860–888.

McKinnon, S., and F. Cannell, *Vital Relations: Modernity and Persistent Life of Kinship*. Santa Fe, NM: School for Advanced Research Press.

Merry, S. E. 2009. 'Legal Transplants and Cultural Translation: Making Human Rights in the Vernacular'. In *Human Rights: An Anthropological Reader*. Edited by M. Goodale, 265–302. Chichester, UK: Wiley-Blackwell.

Meyer, B. 2010. 'Aesthetics of Persuasion: Global Christianity and Pentecostalism's Sensational Forms'. *South Atlantic Quarterly* 109, no. 4: 741–763.

Minnery, T. 2001. *Why You Can't Stay Silent: A Biblical Mandate to Shape Our Culture*. Wheaton: Tyndale House Publishers, Ltd.

Mo, Helen. 2019. 'A Christmas Crisis: Lessons from a Canadian Public School's Seasonal Skirmish'. In *The Public Work of Christmas: Difference and Belonging in Multicultural Societies*. Edited by P. E. Klassen and M. Scheer, 188–211. Montreal: McGill-Queen's University Press.

Montgomery, J. W. 2017. *Defending the Gospel in Legal Style: Essays on Legal Apologetics and the Justification of Classical Christian Faith*. Eugene, OR: Wipf and Stock Publishers.

Morris, R. M. 2009. 'Part One: Establishment in Great Britain Now'. In *Church and State in Twenty-First Century Britain: The Future of Church Establishment*. Edited by R. M. Morris, 15–109. London: Palgrave Macmillan.

Morrison, D. E. 2009. 'Cultural and Moral Authority: The Presumption of Television'. *The Annals of the American Academy of Political and Social Science* 625, 116–127.

Morrison, D. E., and M. Tracey. 1978. 'American Theory and British Practice: The Case of Mrs Mary Whitehouse and the National Viewers and Listeners Association'. In *Censorship and Obscenity*. Edited by R. Dhavan and C. Davies, 37–109. London: Martin Robertson.

Morsink, J. 1999. *The Universal Declaration of Human Rights: Origins, Drafting, and Intent*. Philadelphia: University Press.

Mosko, M. 2010. 'Partible Penitents: Dividual Personhood and Christian Practice in Melanesia and the West'. *Journal of the Royal Anthropological Institute* (N.S.) 26, 215–240.

———. 2015. 'Unbecoming Individuals: The Partible Character of the Christian Person'. *HAU: Journal of Ethnographic Theory* 5, no. 1: 361–393.

Moss, C. 2012. *Ancient Christian Martyrdom: Diverse Practices, Theologies, and Traditions*. New Haven: Yale University Press.

Moustafa, T. 2018. *Constituting Religion: Islam, Liberal Rights, and the Malaysian State*. Cambridge: Cambridge University Press.

Moyn, S. 2015. *Christian Human Rights*. Philadelphia: University of Pennsylvania Press.

Niezen, R. 2010. *Public Justice and the Anthropology of Law*. Cambridge: Cambridge University Press.

Nobles, R., and D. Schriff. 2004. 'A Story of Miscarriage: Law in the Media'. *Journal of Law and Society* 31, no. 2: 221–44.

Office for National Statistics. 2012. 'Religion in England and Wales, 2011'. Office for National Statistics. 11 December. https://www.ons.gov.uk/peoplepopulationandcommunity /culturalidentity/religion/articles/religioninenglandandwales2011/2012-12-11.

Oliphant, E. 2012. 'The Crucifix as a Symbol of Secular Europe: The Surprising Semiotics of the European Court of Human Rights'. *Anthropology Today* 28, no. 2: 10–12.

Orsi, R. A. 2010. *The Madonna of 115th Street: Faith And Community in Italian Harlem, 1880–1950*. New Haven: Yale University Press.

Packer, J. I. 1977. *'Fundamentalism' and the Word of God: Some Evangelical Principles*. Grand Rapids, MI: Eerdmans Printing Company.

Pelkmans, M. E. 2013. 'Outline for an Ethnography of Doubt'. In *Ethnographies of Doubt: Faith and Uncertainty in Contemporary Societies*. Edited by M. Pelkmans, 1–42. London: I.B. Tauris.

Peroni, L. 2014. 'Deconstructing "Legal" Religion in Strasbourg'. *Oxford Journal of Law and Religion* 3, no. 2: 235–257.

Petre, J. and N. Constable. 2010. 'Nurse in Crucifix Row Reveals the Uplifting Story of the Faith It Symbolises and Why It's So Difficult to Stand Up and Be a Christian'. *Mail Online*, 4 April. http://www.dailymail.co.uk/news/article-1263441/Nurse-crucifix-row -reveals-uplifting-story-faith-symbolises-difficult-stand-Christian.html.

Pitt-Rivers, J. 1992. 'Postscript: The Place of Grace in Anthropology'. In *Honour and Grace in Anthropology*. Edited by J. G. Peristiany and J. Pitt-Rivers, 215–246. Cambridge: Cambridge University Press.

Plant, R. 2013. 'Religion in a Liberal State'. In *Religion in a Liberal State*. Edited by G. D'Costa, M. Evans, T. Modood, and J. Rivers, 9–37. Cambridge: Cambridge University Press.

Poirier, A. 2019. 'We Watched Notre Dame Burn: Can We Recapture Her Spirit?' *The Guardian*, 20 April. https://www.theguardian.com/global/2019/apr/20/i-watched-notre -dame-burn-then-ran-home-and-wept.

Pojman, L. P. 1991. 'A Critique of Contemporary Egalitarianism: A Christian Perspective'. *Faith and Philosophy* 8: 4, 481–504.

Povinelli, E. A. 2011. *Economies of Abandonment: Social Belonging and Endurance in Late Liberalism*. Durham, NC: Duke University Press.

———. 2012. 'The Will to Be Otherwise/The Effort of Endurance'. *The South Atlantic Quarterly* 111, no. 3: 453–475.

Quinn, B. 2011. 'Anti-Abortion Groups Raise Stakes by Deploying US Tactics on UK Streets'. *The Guardian*, 30 May. http://www.theguardian.com/world/2011/may/30/anti-abortion -protest-groups.

Rees, C. 2014. 'Yes to Women Bishops—Yes to Women?' *Women's History Review* 23, no. 6: 996–999.

Riles, A. 2006. 'Anthropology, Human Rights, and Legal Knowledge: Culture in the Iron Cage'. *American Anthropologist* 108: 1, 52–65.

Rivers, J. 2010. *The Law of Organized Religions*. Oxford: Oxford University Press.

———. 2012. 'The Secularisation of the British Constitution'. *Ecclesiastical Law Journal* 14, no. 3: 371–399.

Robbins, J. 2003. 'What Is a Christian? Notes towards an Anthropology of Christianity'. *Religion* 33: 3, 191–199.

———. 2004. *Becoming Sinners: Christianity and Moral Torment in a Papua New Guinea society*. Berkeley: University of California Press.

———. 2007. 'Continuity Thinking and the Problem of Christian Culture: Belief, Time, and The Anthropology of Christianity'. *Current Anthropology* 48: 1, 5–38.

Rozenberg, J. 2011. 'Fostering Discrimination'. *Standpoint Magazine*, 23 March. https:// standpointmag.co.uk/issues/april-2011/jurisprudence-april-11-joshua-rozenberg -justice-munby-justice-beatson-christian-campaign-groups-gay-fostering-adoption/.

Rubens, H. M. 2014. '"Something Has Gone Wrong": The *JFS* Case and Defining Jewish Identity in the Courtroom'. *Maryland Journal of International Law* 29, 366–418.

Sandberg, R. 2011. 'The Right to Discriminate'. *Ecclesiastical Law Journal* 13: 2, 157–181.

———. 2011. *Law and Religion*. Cambridge: Cambridge University Press.

Scott, R. 2013. *Christians in the Firing Line*. London: Wilberforce Publications.

Shanahan, D. 1992. *Towards a Genealogy of Individualism*. Amherst: University of Massachusetts Press.

Sharma, A. 2006. *Are Human Rights Western? A Contribution to the Dialogue of Civilisations*. Oxford: Oxford University Press.

Sheldon, S. 1997. *Beyond Control: Medical Power and Abortion Law*. London: Pluto Press.

Sherwood, Y. 2012. *Biblical Blaspheming: Trials of the Sacred for a Secular Age*. Cambridge: Cambridge University Press.

Smith, C. 1998. *American Evangelicalism: Embattled and Thriving*. Chicago: University of Chicago Press.

Smith, J. Z. 1998. 'Religion, Religions, Religious'. In *Critical Terms for Religious Studies*. Edited by M. C. Taylor, 269–284. Chicago: University Press.

Soper, J.C. 1994. *Evangelical Christianity in the United States and Great Britain: Religious Beliefs, Political Choices*. London: Palgrave Macmillan.

Strathern, M. 1997. 'Enabling Identity? Biology, Choice and the New Reproductive Technologies'. In *Questions of Cultural Identity*. Edited by S. Hall and P. Du Gay, 37–53. London: Sage Publications.

Strhan, A. 2012. 'Discipleship and Desire: Conservative Evangelicals, Coherence and the Moral Lives of the Metropolis'. Ph.D. thesis. University of Kent.

———. 2015. *Aliens and Strangers? The Struggle for Coherence in the Everyday Lives of Evangelicals*. Oxford: Oxford University Press.

———. 2016. 'English Evangelicalism and the Claims of Equality'. In *Religion, Equalities and Inequalities*. Edited by D. Llewellyn and S. Sharma, 163–176. London and New York: Routledge.

Strudwick, P. 2010. "The Ex-Gay Files: The Bizarre World of Gay to Straight Conversion'. *The Independent*, 1 February. http://www.independent.co.uk/news/uk/this-britain/the -exgay-files-the-bizarre-world-of-gaytostraight-conversion-1884947.html.

Stychin, C. 2009. 'Closet Cases: "Conscientious Objection" to Lesbian and Gay Legal Equality'. *Griffith Law Review* 18, 17–40.

Su, A. 2016. *Exporting Freedom: Religious Liberty and American Power*. Cambridge: Harvard University Press.

Sugirtharajah, R. S. 2001. *The Bible and the Third World: Precolonial, Colonial and Postcolonial Encounters*. Cambridge: Cambridge University Press.

Sullivan, W. F. 1996a. 'Competing Theories of Religion and Law in the Supreme Court of the United States: An Hasidic Case'. *Numen* 43, no. 2: 185–212.

———. 1996b. 'Religion, Law and the Construction of Identities: Introduction'. *Numen* 43: 2, 128–138.

———. 1998. 'Judging Religion'. *Marquette Law Review* 81, no. 2: 441–460.

———. 2005. *The Impossibility of Religious Freedom*. Princeton: Princeton University Press.

———. 2006. 'Comparing Religions, Legally'. *Washington & Lee Law Review* 63, no. 3: 913–930.

———. 2009. 'We Are All Religious Now. Again'. *Social Research* 76, no. 4: 1181–1198.

———. 2010. 'Religion Naturalised: The New Establishment'. In *After Pluralism: Reimagining Religious Engagement*. Edited by C. Bender and P. E. Klassen, 82–97. New York: Columbia University Press.

Sullivan, W. F., R. A. Yelle, and M. Taussig-Rubbo. 2011. 'Introduction'. In *After Secular Law*. Edited by W. F. Sullivan, R. A. Yelle, E. Hurd, M. Taussig-Rubbo, 242–260. Stanford: Stanford University Press.

Sullivan, W. F., E. S. Hurd, S. Mahmood, and P. Danchin, eds. *Politics of Religious Freedom*. Chicago: University of Chicago Press.

Sullivan, W. F. and E. S. Hurd. 2017. 'Theologies of American Exceptionalism: Introduction'. *The Immanent Frame*, 13 February. https://tif.ssrc.org/2017/02/13/american -exceptionalism-introduction/.

Tarlo, E. 2010. *Visibly Muslim: Fashion, Politics, Faith*. Oxford: Berg.

Tarusarira, J. 2019. 'The Anatomy of Apology and Forgiveness: Towards a Transformative Apology and Forgiveness'. *International Journal of Transitional Justice* 13, no. 2: 206–224.

Taylor, C. 2007. *A Secular Age*. Cambridge: Belknap Press of Harvard University Press.

———. 2011. 'Why We Need a Radical Redefinition of Secularism'. In *The Power of Religion in the Public Sphere*. Edited by E. Mendieta and J. VanAntwerpen, 34–59. New York: Columbia University Press.

Thompson, D. 2005. *Waiting for Antichrist: Charisma and Apocalypse in a Pentecostal Church*. Oxford: Oxford University Press.

Tomlinson, M., and M. Engelke, eds. 2006. *The Limits of Meaning: Case Studies in the Anthropology of Christianity*. New York: Berghahn Books.

Tomlinson, M., and M. Engelke. 2006. 'Meaning, Anthropology, Christianity'. In *The Limits of Meaning: Case Studies in the Anthropology of Christianity*. Edited by M. Engelke and M. Tomlinson, 1–37. New York: Berghahn Books.

Topping, A. 2007. 'Girl Takes School to Court Over Right to Wear "Purity" Ring'. *The Guardian*, 23 June. http://www.theguardian.com/uk/2007/jun/23/schools.religion.

Troeltsch, E. 1991 [1925]. *The Christian Faith*. Translated by G. E. Paul. Minneapolis, MI: Fortress Press.

Turnbull, R. 2010. *Shaftesbury: The Great Reformer*. Oxford: Lion Hudson.

Vallely, P. 2014. 'Christians: The World's Most Persecuted People'. *The Independent*, 27 July. http://www.independent.co.uk/voices/comment/christians-the-worlds-most-persecuted-people-9630774.html.

Vilaça, A. 2011. 'Dividuality in Amazonia: God, the Devil, and the Constitution of Christian Personhood in Wari' Christianity'. *Journal of the Royal Anthropological Institute* 17, no. 2: 243–262.

Walton, A., A. Hatcher, and N. Spencer. 2013. *Is There a 'Religious Right' Emerging in Britain?* London: Theos.

Warner, M. 1999. *The Trouble with Normal: Sex, Politics and the Ethics of Queer Life*. New York: The Free Press.

———. 2002. *Publics and Counterpublics*. New York: Zone Books.

Warner, R. 2007. *Reinventing English Evangelicalism, 1966–2001: A Theological and Sociological Study*. Milton Keynes, UK: Paternoster.

Weber, M. 1967 [1918]. 'Science as a Vocation'. In *From Max Weber: Essays in Sociology*. Edited and translated by H. H. Gerth and C. Wright Mills, 129–156. London: Routledge.

Webster, J. 2017. *The Anthropology of Protestantism: Faith and Crisis among Scottish Fishermen*. New York: Palgrave Macmillan.

———. 2016. 'Praying for Salvation: A Map of Relatedness'. *Religion* 47, no. 1: 19–34.Weiner, I. 2017. 'Corporately Produced Conscience: Emergency Contraception and the Politics of Workplace Accommodation'. *Journal of the American Academy of Religion* 85, no. 1: 31–63.

Wenger, T. 2017. *Religious Freedom: The Contested History of an American Ideal*. Chapel Hill: University of North Carolina Press.

Williams, A. M. 2011a. 'Permanent Exclusion and the Johns'. Christian Concern, 8 March. http://christianconcern.com/blog/permanent-exclusion-and-the-johns.

———. 2011b. 'Is This Equality? As a Lawyer, I Never Thought I'd Have to Defend Christians in a Christian Nation'. *Mail Online*, 23 April. http://www.dailymail.co.uk/debate/article-1379970/Is-equality-As-lawyer-I-thought-I-d-defend-Christians-Christian-nation.html.

———. 2011c. 'Modern Legal Thought Eliminates Christian Morality'. *Law Society Gazette*, 28 April. http://www.lawgazette.co.uk/analysis/modern-legal-thought-eliminates-christian-morality/60262.article.

———. 2019. 'Church Teaching Used as Evidence Against Christian in Court'. Christian Concern, 12 July. https://christianconcern.com/comment/church-teaching-used-as-evidence-against-christian-in-court/.

Williams, B. 1993. 'Moral Incapacity'. *Proceedings of the Aristotelian Society* (N.S.) 93: 1, 59–70.

Wilson, A. 2011. 'Homosexuality, Christianity and Child Welfare'. *The Guardian*, 5 March. http://www.theguardian.com/commentisfree/belief/2011/mar/05/views-on-homosexuality-children-welfare.

Wintour, P., and L. Davies. 2012. 'David Cameron: Church of England Should "Get On with It" on Female Bishops'. *The Guardian*, 21 November. http://www.theguardian.com/world/2012/nov/21/david-cameron-church-female-bishops.

Wolterstorff, N. 1987. 'Christianity and Social Justice'. *Christian Scholars Review* 16: 3, 211–228.

———. 2008. *Justice: Rights and Wrongs*. Princeton: Princeton University Press.

YouGov. 2014. British Empire Poll. http://cdn.yougov.com/cumulus_uploads/document/6quatmbimd/Internal_Results_140725_Commonwealth_Empire-W.pdf.

Legal Cases Referenced

Chaplin v Royal Devon and Exeter NHS Foundation Trust [ET/1702886/09].

Core Issues Trust v Transport for London [2013] EWHC 651 (Admin).

Eweida v British Airways Plc [2010] EWCA Civ 80.

Eweida & Others v UK [2013] ECHR 37 (15 January 2013).

Greater Glasgow Health Board v Doogan & Another [2014] UKSC 68.

Hall & Preddy v Bull & Bull [2011] EW Misc 2 (CC).

Hammond v DPP [2004] EWHC 69 Admin.

Johns v Derby City Council [2011] EWHC 375.

Ladele v London Borough of Islington [2009] EWCA Civ 1357.

Lautsi v Italy [2011] ECHR 2412 (18 March 2011).

Mba v London Borough of Merton [2013] EWCA Civ 1562.

McFarlane v Relate Avon Ltd [2010] EWCA Civ B1.

R (Begum) v Governors of Denbigh High School [2006] UKHL 15.

R (Playfoot) v Millais School Governing Body [2007] EWHC 1698.

R v Stephenson & Sloane [2012] Unreported.

R (E) v Governing Body of JFS [2009] UKSC 15.

R (Watkins-Singh) v Governing Body of Aberdare Girls' School [2008] EWHC 1865.

R (X) v Head Teacher of Y School [2008] 2 All ER 249.

A NOTE ON THE TYPE

{ᴀᴛᴛ⟩ᴡⲅᴅᴅᴅ⟩

THIS BOOK has been composed in Miller, a Scotch Roman typeface designed by Matthew Carter and first released by Font Bureau in 1997. It resembles Monticello, the typeface developed for The Papers of Thomas Jefferson in the 1940s by C. H. Griffith and P. J. Conkwright and reinterpreted in digital form by Carter in 2003.

Pleasant Jefferson ("P. J.") Conkwright (1905–1986) was Typographer at Princeton University Press from 1939 to 1970. He was an acclaimed book designer and AIGA Medalist.

The ornament used throughout this book was designed by Pierre Simon Fournier (1712–1768) and was a favorite of Conkwright's, used in his design of the *Princeton University Library Chronicle*.

CPSIA information can be obtained
at www.ICGtesting.com
Printed in the USA
LVHW090530220820
663805LV00002B/4

9 780691 193632